# The
# Imagery of
# John Donne's
# Sermons

# The Imagery of John Donne's Sermons

WINFRIED SCHLEINER

BROWN UNIVERSITY PRESS *Providence*

*Standard Book Number: 87057–116–8*
*Library of Congress Catalog Number: 70–91655*
*Brown University Press, Providence, Rhode Island 02912*
*Copyright © 1970 by Brown University. All rights reserved*
*Published 1970*
*Printed in the United States of America*

*Designed by Richard Hendel*
*Type set in Janson and Caslon*
*Printed by Crimson Printing Company*
*On Warren's Olde Style, laid finish*
*Bound by Stanhope Bindery*

*For Louise*

# Contents

# Preface

N his elegy on John Donne, Thomas Carew asks, "Why yet dare we not trust / Though with unkneaded dowe-bak't prose thy dust?" Since then very many have enshrined the poet-preacher's literary remains in "dowe-bak't prose," and I also have dared. Many friends have tried to help me knead at least a little—if not with success, the fault is entirely mine.

I am grateful to Brown University for supporting me for three years as a graduate student. A grant from the Fels Fund gave me the freedom to finish an earlier draft of this study (accepted as a doctoral dissertation at Brown in 1968) in Cambridge, Massachusetts. I am also grateful to Harvard University for generously allowing me the use of its libraries for a whole year.

This study owes much to my earlier student years at Kiel, where my interest in Donne was first kindled in Professor Paul G. Buchloh's classes, and where Professor Harald Weinrich was exploring that interesting realm between linguistics and the history of literature. My greatest obligation, however, is to Professor Barbara K. Lewalski of Brown University for the care and the critical sense with which she read my first attempts. Only she knows what they were like. Sometimes her marginal notes were so much to the point that I surreptitiously incorporated them into my text. I also owe much to Professor Leicester Bradner and Professor W. Nelson Francis, both of Brown University, who read earlier versions of the manuscript and made valuable comments.

Finally, I would like to express my indebtedness to those helpers, named or unnamed, who (like my wife) never despaired in the task of kneading away the lumps of Germanic syntax.

# The
# Imagery of
# John Donne's
# Sermons

# 1. Introduction

OR a long time scholars used Donne's sermons chiefly as a mine from which to extract passages that might serve as a commentary to his poems. In spite of the renaissance of Donne studies in this century, scholars were slow to turn to his prose, by which he himself expected to be remembered. However, the Simpson-Potter edition of his sermons[1] is indicative of a new interest in them, which has probably reached a climax in Joan Webber's excellent study of his prose.[2]

Yet when critics began to take a keener interest in Donne's prose, they often saw it in terms of what they understood to be the essence of metaphysical poetry, a conception which, as more recent critics such as Rosemond Tuve and Louis Martz have shown,[3] was often inadequate if not erroneous. The metaphysical preacher was believed to derive unusual and whimsical images from a background of remote learning and adapt them to use "by a curious transmutation effected by means of [his] peculiar temperament." [4] The "witty" style of Donne and Andrewes was defined as follows:

> In prose as in verse wit involved not merely verbal tricks and surprises but the bringing together of dissimilar objects, symbols, and ideas philosophized and fused by intellectual and spiritual perceptions and emotions, weighted by frequently abstruse and scientific learning.[5]

Although this is a complex description making use of critical insights that have awakened in a generation of students a taste for the Metaphysicals, behind it stands the simpler, time-honored definition of the metaphysical style as characterized by heterogeneous ideas "yoked by violence together." [6] One writer endeavored to support this critical perspective with statistical evidence.[7] He did so by tearing tropes in half and grouping them according to vehicle in new, often arbitrary units. The conclusion of the analysis, which again stressed disparity, was bound to be misleading.

In recent years a number of studies have been devoted to Donne's prose. Some scholars have selected a number of sermons in order to investigate how they relate to traditions of rhetoric or of biblical exegesis, or how they are linked with Donne's own time and place.[8] Other readers of Donne have studied all his sermons (or his prose) to observe how certain features of his style relate to each other and to critical concepts such as "the baroque," or to describe changes of theme and tone during the course of Donne's preaching career.[9] The author of one thesis describes all Donne's images of roundness and interprets them as belonging to one archetype.[10] This work is the only recent extensive study devoted exclusively to Donne's imagery. Its limitation of scope is deliberate. But even if we accept the Jungian premise and grant that "the circle, in terms of the individual, is a symbol of the self as a psychic totality," [11] not every reader will be convinced that crown, egg, sphere, hemisphere, map, womb, and coin images have enough in common to justify their treatment as a meaningful unit. The approach is highly original, but any method that removes the metaphorical part of the image so far from what it signifies in a specific context must remain open to question.[12]

Combining close attention to the text with awareness of traditions of rhetoric, recent publications have contributed much to our understanding of Donne's prose. But although they avoid the fragmentation of earlier studies, they still sometimes hold that it is the linking of the secular with the sacred that constitutes the vice or virtue of metaphysical poetry.[13]

My purpose in this study is mainly descriptive, but I also want to reconsider such judgments insofar as they concern the imagery of Donne's sermons. Imagery is here understood—as it is by

Stephen Ullmann,[14] among others—to include all forms of figurative discourse, among them, metaphor, simile, and allegory.
To try to give a definition of Donne's figures here at the outset
would be to attempt the impossible; if it were possible to give
such a definition, this study could hardly be justified. Some terms,
however, that will be used in the analysis will have to be defined.
The justification for this is purely heuristic. In a study of this
type I cannot attempt to grapple with a problem that a number
of monographs have addressed, so far without reaching agreement—the problem of the nature of figurative discourse.[15]

One question any analysis will have to raise and answer is
that of the particularity, or uniqueness, of the matter described.
Implicitly this has been one of the purposes of all the major
studies of Donne's prose. As far as the imagery is concerned, this
question can only be answered by a broad-based analysis. Yet,
all too often critics have been struck by one figure or another,
often because it fit their expectations of what the poet would be
like as a preacher, and have then generalized their impressions. It
must be admitted that ten volumes of sermons are a challenge and
that the temptation is great to choose those images that support a
particular theory and to leave out the rest. What is sought, then,
is a method that will allow us to include as many images as possible in the discussion. If the majority of all the tropes an author
uses are conventional, we should not hesitate to say so, nor should
we in our descriptions passionately push forward those few that
allow for a witty comment. A balanced description will neglect
neither kind; it will say what the rule is and what the exception.
Its theory should make room for that first group and at the same
time provide an explanation of why such images are "conventional" or "not very striking" or "of limited originality." If ped-
antry is to be avoided, the requirement of inclusiveness will of
course have to be tempered by the principle of economy.

The task of mapping out Donne's tropes raises the question of
what map to use. On what co-ordinates should they be plotted?
How can one compare one metaphor with another?

A dimension in which all tropes compare is one that for lack of a more convenient term may be called their degree of boldness, novelty, or originality. As I make explicit this yardstick—which is applied in many studies but is seldom evaluated as a criterion—I hasten to reject the charge that this might represent an anachronistic and highly subjective or, worse, normative approach. No one will seriously hold that the seventeenth-century preacher sought originality in the sense of the word with which we have become familiar since the romantic age; nor can it be the purpose of this study to use boldness as a criterion for judging the excellence of Donne's figures, though I do intend to describe some of the factors that determined how bold or how conventional they probably seemed to a seventeenth-century audience; what seems bold to one age may not seem so at all to another, and furthermore, boldness may be either censured or praised or given more complex evaluation, depending on the literary climate.

The dimension here intended is much larger than novelty or boldness as a criterion of excellence; in fact, it may be called the largest common denominator of all theories of metaphor. It seems that a trope, particularly a metaphor, has at all times been considered as some kind of transgression of the ordinary rules of signification. The psychologist Wilhelm Stählin speaks in this context of a peculiar "state of consciousness of double meaning." [16] He explains that there is always a certain tension between the metaphorical expression and its context.[17] This element of tension has not gone unnoticed even in the earliest explanations of figurative discourse. Aristotle remarks that "metaphors should be drawn from objects which are proper to the object, but not too obvious; just as, for instance, in philosophy it needs sagacity to grasp the similarity in things that are apart." [18]

The feeling that metaphors strain the ordinary use of language has led some observers, ancient and modern, to give the discussion of figurative discourse a moralistic turn. Aristotle had at least prepared the ground when he wrote, "Most smart things are derived from metaphor and also from misleading the hearer beforehand." [19] In the late nineteenth century Brinkmann went so far as to find an element of deception in every metaphor and to oppose it to the "language of the heart." [20]

Without accepting the moral implications or, for that matter, the final evaluation, which is brought in here only for its symptomatic value, we can easily see some truth in the observation that there is an element of deception in all metaphorical language. In a recent monograph on the phenomenon of linguistic deception, a linguist draws on information theory in his discussion of metaphor.[21] Information, he reminds us, always consists in the reduction of possibilities. Information is zero, that is, the number of possibilities is greatest, when nothing has been said. From the point of view of the single word, information has two dimensions. On the one hand it relates to the world, to the total number of possibilities. Once the word has been uttered it informs us about what has been excluded from this total. But on the other hand, another dimension relates to the signals, or words, that are now to be expected, that is, to the sequence in the communication. After the first word has been uttered, certain kinds of words are not very likely to follow. Although such a determination through probabilities does not attain the degree we call certainty, it is a linguistic reality. If, say, the word *fire* is uttered, the expectation is determined in the sense that now a message about flames, ruins, campfires or fireplaces will be expected. Expectation has now a direction, which can be indicated through a bundle of associations. In most cases our expectation is realized—after all, this is why we can acquire linguistic habits, learn a language. But if, instead, speech switches to a different sphere, if the message turns out to be about a "fire of love," and not fireplaces, our reckoning is disturbed and we have to revise our expectations. In this, according to the author, lies the metaphorical tension.

If there is evidence that Aristotle found some kind of tension within the trope, Cicero makes this explicit in his discussion of metaphorical discourse. Leaning on Aristotle's theory of genius he even suggests that it might be a manifestation of genius to leap over such expressions as lie near and to catch others that are at a farther distance ("ingeni specimen est quoddam transilire ante pedes posita et alia longe repetita sumere").[22] Nevertheless, there is no reason to suppose that either Aristotle or Cicero considered such statements to constitute an invitation to make metaphors bold and striking. It has been rightly pointed out that Cicero also objected to the trope that is farfetched ("videndum est ne longe simile sit ductum").[23] In order to soften any possible harshness he recommended the use of the formula *ut ita dicam,* and we may agree with Harald Weinrich's pointed remark that the lexical honors that all European languages have bestowed on the loan translations of the formula—for instance, *as it were, pour ainsi dire, sozusagen*—attest to the success of the recommendation.[24] Cicero's warning, then, is additional proof to us that some tension is felt to exist in tropes, although his explanation of metaphor is of little help in specifying where unpleasant harshness begins.

The foregoing remarks should be sufficient to show the relevance of the concept of boldness in the study of imagery. We can now go on unfolding the traditional theory of metaphor, drawing on modern linguistics whenever it may help to qualify or to clarify. The object is to find a framework for the description of Donne's imagery, a framework that is at once historical and in accordance with linguistic fact.

Cicero's "leaping" metaphor for the image-making mind suggests that two elements go into the making of an image. They may both be expressed, as in the simile, or one of them may be omitted in favor of the other. Similarly, Aristotle had spoken of two objects between which some similarities would exist. The duality yields the two parts of an image, which I. A. Richards, in some respects echoing medieval usage, has called *tenor* (the *designatum,* or principal subject) and *vehicle* (the *res designans,* or what the subject resembles).[25] Cicero's model, the leap, further suggests that the boldness of the image can somehow be measured in terms of the distance between tenor and vehicle.

It can easily be seen that the model, if interpreted this way, is simplistic, since it reduces boldness to being the function of just one criterion, and that an extremely uncertain one. Nonetheless,

it has been highly influential. The neoclassical view of "heterogeneous" elements "yoked by violence together" is but one of
many restatements of the idea. The framework for the Renaissance criticism of metaphor can to some extent be called ontological, since the distance the critics have in mind is the "real"
distance between things in a supposed hierarchy of being. Little
would of course be achieved by calling such a hierarchy a mere
fiction. Even Harald Weinrich, whose concern is not historical,
admits that in our understanding of the world there may be
some sense of a hierarchical structure.[26] Man and animal seem
closer than man and plant. Yet, though we cannot quite disregard
such a hierarchy, it is not safe, in the analysis of imagery, to
rely on such an ordering scheme as the *Arbor Porphyriana*, so-
called after the Neoplatonic philosopher Porphyry, who tried to
order all being in a large system by means of *genus* and *genera
specifica*.[27] Important as is the question whether Donne's use of
imagery rests on the belief in the existence of such an order, a
simple reflection may show that the ontological distance alone
does not determine the boldness of an image. On any "tree" or
"ladder" of realities river and speech are fairly far apart, and
yet a metaphor like "his words flowed" is hardly very striking.[28]
Metaphors like this one, which encompass the whole *Arbor Porphyriana* and which link the spiritual and the material, are so
common that we have to make a deliberate effort if we want to
avoid them.

It seems evident, then, that Cicero's explanation is too sketchy.
No single factor decides whether an image is striking, but there
is a whole group of factors whose presence or absence deter-
mines the relative boldness of an image. In this study I shall
proceed by a *via negativa* and describe the factors that help to
integrate Donne's images.

It is important in the study of imagery not to isolate images
artificially from the context in which they occur, but rather to
observe and describe the nature of the context. The requirement
is not particular to the study of tropes; it is in fact derived from
the nature of any semantic situation. It need hardly be proven

that words are not normally written or understood except in sentences. As Stählin said, "The normal thing is not the bare occurrence of the experience of meaning, an occurrence delimited by no specification, but rather it is such an experience of meaning as is effectively determined by situation and context." [29] The influence of context on tropes differs from its influence on single words not in kind but in degree. The following definition is borrowed from Weinrich: "A metaphor, and this is basically the only possible definition of a metaphor, is a word in a context by which it is so determined that it signifies something other than what it means," [30] or, to paraphrase, a word used in such a way that its contextual meaning is noticeably different from its lexical meaning. It is the determination through context, of which we can now distinguish several kinds, that regulates the boldness of an image.

A homely word in a sublime context can seem extremely daring. Erich Auerbach has shown in his *Mimesis* that it took some courage for Victor Hugo to write in *Hernani* the seemingly innocent line, "On entendit un roi dire: Quelle heure est-il?" [31] With the question "What time is it?" Hugo became engaged in a violent polemic, since details of everyday living, references to sleeping, eating and drinking, the weather, and the time of day were incompatible with the sublime style of classical drama. Extreme as it may be, the example shows how rules of genre structure the content. Every particular utterance derives its value from its position in that structure. In the case of Donne's sermons we will see that images have different values according to position, that is, according to whether the tone of the passage is, for example, satirical or eulogistic. The principle involved here is the principle of decorum, which, according to classical rhetoric, regulates the fittingness of all discourse. In the literary treatises of the Renaissance it is the prime instrument in critical analysis, and it has therefore received some recent scholarly attention.[32] I shall attempt to show how Donne's tropes measure up to that principle.

But it is not only the speaker's perspective that integrates a trope. Every trope stands in some kind of relation to all the tropes ever formed, or at least to those known to the speaker and his audience. Taking the synchronic point of view we can say that language, in the sense of Saussure's abstract *langue*, which he distinguishes from *parole*, the actualization of *langue*,[33] is already structured: there are metaphors that are more familiar than others, and there are clichés. A cliché, by definition, cannot be novel. But between the overused figure and a truly original coinage there is a wide range of possibilities. In order to describe them I shall posit the existence of "fields of imagery" in the social system of the *langue*, which is objective and potential.

A *field of imagery*, which will be defined in the third chapter in more detail, is constituted by the analogical link between two areas of meaning. Love and sickness are such areas; their combination can be expressed by the word *lovesickness*. The poets of the sixteenth and seventeenth centuries are particularly fond of this field; they invoke many kinds of love (divine, profane, courtly) in terms of innumerable sicknesses. If we combine the synchronic with the diachronic view, it is often possible to see an individual image as a variation of a traditional metaphor. So, to pursue the above example, if we were to examine some love sonnet containing such a metaphor, we would try to determine how the sixteenth-century poet's use of metaphor compares with the imagery of Petrarch (and further back, with the poetry of the troubadours and trouvères) who firmly established the field of love as sickness. Many of Donne's images will be found to relate to such structures, or fields of imagery, which support them and help to integrate them.

The fields of imagery are abstract constructs. One can describe them as they exist in Donne's sermons. Their existence is of the nature of a paradigm, which "is there" but is never enunciated. As we direct our attention to the syntagmatic level, we notice that tropes are also supported by other tropes in their neighborhood in the text. If these neighboring figures happen to belong to the same field of imagery, they form extended analogies. The analogy may be so consistent that it approaches formal allegory.

But a number of figures will remain that are not sufficiently described or explained in any of the foregoing ways. They seem hard to justify by the principle of decorum, which is foremost in the critical sensibility of Renaissance writers. Their terms—tenor and vehicle—bridge a wide range on any hierarchical scale of reality, and yet no intention of meiosis or amplification is noticeable. Nor can they be sufficiently accounted for by the existence of any fields of imagery to which they might relate.

This will necessitate broadening our concept of context and situation to include theological beliefs and exegetical conventions to which the preacher adhered and which he possibly to some extent shared with his audience. I will try to show that some tropes reflect a view of reality to which the *Arbor Porphyriana* has no relevance. It is a view having some similarities to the sense of reality that allowed a medieval poet to compare Christ to a nut: "Nux est Christus." [34] The best frame of reference for these figures is the medieval semantic theory of the word in the Holy Scriptures, a theory that is also at the basis of the threefold or fourfold interpretation of the Bible according to historical, allegorical, moral, and anagogical senses. According to this conception a word has as many potential meanings as the *res* that lies behind its *vox* has properties. Although many tropes that are related to this view are clearly embedded in the sermons' structure, which sometimes consists simply of the steps of traditional exegesis, there are other images that would appear incongruous and unduly audacious if it were not recognized that they relate to such theories.

I shall therefore proceed in this study by the four steps that have briefly been indicated: I shall analyze Donne's imagery in relation to the concept of decorum, establish certain fields of imagery, then give attention to metaphors in the textual neighborhood of a trope, and finally try to place certain tropes against the background of some medieval semantic theories. Thus it will be necessary to draw on modern as well as old semantic theories and to adopt now a synchronic and then a diachronic view. But this seeming inconsistency should not be embarrassing, since my purpose is to place the imagery of Donne's sermons between the co-ordinates of tradition and originality.

# 2. Imagery and Decorum

RITING about Renaissance poetic, Rosemond Tuve contended that the question Is it decorous? was not like the other questions in the mind of the Renaissance reader when he judged the excellence of an image, or of the poet when he decided whether to omit or to change an image. "For," she held, "this is the question which helped to determine his answer to all the others. Propriety or decorum was the basic criterion in terms of which all the others were understood." [1] For the poetry of the sixteenth century this view seems to be widely accepted by the critics; yet for the literature of the Metaphysicals the role of the criterion of decorum is still contested. At least two views, carrying different degrees of conviction, have been held. According to one the Metaphysicals adhered to essentially the same rhetoric and poetic as the Spenserians, but exploited them for new effects; the other position contends that they boldly rebelled against the traditional rules of propriety and drew their effects from a deliberate breach of decorum.

In her very suggestive chapter on decorum, documented with passages from contemporary books of rhetoric and poetic, Rosemond Tuve tried to prove that the principle of decorum held also for metaphysical poetry. She argued that imagery can be entirely consistent with orthodox pronouncements on decorum even though it be unconventional, homely, rough, or difficult to understand.[2]

According to a different opinion, still widely held and persuasively argued in literary criticism, it was characteristic of the

Metaphysicals that they "deliberately produced poetic shocks by coupling what was sacred, august, remote, or inhuman with what was profane, hum-drum, familiar, and social." [3] In producing such effects the Metaphysicals were not, according to this view, making an absolute innovation. The novelty consisted in producing these effects more often and more violently than previous poets had done, and indeed in making them almost "the mainstay of their poetics." [4] It is clear that even if poetry is seen as such a *discors concordia*, the role of decorum cannot be disregarded, for the special effects of this literature rest on a deliberate breach of those rules. The effects are missed if decorum is not recognized first. The poets were not "ignoring poetic decorum but exploiting it, so to speak, in reverse." [5] Therefore metaphysical poetry is "twice born," no literature could begin with it: it uses discords "on the assumption that your taste is sufficiently educated to recognize them"; it presupposes other literature and therefore may in a sense be called "parasitic." [6]

There is no need for me to take a position in a controversy over a matter that is not the subject of this study. The controversy about metaphysical poetry is indirectly relevant, however, since it has been the latter opinion alone that has, as I indicated in my introductory remarks, for many years influenced discussions of metaphysical prose style. The problems to which I will limit my discussion may be summarized in three questions: What role does the criterion of decorum, which Rosemond Tuve derived chiefly from the poetics of the time, play in such handbooks on the *artes concionandi* as a preacher might have consulted? Does Donne indicate any awareness of the principle? Do the tropes in his sermons conform to it?

# Decorum and the *Artes Concionandi*

The history of the *artes concionandi* has not yet been written. Dorothea Roth's dissertation comes closest to such an attempt, but her survey extends only as far as Ulrich of Surgant's *Manuale Curatorum*, which was published in 1503. The chapter on Erasmus's *Ecclesiastes* (1535) that she appends is very sketchy and not as suggestive as the rest of her book.[7] Miss Roth is of course well justified in making Ulrich of Surgant the focal and final point of her study, for the *Manuale* was actually about the last well-known homiletic treatise in the medieval scholastic mold. Yet, as far as Donne studies are concerned, it would be deceptive to follow the critics who have relied almost exclusively on the treatises on preaching made more readily accessible through the work of Etienne Gilson, Harry Caplan, and Dorothea Roth.

When Poggio, on his way to the Council of Constance (1414), recovered the complete Quintilian in the tower of the Abbey of St. Gallen, and Gherardo Landriani in 1425 came upon Cicero's treatises in the Duomo at Lodi, it was almost predictable that these finds, through the Renaissance enthusiasm for classical rhetoric, would influence the theory of preaching.[8] The new treatises on preaching, modeled on these examples, tended to treat in some fashion the five parts of traditional rhetoric: invention and its tools, the *topoi*, or commonplaces; disposition (arrangement of exordium, narration, division, confirmation, confutation, and peroration); elocution (the figures of thought and figures of words); aids to memory; and delivery (voice and action). These facts are so well known that they would not be repeated here if these treatises did not also indicate a new concern for two problems that are not mentioned in the handbooks and encyclopedias: the function of figurative discourse (the use and purpose of tropes) and the role of decorum in preaching.

Some of the most successful authors were Spanish and Italian. The fact that they were Catholic should not cause us to exclude them from our consideration, for we know from Donne's own testimony that books by Spanish authors made up a large part of his library.[9]

In one of the most widely used of all the books on preaching, *Ecclesiasticae rhetoricae, sive de ratione concionandi, libri sex*, by Luis de Granada,[10] the chapter headed "De apte dicendo" deals with the nature of decorum:

Yet there are four rules which ought to be observed by whoever wants to speak aptly, namely, that his speech should fit perfectly the speaker, the audience, the subject matter, and the purpose which it intends. That is, who speaks, who is addressed, and what is above all to be achieved by the speech. In all this one has to consider what is most fitting; yet this pertains not only to the rules of this art but principally to the sense of prudence which is the guide of all actions and so also of our speech. But of the functions of this guide the greatest as well as the most difficult one is to understand what is fitting in any place. For from here arises the decorum which has to be kept in everything.[11]

Surely this principle is not really revolutionary, for it stems, as the author himself indicates, from the most general rules of behavior. But one has only to read similar passages in medieval treatises to note the new emphasis. In his *Regula pastoralis* Gregory the Great had stressed the rule that even though the preacher should have one doctrine, he should vary his sermons according to the audience,[12] just as the musician will pluck the strings of his instrument differently, though using one plectrum. Dorothea Roth points out that he arranged his examples according to a possible audience, which he groups as *juvenes et senes, laeti et tristes, servi et domini, benevoli et inviti.*[13] Yet as one goes down the long list of possible audiences and the corresponding examples and quotations from Scripture, it becomes apparent—and this Dorothea Roth omits to tell us—that the author has in mind a thematic rather than a stylistic accommodation. It is true that in his treatment of the art of dividing a theme, when he recommends taking into consideration the comprehension of the audience for which a sermon is preached, he comes somewhat closer to what later books on preaching will understand as the principle of decorum.[14] But I cannot find anything comparable to the insistence on decorum of the Renaissance writers as they unfold in great detail the conditions they have set up as constituting the elements of that principle. Luis de Granada, for example, sets forth the styles suitable for various possible audiences as follows:

> The same reason demands that not only the identity of the speaker but also the audience be taken into consideration. For there is one way to speak to the plain and uneducated people, and another to the educated, to noblemen and princes, and to delicate ears. In the case of the latter the sermon must be sublime; in the case of the former, more vehement. Moreover there is one way before monks and maidens dedicated to theology and contemplation, and another before those who without fear of divine retribution rush into crimes.[15]

This theory of decorum is the framework within which the excellence of tropes is discussed in the *artes concionandi* that I have consulted. Their model is not hard to find. In his *Rhetorica ecclesiastica*, which was widely used, the Protestant Bartholomew Keckermann several times refers his clerical readers to the second chapter of the third book of Aristotle's *Art of Rhetoric*, in which the fittingness and proportion of style and the fittingness of metaphor is treated.[16] Aristotle writes there:

> It is metaphor above all that gives a foreign air and it cannot be learnt from anyone else; but we must make use of metaphors and epithets that are appropriate. This will be secured by observing due proportion; otherwise there will be a lack of propriety, because it is when placed in juxtaposition that contraries are most evident.[17]

Any trope consists of such a juxtaposition of two terms, expressed or understood. Recognition of this reveals the working model in the back of the minds of most writers on ecclesiastical rhetoric when they judge the fittingness of a trope. Each of the two terms of the figure (tenor and vehicle) exists somewhere in a supposed hierarchy. In a metaphor or simile that is used for explanation or elucidation, the two terms have to be of the same rank on this ladder. In coining images the preacher's art consists in his adjusting the two terms, for he has it in his power to shift the scales ever so slightly: Under certain circumstances he can choose a vehicle of a slightly higher or lower rank than is expected. The disproportion is not indecorous so long as it is governed by his purpose. In a sense the coining of an image thus comes close to what logicians call a predication.

The writers on pulpit oratory agree on the point that tropes contribute more than any other device of rhetoric to the "ornament" of the sermon.[18] Modern objections to the idea of style as the dress of thought should not keep us from seeing that the concept of *ornamentum* was so wide as to embrace a number of important functions of images. Again Luis de Granada is most elaborate on this point: "So much may be said about tropes, which, as we said before, contribute most of all to the ornament of speech and of all of which the nature and reason is one: namely, to replace the known and proper name of a thing by another which is more accomplished, more expressive, or which has more force of proof and argument." [19] That the delight a figure or trope gives to the audience is thought of as functional is also indicated by Keckermann in the brief statement that introduces his section on tropes: "The ornament of simple words is by tropes, of which the preacher will preferably use metaphor; since indeed this is the most effective of all tropes and suitable to move and to delight." [20] When he speaks about the explanatory power of metaphor, Keckermann can again quote Aristotle as saying that "it is metaphor above all that gives lucidity and pleasure." [21]

Such reflections on the nature of metaphor are invariably followed by the traditional caveat that the preacher should in his tropes avoid *dissimilitudo*,[22] which, according to the Protestant Keckermann, who follows Aristotle even more closely than most rhetoricians, results in harshness. Nor should metaphors be too light or too base.[23] Luis de Granada, who knows from Cicero that harshness can be reduced by using the word *ut*, moreover adds a warning that not everything that is allowed the poet is permitted the preacher,[24] whereas Keckermann has a more specific *ne quid nimis*.[25]

The writers on rhetoric do not give explicit standards for judging *dissimilitudo*, harshness, or farfetchedness; but it seems that behind their recommendations and warnings is some kind of scale on which the two terms of a metaphor are distributed. Although Luis de Granada recommends that if one wants to make something lively for an audience he should show the object as the greatest of its kind,[26] he is not violating the criterion of equal rank for tenor and vehicle, because in that case he is giving not a trope, which will normally link objects of different kinds, but only a description. In the case of tropes the hierarchy in which the two terms are ranked may be some general scheme such as gradations of excellence, from high to low, as suggested in Keckermann's "base metaphor," or a scale from "good" to "bad" on which things are distributed according to their "nature." In his chapter entitled "Uti comparationes inveniantur," Didacus Stella explains at length how to make a similitude congruent (*congrua similitudo*).[27] He combines a hierarchy of being (indicated by such examples as sun, firmament, slime, and mud) with a scale of value:

Therefore the likening itself and the thing which is taken over should communicate, so to speak, completely or in part that which they symbolize by nature, whether this object is good or bad. Not less in the case of diverse kinds of creatures of base and harmful quality than in the case of those of good grace and nature, so that the comparison is made complete or partly so. In the example given we will devise a subject, which is man, and that is something good; and a predicate, which is sin, and that is something bad or harmful. But the things that must be compared to something bad are generally of a base degree or quality, which are likened completely or in part. Such are filth, poison, viper, venom, captivity, ulcer, slime, snake, etc. To signify an honest man, the things to which one may compare his life in part are generally of a high nature. Such are the sun, firmament, prince, and others which indicate something good completely or in part.[28]

# High and Low Metaphor

It cannot be proven that Donne used the *artes concionandi* that have been adduced so far; indeed, there is no proof that he used any of them. No one will seriously hold that Donne had to go to the rather pedestrian Didacus Stella to be taught how to construct a metaphor or a simile. But what can be shown is that Donne is aware of the theory of fittingness of tropes that is expounded in such books and that his tropes for the most part conform to it.

With the writers on pulpit oratory Donne shares a feeling for the relative "height" of metaphors and other tropes. This can be shown by looking at some of his critical remarks about style.

It has often been noticed that he holds up the Scriptures as models of style, a common practice among authors of books on preaching of the time, who liked to use quotations from the Scriptures and the church fathers to exemplify their figures and tropes. What is more important in this context is the awareness shown in his comments on the rhetorical excellence of the Bible of the relative "height" of its metaphors:

> Accept those names of Tropes and Figures, which the Grammarians and Rhetoricians put upon us, and we may be bold to say, that in all their Authors, Greek and Latin, we cannot finde so high, and so lively examples, of those Tropes and those Figures, as we may in the Scriptures. [2:170, 7:242] [29]

All through his ministry Donne praises the "eloquence" of the Scriptures. According to contemporary ideas of style, the eloquence resides in embellishments. In a very similar passage of a later sermon he comments again on the excellence of the tropes found in the Bible and insists that they are "higher" than tropes that commonly illustrate the books on secular rhetoric:

> So, howsoever the Christians at first were fain to sink a little under that imputation, that their Scriptures have no Majesty, no eloquence, because these embellishments could not appear in Translations, nor they then read Originalls, yet now, that a perfect knowledge of those languages hath brought us to see the beauty and the glory of those Books, we are able to reply to them, that there are not in all the world so eloquent Books as the Scriptures; and that nothing is more demonstrable, then that if we would take all those Figures, and Tropes, which are collected out of secular Poets, and Orators, we may give higher, and livelier examples, of every one of those Figures, out of the Scriptures, then out of all the Greek and Latine Poets, and Orators; and they mistake it much, that thinke, that the Holy Ghost hath rather chosen a low, and barbarous, and homely style, then an eloquent, and powerfull manner of expressing himselfe. [6:56, 1:632]

It would be beside the point to argue that biblical language can also at times be very homely, for we are here concerned not with what is, but with Donne's interpretation of it. The charge he rejects, that the Scriptures must be despised "because of the poore and beggerly phrase, that they seemed to be written in," (6:55, 1:607) is equivalent to a charge of indecorum, or lack of propriety. The criterion of propriety is expressly referred to in the same sermon:

> Let me note thus much . . . that the Holy Ghost in penning the Scriptures delights himself, not only with a propriety, but with a delicacy, and harmony, and melody of language; with height of Metaphors, and other figures, which may work greater impressions upon the Readers, and not with barbarous, or triviall, or market, or homely language. [6:55, 1:600]

The single dimension of "high" and "low" metaphors is of course a rather rough gauge. One might conjecture that it may have seemed suitable to the preacher in his exposition just because of its simplicity; one might also hold that it would be unfair to expect a preacher to expound in detail his rhetorical creed, let alone a complete theory of metaphor. I have tried to show that we are justified even from Donne's remarks on style in coupling the dimension of "high" and "low" with the principle of propriety. If this single dimension is set, as it should be, within the framework of the general rules of decorum, the result is quite a large and powerful theory.

In the middle of a comparison Donne inserts a parenthesis that is interesting in this context:

> How much more is God grieved now, that we will make no benefit of that bloud which is shed for us, then he was for the very shedding of that bloud! We take it not so ill, (pardon so low a comparison in so high a mystery; for, since our blessed Saviour was pleased to assume that metaphor, and to call his passion a *Cup*, and his death a *drinking*, we may be admitted to that Comparison of drinking too) we take it not so ill, that a man go down into our Cellar, and draw, and drinke his fill, as that he goe in, and pierce the vessells and let them runne out, in a wastfull wantonnesse.
> [3:162, 6:223]

The parenthesis here is more than Cicero's softening *ut ita dicam*; Donne is aware of the fact that his comparison disregards certain hierarchical levels; he notices that it is in a sense indecorous. In order to give it a minimum of decorum he points to a similarity with metaphorical usage in the Scriptures. Using the terms that were suggested earlier one may say that he is obliged to supply an additional context by means of which he hopes to integrate the image.

Apparently some of the discordant elements are neutralized in longer comparisons or analogies if the image points to a complex spiritual meaning. To some extent this seems to be true of the literary genre of the beast fable. If one were to follow Aristotle, to whom the valor of a slave seemed appropriately dealt with only in the comic genre, animals as agents would, according to his ideas of decorum, necessarily relegate the genre to a very low position; it is a well-known fact that this low position in turn allowed writers of classical eras, as, for instance, La Fontaine, to treat the social and political scene under the guise of animal lore. But since animals in a fable, by the nature of the genre, are not just animals, but speak and understand speech like human beings, and since their actions consistently point to a moral meaning, the function of a fable in a discourse need not reflect the low rank it occupies in the rather wooden classification of classical poetics. In the following passage, though, Donne prefers to call the story he narrates a parable rather than a fable. According to Puttenham, fables like Aesop's differ from parables in that they are "fayned as true." [30] Maybe Donne would not claim that his little story was consistent enough even on the fictional level to deserve that name. He possibly also wanted his congregation to cast out of their minds the irrelevant question as to the veracity of his story and to point to the "resemblence misticall," which according to Puttenham is the distinguishing feature of the parable.[31]

> Wee need not call that a *Fable*, but a *Parable*, where we heare, That a Mother to still her froward childe told him, she would cast him to the Wolf, the Wolf should have him; and the Wolf which was at the doore, and within hearing, waited, and hoped he should have the childe indeed: but the childe being still'd, and the Mother pleased, then she saith, so shall we kill the Wolf, the Wolf shall have none of my childe, and then the Wolf stole away.[7:369, 14:725]

The sense Donne derives from his parable is "misticall" indeed:

> God bids your Mother the Church, and us her Servants for your Souls, to denounce his judgements upon your sinnes, and we do it; and the executioner *Satan*, beleeves us, before

you beleeve us, and is ready on his part. Be you also ready on your part, to lay hold upon those conditions, which are annext to all Gods maledictions . . . to . . . disappoint that *Wolf*, that roaring *Lion*, that seeks whom he may devour. [7:369, 14:733]

If the modern reader seems somewhat uneasy about the whole passage it is mainly because of the sense; the devil lying ready to act at the request of the preacher is a strange idea indeed. Yet here Donne wants it this way. If anything, it is the seeming indecorum of the passage that bothers him. The scene depicted is homely. The wolf of the fable or fairy tale who understands human speech, retains enough real wolfishness to serve as a contrast to the homey milieu of mother and child. The mixture of the fabulous and the real that results reminds one of some of the moralizing miniatures by Hieronymus Bosch. It is therefore to forestall any criticism of indecorum that Donne inserts between the two passages quoted the sentence: "No metaphor, no comparison is too high, none too low, too triviall, to imprint in you the sense of Gods everlasting goodnesse towards you" (7:369, 14:731). Finally Donne tries again to make his parable conform to the use of metaphor in the Bible; the wolf, who at that point has become a mere abstraction of evil and danger, is easily dropped and replaced by "the roaring Lion that seeks whom he may devour."

Donne's excuse that "no metaphor, no comparison is too high, none too low, too triviall, to imprint . . . the sense of God's everlasting goodnesse" is here quoted not for what it says—it would be hazardous indeed to consider it as his metaphorical manifesto —but as an indication of the critical theory within which the preacher thinks and of the kind of criticism he reckons with. The same theory is apparent when he excuses the seeming indecorum of a later passage:

It is but a homely Metaphor, but it is a wholesome, and a usefull one, *Confessio vomitus*, Confession works as a vomit; It shakes the frame, and it breaks the bed of sin: and it is an ease to the spirituall stomach, to the conscience, to be thereby disburdened. [9:304, 13:307]

The audacious metaphor is given as a quote from so prestigious an authority as Origen. Furthermore Donne presents it in Latin first, the jargon of the specialist, just as a medical doctor will easily talk about an *exitus* when certain taboos will make him hesitate to pronounce the word *death*. Finally, and this will call for special attention in chapter 3, the metaphor is congruent with a whole field of imagery in which sin is spoken of as an ugly sickness, for Donne's point in the whole passage is that confession is a therapy to ease the "spirituall stomach."

It may not be without interest in this context that a similar awareness of the suitability of metaphor and comparison can be found in such a famous Spanish preacher as Juan de Avila. Again the critical awareness is most apparent in those exceptional cases in which ordinary usage is felt to be somewhat strained:

> Haven't you seen when a little pimp walks by a woman, haunting her door and spending sorrowful nights for her sake, and he says in his heart: "I will make you undergo what I underwent, and will make you wander after me as I wandered after you"? Well, thus it happens, although the comparison may not be very exact because the person is good here and bad there. Thus Jesus Christ says, "Let her go, because what she made me suffer so that I attract her to me, this person will now pay for it, for I will have this person see for herself what I suffered for her sake. *Ego ostendam illi quanta oporteat eum pati pro nomine meo.* Because as many times as I called and you did not hear me, you will call and it will seem to you that I do not hear you." [32]

The comparison is felt to be audacious because it seems to violate the requirement for a congruent comparison that we found formulated in the *De ratione concionandi* by Didacus Stella.[33] And yet, in paralleling a *rufiancito* with Christ, Juan de Avila disregards the incongruence only seemingly, since he established it firmly in the concessive clause: "although the comparison may not be very exact [suitable? decorous?] because the person is good here and bad there."

Now the question might be raised, If the comparison is felt to be inadequate in some respect, what justifies the use of such analogies as Donne's wolf story or Avila's frustrated lover? The question has been answered in part already, but a brief consideration of contemporary rhetoric and logic may add some precision.

"Nobody is of so clear a mind," Ioannis Hepinus reminds the preacher, "that he could teach or learn without the help of dialectics or rhetoric."[34] The theory and practice of preaching rest on this assumption. Some writers on pulpit oratory simply refer the preacher to the commonplaces, the traditional *topoi* or *loci communes*,[35] of which Cicero's *Topica* is the classical treatment; others, like Johann Reuchlin, with whose works Donne was well acquainted, give a digest of the places that they think most useful for the preacher.

From their treatment of comparison, which is one of these *loci*, it becomes apparent that a comparison has other than purely decorative functions. The *loci communes*, as Reuchlin holds, quite in accordance with tradition, are *sedes argumentorum;* arguments to prove or to disprove are derived from them or formed by means of them. The place *comparatio*, as described by Reuchlin, has some resemblance to a logical inference:

> The comparison of the larger is whenever that which is smaller is compared to the larger. We will argue from this place as follows: John 15[:20]. The servant is not greater than his lord. If they have persecuted me, they will also persecute you; if they have kept my saying, they will keep yours also. This is the argument from the larger. A larger statement is the following: What holds in the larger instance holds in the smaller. Likewise, if the larger is present, then the smaller is too.
>
> The comparison of the minor is whenever the larger is compared to the smaller. From here an argument is taken

like this: Heb. 9[:13]. For if the blood of bulls and goats, and the ashes of an heifer sprinkling the unclean, sanctifieth to the purifying of the flesh: How much more shall the blood of Christ, who through the eternal Spirit offered himself without spot to God, purge your conscience from dead works to serve the living God? This is the *locus* from the smaller. A larger statement is: What holds in the smaller case should also hold in the larger. Likewise, when the smaller is absent, the larger also seems absent.

Those are called equal which are of the same rank. From this *locus* the argument in 1 Cor. 9[:5] is derived: Have we not a right to take about with us a sister, a wife, as do the other apostles, and the brethren of the Lord, and Cephas? Is it only Barnabas and I who have not the right to do this? This is an argument from the comparison of equals. A larger statement is the following: Of equal things the judgment is the same.[36]

All three kinds of *comparatio* have some resemblance to the process of deduction. Of course the criterion is not that an item is a member of a class, as in a syllogism, for the division into classes and species is only one way of arranging things in a hierarchy; one can base the arrangement on other differences, such as the difference between lord and servant, between the sacrificial blood of steers and goats, and the sacramental blood of Christ. Reuchlin's passage can be understood only in terms of a supposed existence of some hierarchical order. The inference the preacher is to make by his comparison rests on the previous establishment of the relative rank of the things compared; he can achieve the purpose of the figure only if the audience accepts his evaluation and follows him in such a conclusion as the author of the epistle to the Hebrews introduces by his "how much more."

Donne's wolf story and Avila's lover analogy are *comparationes minoris*. In both cases the "lower" sphere is adduced for explanation and the audience is made to see "how much more" the point holds on the higher level. In Donne's story the wolf, by its nature, is bad, which is true also of the devil, who seeks whom he may devour; in this respect at least the passage is congruent. If it is not entirely successful, this is because of the inadequacies that were pointed out above. Juan de Avila, on the other hand, spells out exactly why he thinks his comparison is deficient: not that the difference in degree is in itself a deficiency, but that the person is "good here and bad there." Surely the indecorum, if there is indecorum at all, is very slight, since the preacher acknowledges the deficiency. It is fairly safe to say that Donne does not use any such manifestly or even seemingly indecorous figures. An indecorous figure is of course "bad"; it results in a failure to persuade. Robert Cawdrey, who compiled a handbook of similes "for all estates of men in generall" and for preachers in particular, is less judicious in the application of the rules of decorum when he writes that "as where the dead carkasse is, thither resort the Eagles: Euen so where are men that truly beleeue in Christ, there is the Church." [37]

The following passage from Donne, which is typical of his use of imagery, is completely in keeping with the precepts found in such books on ecclesiastical rhetoric as Reuchlin's:

As gold whilest it is in the mine, in the bowels of the earth, is good for nothing, and when it is out, and beaten to the thinnesse of leafgold, it is wasted and blown away, and quickly comes to nothing; But when it is tempered with such allay, as it may receive a stamp and impression, then it is currant and usefull: So whilest Gods Justice lyes in the bowels of his own decree and purpose, and is not executed at all, we take no knowledge that there is any such thing; And when Gods Justice is dilated to such an expansion, as it overflowes all alike, whole Armies with the sword, whole Cities with the plague, whole Countryes with famine, oftentimes we lose the consideration of Gods Justice, and fall upon some naturall causes, because the calamity is faln so indifferently upon just and unjust, as that, we thinke, it could not be the act of God: but when Gods Justice is so allayd with his wisedome, as that we see he keeps a Goshen in Aegypt, and saves his servants in the destruction of his enemies, then we come to a rich and profitable use of his Justice. [3:148, 5:536]

What is popularly considered as the token of value is here compared to something the preacher considers valuable. In this sense the simile is a *comparatio parium*. The analogy between God's justice and gold is maintained to the end. But within this simile a scale of values expressing various degrees of justice is defined by the techniques of processing the gold.

Donne's imagery indicates his concern with ordering the universe through evaluation. It is and must be his intent as a preacher to exalt the spiritual, an intent that he once expressed by the programmatic statement, "A dram of spirituall is worth infinite talents of temporal" (3:85, 2:435). But a mere duality between the spirit and the flesh, between this world and the next, is neither intellectually satisfying nor rhetorically effective. Donne has a strong feeling for "degree," not unlike that articulated by Robert Bellarmine in a passage from *The Ascent of the Mind to God: By a Ladder of Things Created*:

But although the multitude of creatures is admirable and declareth the manifold perfections of God, yet more admirable is the variety of things which is seen in that multiplication. For it is not hard, with one seal to express many figures alike, or with the same mould to print innumerable letters; but to distinguish the former's almost infinite ways, as God did in the creation is plainly a divine work, most worthy of admiration. To omit those things which are most indifferent and unlike; in the individuals of herbs, plants, flowers and fruits, what great variety there is: Their figures, colours, odours, tastes, how wonderfully distinguished! And is not the like also in living creatures that have sense? But what shall I say of men, since in a great army there can hardly be found two men alike. Which is also verified in the stars and in the angels: *For one star differeth from another in bright-*

*ness* [1 Cor. 15:41] as the Apostle witnesseth in the first to the Corinthians. And St. Thomas saith that the angels, although they exceed corporal things in number, yet they all differ among themselves, not only in individual number but also in specifical form.

Lift up then, my soul, thine eyes to God, in whom are the causes of all things; and from whom, as from a fountain of infinite plenty, this almost infinite variety did flow.[38]

As Arthur O. Lovejoy points out, Bellarmine sums up a long Neoplatonic and Christian tradition.[39] It is impossible to point to any single work that might particularly have impressed the importance of hierarchical principles on Donne's mind: it might have been Thomas Aquinas's *Summa* or Bellarmine's *Ascent* or a number of other works. At least twice Donne quotes Augustine for a witty comparison based on a typical hierarchial distinction: "*Musca Soli praeferenda, quia vivit*, A Fly is a nobler creature than the Sunne, because a fly hath life" (2:341, 17:237 and 3:329, 15:598).

The universe is an articulated whole in which all being is well arranged according to higher genera and lower species, as in a chain, tree, or ladder. A similar reduction to one dimension, to a span or distance between things, is expressed in Bellarmine's paraphrase of Ecclesiasticus 1:3: "If, therefore, Ecclesiasticus said: *Who hath measured the breadth of the earth and the depth of the abyss?* what would he have said of the compass of the highest heaven, and distance thereof unto the lowest hell?" [40] The scale begins with inorganic matter, encompasses the animal world, in which the order and degree of human society is reflected, and ends with the hierarchical levels of those who dwell in heaven. This structure is seen as instituted by God, and is constantly asserted by Donne's metaphors.

The hierarchical structure of the world, for instance, serves Donne as the basis for arguing that individual man should keep to his station:

A *dogge* murmures not that he is not a *Lion*, nor a *blindeworm* without eyes, that he is not a *Basilisk* to kill with his eyes; *Dust* murmures not that it is not *Amber*, nor a *Dung-hill* that it is not a *Mine*, nor an *Angell* that he is not of the *Seraphim.* [7:420, 17:196]

The logic of this hierarchy should of course not be pressed too far. It does not have the consistency of a system like Linné's. Some of the passages quoted above show that there is a clear line between organic and inorganic matter. But superimposed are standards that are essentially anthropomorphic. The lion, as the king of the animals, dominates all the others; gold and amber, because of their value in human society, are on one end of a scale of which the other is occupied by dust.

The hierarchy in human society is the type and model of all others, and Donne's images attest to his strong feeling for what is proper to the position, rank, or dignity of a person:

It is a lamentable thing to fall under a necessity of suffering in our age. *Labore fracta instrumenta, ad Deum ducis, quorum nullus usus?* wouldest thou consecrate a Chalice to God that is broken? no man would present a lame horse, a disordered clock, a torn book to the King. *Caro jumentum,* thy body is thy beast; and wilt thou present that to God, when it is lam'd and tir'd with excesse of wontonness? [2:244, 11:339]

Here Basil supplies Donne with the basic argument, but the analogies drawn from the decorum of a royal court are his own. Similarly, the idea of looking at Augustine's *caro iumentum* as a present for God is Donne's own.

Additional proof for the argument presented in these pages can be found in Donne's comments on scriptural style:

Certainly in those passages, which are from lower persons to Princes, no Author is of a more humble, and reverentiall, and ceremoniall phrase, than the phrase of the Scripture is. Who could goe lower than *David* to *Saul,* that calls himselfe a *flea,* and a *dead dogge?* Who could goe higher, then *Daniel* to *Nebuchadnezzar, O King, thou art King of Kings; In all places, the children of men, the beasts of the field, the fouls*

*of the ayre are given into thy hand; Thy greatnesse reacheth
to heaven, and thy dominions to the end of the earth.* So it
is also in persons nearer in nature, and nearer in ranke, *Iacob
bowes seaven times to the ground,* in the presence of his
brother *Esau,* and *My Lord,* and *My Lord,* at every word.
[9:358, 16:292]

What Donne points out here and praises is that in dialogue the
style of the Scriptures varies according to the speaker's distance
"in nature" and "in ranke" from the person addressed. David in-
dictates his submission by the "low" metaphors that he uses to
humble himself, Daniel by the hyperboles that praise Nebuchadnezzar. Donne sums up his admiration in the sentence, "The
Scripture phrase is as ceremoniall and as observant of distances,
as any, and yet full of this familiar word too, *Tu* and *Tuus,*
*Thou* and *Thine*" (9:358, 16:302).

Decorum, then, is a flexible principle. According to the subject
matter it may demand that the style be lowered or that it be
elevated.[41] How this works in Donne's sermons remains to be
studied in greater detail.

# The Lowering of Style

The books on ecclesiastical rhetoric allow for a variety of modes
of preaching. Nowhere do they say that the preacher's words
should be uniformly bland. Agostino Valerio writes:

> It is the decorum of the sermon that it be agitated or calm
> as is fitting for the subject matter; it will be agitated, however,
> if the preacher himself conceives those emotions and feelings
> to which he tries to bring his audience; so that if the crimes
> and disgraceful acts of men are to be inveighed against,
> which is often necessary, he shall speak sharply, impetuously,
> vehemently; if the compassion for [of?] the people is to be

roused, if the troubles and miseries of the poor are to be explained, if Christ's sufferings are to be expressed by the sermon, especially on the sixth feast day of Holy Week, if the violence and greatness of the Holy Virgin's sorrows at that time and often are to be commended; the preacher shall adapt himself to his subject matter by his words . . . sentences, voice, features, and finally by his tears.[42]

It has been observed that Donne sometimes moved himself to tears, that he seemed to preach to himself,[43] that he assumed the role of the sinner, speaking with the words and in the manner of such converts as Paul and Augustine. The passage from Valerio is adduced here not in order to reduce his personal way of preaching to some common and accepted pattern but simply to show that there existed at the time of the Counter Reformation a theory of preaching that justified perfectly what in later centuries would have been mere eccentricity.

It is one of the duties of the preacher to inveigh against sin and sinners; to do so he will have to choose appropriate images. The lowering of one subject, then, is as decorous as the commendation of another, as is borne out by the following words of George Puttenham:

After the Auancer followeth the abbaser working by wordes and sentences of extenuation or diminution. Whereupon we call him the *Disabler* or figure of *Extenuation:* and this extenuation is vsed to diuers purposes, sometimes for modesties sake, and to auoide the opinion of arrogancie, speaking of ourselues or of ours, as he that disabled himselfe to his mistresse, thus . . . It may be also done for despite to bring our aduersaries in contempt.[44]

Using sin (as something *malum* and *nocivum*) as an example, Didacus Stella had given the clear if somewhat commonplace precept for the coining of tropes that I quoted earlier: "But the things that must be compared to something bad are generally of a base degree or quality, which are likened completely or in part.

Such are filth, poison, viper, venom, captivity, ulcer, slime, snake, etc." If the reader wonders how a sinner shall be compared to *lutum* ("mud") and *limus* ("slime") he may find an example in Donne:

> I came to a feeling in my selfe, what my sinfull condition was. This is our quickning in our regeneration, and second birth; and till this come, a sinner lies as the Chaos in the beginning of the Creation, before the *Spirit of God had moved upon the face of the waters, Dark, and voyd, and without forme;* He lies, as we may conceive, out of the Authors of Naturall Story, the slime and mud of the River *Nilus* to lie, before the Sun-beames strike upon it. [9:299, 13:95]

Donne likes the saying of the Psalmist, "Vermis ego et non homo" (Ps. 22:6), which perfectly agrees with Stella's precept, since it compares the sinner to the lowest form of life. Donne quotes it (2:243, 11:289), elaborates it: "They who being but worms, will look into Heaven" (1:170, 2:66), and even tries to surpass it: "Thou wast worse than a worm, there's matter of humiliation" (2:247, 11:450). Using a quote from Origen as a motto, he illustrates it, along Stella's lines, by a number of metaphors for the sinner that are meant to show the various forms of his depravity:

> *Nam quem Daemones possident, non unus sed multi. . . .* The same sinner is not the same thing; still he clambers in his ambitious purposes, there he is an Eagle; and yet lies still groveling, and trodden upon at any greater mans threshold, there he is a worme. He swells to all that are under him, there he is a full Sea; and his dog that is above him, may wade over him, there he is a shallow, an empty River. In the compasse of a few dayes, he neighes like a horse in the rage of his lust over all the City, and groanes in a corner of the City, in an hospitall. [3:228, 10:110]

The terms of the various comparisons are chosen so as to contrast with each other to show the many sides of sin. There is the contrast between high and low, swollen and empty, and finally the ingenious and cruelly effective contrast between the sinner's cries of joy—likened to the neighing of a horse, traditionally the embodiment of lust—and his groaning in the hospital.

It is of course significant that Donne likes to quote passages that already contain radically diminishing tropes. These then provide him with the key for subsequent elaboration in which he carries diminution one step further:

> *Erubesce vas stercorum,* says good Saint *Bernard,* If it be a vessell of gold, it is but a vessell of excrements, if it be a bed of curious plants, it is but a bed of dung. [5:172, 8:151]

Not satisfied with the neutral "vessell" which translates Latin *vas,* Donne eventually changes it to "barrell of dung" (5:172, 8:156).

In general, though, Donne does not go far beyond Stella's menagerie. The following passage deals with the hubris of man:

> Hee reproaches that God who made him rich, his owne Maker. Now, doth he consider, that the Devill hath superinduced a *half-lycanthropy* upon him, The Devill hath made him halfe a *wolfe,* so much a wolfe as that he would tear all that fall into his power, And half a *spider,* so much a spider, as that hee would entangle all that come near him, And half a *Viper,* so much a Viper, as that he would envenome all that any way provoke him. Does he consider that the Devill hath made him half a wolfe, halfe a spider, half a viper, and doth hee not consider that that God that is his Maker, could have made him a *whole Wolfe,* a whole Spider, a whole Viper, and left him in that rank of ignoble, and contemptible, and mischievous creatures? [8:284, 12:518]

The passage is framed according to some such rule as Stella's. One creature of "base order or quality" after another is paired with the sinner and the resemblance pointed out. To suit his purpose Donne sometimes varies his zoo slightly and uses wolf, serpent, and goat (9:58, 1:410).

Maybe such figures are not Donne's best. One can find more effective debasing tropes in his epistles, his *Songs and Sonnets*, and even his *Ignatius*. And yet, in a study of his tropes they are particularly interesting, since they represent, as it were, a slow-motion picture of how he forms his images. What contributes to this effect is that in his sermons he often first indicates the logical place around which he will frame the image, that is, he states the theme in some way before "laying on colours." Of course he is thereby directing the attention of the audience; but this feature is responsible for the mechanical impression that many of these images make, compared with those of his poetry. In the passage quoted below he sets up the difference between God's positive and man's negative ways and then systematically diminishes the man, who is in Goethe's words "der Geist, der stets verneint":

> Gods way is positive, and thine is privative: God made every thing something, and thou mak'st the best of things, man, nothing; and because thou canst not annihilate the world altogether, as though thou hadst God at an advantage, in having made an abridgment of the world in man, there in that abridgment thou wilt undermine him, and make man, man, as far as thou canst, man in thy self nothing. He that qualifies himself for nothing, does so; He whom we can call nothing, is nothing: this whole world is one intire creature, one body; and he that is nothing may be excremental nailes, to scratch and gripe others, he may be excremental hairs for ornament, or pleasurableness of meeting, but he is no limb of this intire body, no part of Gods universal creature, the world. [8:177, 7:119]

The argument is that the sinner reduces himself to nothing; Donne diminishes him to "excremental nailes" and "excremental hairs." Taken out of their context, these figures might be felt to be shocking if not in bad taste. Yet they are the result of radical diminution and the telescoping of the macrocosm of the world into the microcosm of man.

It is probably not the whole truth to interpret Donne's forth-right statement of the intellectual purpose of the figure, which accounts for the slow-motion effect mentioned above, as a mere concession to the powers of comprehension of the congregation. At times it seems as if Donne would like to stimulate his audience to diminish the subject along a suggested line. This would accord with the contemporary interest in meditational techniques, which Louis Martz has traced from Ignatius of Loyola to such an un-compromising Protestant as Baxter.[45] The appeal to the con-gregation or to the readers to direct their imagination along a suggested line is as apparent in Donne as it is in Bellarmine, one of the most successful preachers of the Counter Reformation:

> And surely of the matter of our bodies there can be no doubt, but that it is *that Nothing*, than the which what can be imagined more vacant and vile? The immediate matters of the body, what is it but menstruous blood?[46]

> If thine imagination could carry thee so low, as to think, not onely that thou wert become some other thing, a fish, or a dogge that had fed upon thee . . . [3:97, 3:214]

Only by stretching the concept, and maybe overstretching it, can the passage from Donne be treated under the heading of figurative discourse. In its form it is close to a straight predica-tion. Yet the subjunctive mood has some of the value of an *ut ita dicam*, and so there may be some justification for seeing the pas-sage as containing metaphors in an embryonic state, or as supply-ing us with the two constituents of a metaphor (tenor and vehicle) and at the same time also with the method by which these are derived: ". . . if thine imagination could carry thee so low . . ."

It is possible, though, to find even in Donne's sermons the kind of brisk diminishings that Rosemond Tuve observed in his poetry.[47] One of the uses of Puttenham's "disabler" is "in de-rision and for a kind of contempt," and Donne uses the figure effectively. Sects, to him, "are not bodies, they are but rotten boughes, gangrened limmes, fragmentary chips, blowne off by their owne spirit of turbulency" (3:87, 2:540). Sometimes he gives his figures a sudden twist, as in the following example:

> Look upon the *water*, and we are as that, and as that spilt upon the ground: Looke to the *earth*, and we are not like that, but we are earth it self: At our Tables we feed upon the dead, and in the Temple we tread upon the dead. [3:202, 8:569]

The diminution is here not quite obvious in the initial simile, but it is accomplished in another clause with unexpected suddenness.

According to Puttenham, the "disabler" is used "for despite to bring our adversaries in contempt." [48] It is the prime instrument for satire, which Donne directs against various sins and sinners. The hypocrite, for instance, "hath no true joy at all; his joy is but dunge, and in a moment comes a Cart, and fetches away that dunge, sweeps away even that false joy" (1:190, 3:254). It can be directed against magistrates who betray their calling: "And then, if the *Magistrate* stops his Eares with *Wooll*, (with staple bribes, profitable bribes) and with *Cyvet* in his wooll, (perfumes of pleasure and preferment in his bribes) hee falsifies *Gods* Word . . ." (6:244, 12:131). Its target may be an idle prelate who is "a spunge, to drinke up the sweat of others and live idly" (10:143, 6:103), or, more generally, "men that make themselves but pipes to receive and convay, and vent rumors, but spunges to sucke in, and powre out foule water" (4:190, 7:396). The vehicles used in such diminishing tropes are far from uncommon in homiletic literature. One may compare Donne's sponge metaphor with Cawdrey's simile, "As a Spunge gathereth up all liquor, whether it be good or bad: Euen so som Hearers of Sermons, receiue all that is spoken good and evill." [49] Donne, however, lays on some extra colors by stressing the foulness of the water, and he gives the false joy-dung figure a final twist.

Occasionally there is a touch of irony, as when Donne assumes the role of a "curious" man, that is, of someone whom he accuses of the sin of curiosity in theology:

> Let me know the Cabal, that which passed betweene God and him [Moses], in all the rest of the forty dayes. I care not for Gods revealed Will, his Acts of Parliament, his publique Proclamations, Let me know his Cabinet Counsailes, his bosome, his pocket dispatches. [3:330, 15:636]

A chief target of Donne's satire is the Church of Rome and her most efficient representatives during the Counter Reformation, the Jesuits:

> A Carthusian is but a man of fish, for one Element, to dwell still in a Pond, in his Cell alone, but a Jesuit is a usefull *ubiquitary*, and his Scene is the Court, as well as the Cloister. [3:169, 6:488]

Sometimes Donne is not even witty, but just caters to cruder tastes, as when he calls the Roman church a "pest-house":

> for the Pest-house is a house, and theirs is such a Church; But the Pest-house is not the best ayre to live in, nor the Romane Church the best Church to die in. [9:344, 15:372]

On the subject of the "Italian Babylon" there is a curious passage in which he satirizes the excesses of some Italian preachers, whom unfortunately he does not name, preachers who filled their sermons with "Soloecismes, the barbarismes, the servilities, the stupid ignorance of those things which fall within the knowledge of boys of the first forme in every School" (10:149, 6:334). His use of the metaphor "God's sheep" in this passage is of course not a figure of meiosis, since the image is firmly established by the biblical parable of the Good Shepherd, but the goose as the animal of proverbial stupidity, here used to represent such preachers, clearly is:

> This was their treading down of grass, not with over-much learning, but with a cloud, a dampe, an earth of ignorance.

After an *Oxe* that oppresseth the grass, after a *Horse* that devours the grass, sheep will feed; but after a *Goose* that stanches the grass, they will not; no more can Gods sheep receive nourishment from him that puts a scorne upon his function, by his ignorance. [10:149, 6:336]

Puttenham explains that the "disabler or figure of extenuation" is used "sometimes for modesties sake, and to avoid opinion of arrogancie, speaking of our selues or of ours, as he that disabled himself to his mistresse, thus. . . ." [50] His book is written for courtiers and ladies in waiting, who might be kissed by the Muses and try their hand at some occasional verses. In the sermon, with its different subject matter, the figure is often used by Donne to diminish man and so bring out the discrepancy between his insignificance and God's greatness. He naturally has a predilection for biblical images which express this disproportion:

He to us, God to man; all to nothing: for upon that we insist first, as the first disproportion betweene us, and so the first exaltation of his mercy towards us. *Man is*, says the Prophet *Esay, Quasi stilla situlae, As a drop upon the bucket.* [9:136, 5:177]

But as far as the ability to diminish goes, Donne is hardly dependent on his models. He can debase or inflate any subject as fast as or faster than the pope, who, he says, can make a cardinal "first a *Giant*, and then a *dwarfe* in an houre" (10:157, 6:645):

And is any one *rationall Ant*, (The wisest *Phylosopher* is no more) Is any *roaring Lyon*, (the most ambitious and devouring *Prince* is no more) Is any *hive of Bees* (The wisest of *Councels*, and *Parliaments* are no more) Is any of these so established, as that, that *God* who by a *word*, by a *thought*, made them of *nothing*, cannot . . . reduce them to *nothing* againe? [7:80, 2:252]

Donne here adopts a superhuman perspective and reduces human society to the level of the animal world. In the context of what

I tried to show earlier, it is interesting to note that this animal world remains well differentiated until Donne finally converts the *ex nihilo* to an *ad nihil*.

Some of those macabre images, which have sometimes been taken as indicating a strange temperament if not a morbid preoccupation with the gruesome, are nothing but the result of such consistent diminution. "The dust of dead kings blowne into the Street" in the following quotation is an example of such radical meiosis:

> To save this body from the condemnation of everlasting corruption, where the wormes that we breed are our betters, because they have a life, where the dust of dead Kings is blowne into the street, and the dust of the street blowne into the River, and the muddy River tumbled into the Sea, and the Sea remaunded into all the veynes and channels of the earth; to save this body from everlasting dissolution, dispersion, dissipation, and to make it in a glorious Resurrection, not onely a Temple of the holy Ghost, but a Companion of the holy Ghost in the kingdome of heaven, This *Christ* became this *Iesus*. [3:302, 14:377]

The presentation of the body in a state in which "the worms that we breed are our betters" is the usual *non plus ultra* of Donne's diminution. It perfectly serves his purpose in this passage, which is to abase the body in its condition before or without sanctification through the Incarnation. At the same time this passage shows once again that diminution does not defy hierarchical principles but makes use of them: They are at the basis of such an argument as that "the worms that we breed are our betters" because they are alive, as well as of Augustine's sentence, "A fly should be preferred to the sun, because it has life." Of course method should not be confused with theme or subject. Donne's theme can be to show that all people, whether of high or of low degree, are reduced to dust:

> As soon the dust of a wretch whom thou wouldest not, as of a Prince whom thou couldest not look upon, will trouble

thine eyes, if the winde blow it thither; and when a whirle-
winde hath blowne the dust of the Church-yard into the
Church, and the man sweeps out the dust of the Church into
the Church-yard, who will undertake to sift those dusts
again, and to pronounce, This is the Patrician, this is the noble
flowre, and this the yeomanly, this the Plebeian bran? [4:53,
1:296]

One will hardly be able to argue that the *presentation* of this
theme, so popular in art, defies hierarchical principles; on the
contrary, such differences as those between nobleman and yeo-
man, patrician and plebeian, are firm elements of that presentation.

The previous pages should have shown that applying the concept of diminution is a convenient way to describe Donne's
method in a number of significant figures. The fact that Donne
effectively abases rhetorically has been firmly established. Moreover, there is little doubt in my mind that Donne, when he formed
such tropes, thought in such terms as diminution or its complement, heightening or amplification, although by the nature of the
question this cannot be proven quite so conclusively.

Normally Donne uses the word *diminution* either in the general
sense of a lessening, as when he speaks of a "diminution of affections" (3:254, 11:494) or in the sense of humiliation (humbling),
as when he talks of "St. *Pauls* diminution, to be changed from
*Saul*, to *Paulus*, (which is *little*)" (1:209, 3:972). But at least two
passages show that the approach to Donne's imagery that is
applied in these pages is in accord with his own way of thinking.
One of the passages is of the kind that readers of anthologies
or selected sermons tend to remember as typical of Donne's
imagery. The theme is once again the discrepancy between man
and God:

Man, whom *Paracelsus* would have undertaken to have made,
in a Limbeck, in a Furnace: Man, who, if they were altogether, all the men, that ever were, and are, and shall be,
would not have the power of one Angel in them all, whereas
all the Angels, (who, in the Schoole are conceived, to be

more in number, then, not onely all the Species, but all the
individualls of this lower world) have not in them all, the
power of one finger of Gods hand: Man, of whom when
*David* had said, (as the lowest diminution that he could put
upon him) *I am a worme and no man* [Ps. 22:6], He might
have gone lower, and said, I am a man and no worm; for
man is so much lesse then a worme, as that wormes of his
own production, shall feed upon his dead body in the grave,
and an immortall worm gnaw his conscience in the torments
of hell. [9:136, 5:199]

The steps of this debunking of man are clear: Donne draws on
the "chemical" theory of Paracelsus with the suggestion of dis-
grace and degradation—in his *Ignatius* he places the inventor of
modern chemistry in hell[51]—then drives home the baseness of man
by pointing to his position, the "lower world," in the hierarchy of all beings; finally he adduces David's word and—this
is the point of interest—analyzes, as it were, its rhetorical function "as the lowest diminution he could put upon him." This
parenthesis interprets David's metaphor and shows at the same
time that Donne is aware of the method he is using himself, a
method that he continues to use as he proceeds to outdo David
in his diminution.

If the last quotation showed Donne's theory and practice, there
is another passage that is more specifically critical in nature. It
is interesting for the terms Donne uses as well as for what it says:

And for the third mariage, the eternall mariage, it is a bold-
nesse to speak any thing of a thing so inexpressible as the
joyes of heaven; it is a diminution of them to goe about to
heighten them; it is a shadowing of them to go about to lay
any colours or lights upon them. [3:250, 11:321]

The expressions *diminution, to heighten, to lay on colours*, are
clearly used in the specific rhetorical sense. At the same time
this is more than a mere rephrasing of what E. R. Curtius has
called the "inexpressibility topos."[52] Donne's rhetorical inability

has theological overtones. This relation between rhetorical heightening and the possible dilemma of the preacher who finds himself unable to speak of the Divine in adequate terms deserves some closer attention.

# The Heightening of Style: How to Speak of God as a Question of Rhetoric

According to some writers, the main function of amplification is to commend a thing.[53] It is the opposite of diminution, which "descends by the same steps that amplification ascends by." [54] Amplification differs from diminution "no otherwise than up-hill and down-hill; which is the same way, begun at several times." [55] Other writers, Hyperius, for example, use *amplification* in a wider sense to mean techniques of both commendation and diminution. What is important, however, is to note that commendation, like its counterpart, is tied to the theory of decorum. Thus Hyperius points out that in amplifying, the preacher should bring his congregation to a sense of the "right scope," which will make any object seem to them "so great as it is meate and requisite." [56]

In practice, Donne's method of amplifying by tropes sometimes consists in simply changing the name of a thing to a higher term denoting the same referent. The figures that result vary from ordinary definitions to tropes, when the change of name is more radical. It is impossible and perhaps not important to say exactly where definition ends and metaphor, properly speaking, begins. Both kinds of figures can be studied in the following passage describing a man at peace with God:

> His Rye-bread is *Manna*, and his Beefe is *Quailes*, his day-labours are thrustings at the narrow gate into Heaven, and his night-watchings are extasies and evocations of his soule

into the presence and communion of Saints, his sweat is *Pearls*, and his bloud is *Rubies*, it is at peace with God. [10:131, 5:455]

Rhetorical heightening may be achieved by other means. In one case Donne introduces the division of his sermon by calling Paul's Epistle to the Romans a "circle," which he then heightens to "ring." Finally he chooses only terms of value that go with a piece of jewelry:

for the circle of this Epistle of S. *Paul*, this precious ring, being made of that golden Doctrine, That Justification is by faith, and being enameled with that beautifull Doctrine of good works too, in which enameled Ring, as a precious stone in the midst thereof, there is set, the glorious Doctrine of our Election, by Gods eternall Predestination, our Text falls in that part, which concernes obedience, holy life, good works. [3:377, 18:27]

The encoding of meaning in the three metaphors *gold, enamel,* and *precious stone,* which are so chosen as to form one larger image, has some obvious similarity to the technique of emblem writers. It is one of many techniques of amplification.

The problem of how to speak of God appropriately could not fail to present itself to a preacher during the seventeenth century. It was a question of rhetoric and also of theology. Although I will deal only with the rhetorical problem, both questions can be viewed as only two aspects of the larger problem of decorum.

On the rhetorical level, the problem presented itself to a Spanish writer on pulpit oratory in this manner:

There are, however, many warnings which the orator must heed in the use of metaphors. First that they be not taken from remote things, as when someone should call Christ "serenissimus" because he is a king, since kings are called by that name. Finally that they do not originate from anything unseemly, as when someone would call God the killer of Christ; for he commanded that he should die for the sins of men so that he satisfy by that death divine Justice and open the gates of Heaven to believing men. He ought not for that reason to be called killer; and, in short, easy metaphors, taken from beautiful things and applied with judgement, which wise men have called the essence of prudence, illuminate the sermon.[57]

Here Valerio enunciates precepts for the right use of metaphor similar to the theoretical statements about imagery contained in other current books of ecclesiastical rhetoric. Such theory prompted the approach used thus far in this study, namely, to observe the nexus between the theory of metaphor and the principle of decorum, and then to examine Donne's imagery in relation to this principle. Valerio repeats the doctrine that tenor and vehicle should not be too far apart. Without probing into the problem of how a metaphor for God can be anything but remote, he then suggests an equally familiar principle: It is not a superficial point of similarity between two things, but their relationship within a hierarchy of values that is the criterion for successful metaphor. Such a hierarchy is the basis of the lowering as well as the heightening of style. In the specific case of finding metaphors for God, Valerio points out that the preacher has to be careful not to take them *ab ulla re turpi*, that is, from anything low, ugly, or unseemly. Unfortunately Valerio's principle, as a caveat, is mainly negative and therefore only of limited value as a point of comparison with Donne's images.

God has created all things but he has also, as Donne once expressed it, "placed his Creatures in divers rankes, and in divers conditions" (7:417, 17:64). Rain seems "but an imperfect, and ignoble creature, fallen from the wombe of a cloud" (7:417, 17:75). Light, on the other hand, as Donne points out in the same paragraph, occupies a very high rank. This fact, along with biblical models, of course, would be a theoretical justification for all those images in which Donne speaks of God in terms of light. Thus he transforms Damascene's bland "Divinum miraculis lucet" very successfully into "The Godhead bursts out, as the Sun

out of a cloud, and shines forth gloriously in miracles . . ."
(3:299, 14:272). It is true that the analogy between God and the
sun is one of the commonest in religious literature. One of the
steps of Bellarmine's *Ascent,* for instance, consists in recognizing
the analogy which is spelled out in the title of one section:
"The Sun Giveth Light and Heat; God also Giveth Wisdom and
Charity." [58] But Donne's image is so much more effective probably because of the little detail of the cloud and because of his
emphasis on action rather than on the analogy in the abstract,
which is motivated by decorum.

The sound figure Son-sun, which Donne is so fond of in his
poetry as well as in his prose, has the same justification. Father Ong
has shown the seriousness and meaning of such wordplay in
medieval hymnody,[59] so that it has become difficult to agree
with one critic of Lancelot Andrewes who calls the preacher's
puns "the most outrageous of his verbal faults." [60]

The following quotation from Donne, which contains the pun,
has the seriousness and beauty that comes from consistent amplification:

> But the Father sent him [the Holy Ghost], and the Son sent
> him, as a tree sends forth blossomes, and as those blos-
> somes send forth a sweet smell, and as the Sun sends forth
> beames, by an emanation from it selfe. [9:240, 10:311]

The images here flow with an ease reminiscent of Crashaw's
poetry.

Donne uses the analogy between God and a king throughout
his years as a preacher. The purpose of the analogy is of course
to explain the invisible in terms of the visible. But it would be
surprising if Donne did not, like other court preachers, such as
Lancelot Andrewes and Paravecino de Arteaga, use the analogy
both ways: as a decorous metaphor for God, since it uses the
highest civil magistrate, and also as a tribute to the king, before
whom he often preaches.

When Donne says, "Christ beats his drum," I doubt that we
have to picture Him as Grass's Oskar sitting behind his tin drum.

It is rather the image of Christ as the warrior or the general, the same idea Juan de Avila expresses when he calls Christ "Capitán." [61] Donne makes that clear when he says that Christ is a general with a difference: "He does not Press men; Christ is serv'd with Voluntaries" (7:156, 5:563).

In ten volumes of sermons there are of course some passages about God that are somewhat more difficult to justify by the principle of rhetorical decorum. Some involve typology and will be examined in that context later. Others may be called anthropomorphic. Consider the following passage in which Donne shows God whetting his arrows:

> Till *Daniel* prayed, there went out no commandment. At the beginning of the sinners sin, God bends his bow, and whets his arrows, and at last he shoots; But if there were no sin in me, God had no mark to shoot at; for God hates not me, nor any thing that he hath made. [8:316, 14:163]

With Donne, blatant anthropomorphism always stands in some relation to Old Testament figures. He observed: "God himself, who is all spirit, hath yet put on bodily lineaments, Head, and Hands, and Feet, yea and Garments too, in many places of Scripture, to appear, that is, to manifest himself to us," and he concluded, "when we appear to God . . . let us put on lineaments and apparel upon our Devotions" (8:338, 15:126). The specific source of the passage quoted above is Psalm 7:12, where God is said to "whet his sword" and to have "bent his bow and made it ready" to shoot the wicked. Donne was certain, as I have shown, that in passages in which "lower persons" address themselves to their superiors the Scriptures were examples of decorum (their language is "ceremoniall" and "observant of distances" [9:358, 16:303]). But although biblical practice elsewhere cannot be said always to agree with the theory of rhetorical decorum, Donne was spared the scruples Augustine, a former teacher of rhetoric, had to overcome before he was able to appreciate the style of the Scriptures. The Bible had become a model in itself, and as long as Donne made it clear that his trope derived from a biblical model,[62] and as long as he set up a suitable context

—in this sermon provided by a number of quotations that credit God with human emotions—his metaphor was not felt to be indecorous.

The arrow, a frequent metaphor in the Bible, is only one of several weapons Donne attributes to God. When he speaks of prayer as God's cannon directed upon Himself, he takes care to introduce the passage by referring to Samson's unusual weapon. The complex idea of the working of prayer is expressed by paradoxical images:

> The jaw-bone of an Asse, in the hand of Samson, was a devouring sword. The words of man, in the mouth of a faithful man, of *Abraham*, are a Canon against God himselfe, and batter down all his severe and heavy purposes for Judgements. Yet, this comes not, God knows, out of the weight or force of our words, but out of the easiness of God. God puts himselfe into the way of a shot, he meets a weak prayer, and is graciously pleased to be wounded by that: God sets up a light, and we direct the shot upon him, he enlightens us with a knowledge, how, and when, and what to pray for; yea, God charges, and discharges the Canon himself upon himselfe; He fils us with good and religious thoughts, and appoints and leaves the Holy Ghost, to discharge them upon him, in prayer, for it is the Holy Ghost himselfe that prayes in us. [3:152, 5:680]

The first sentence of the quotation sets the tone for the whole passage: What is not credible in terms of human experience is possible by the power of God. Similarly the working of prayer, when expressed in human language, must sound paradoxical; the paradoxes can be resolved only on a higher level. Donne's images of God being shot at and shooting are deliberately so framed as to be impossibilities on this literal level. The analogy does not simply bring divinity down to the level of human experience; through the reduction it shows at the same time that this level provides but a poor analogue, that the Divine is beyond human motivation.

There is one passage in Donne's sermons in which God's actions are compared to such a profane occupation as playing with a ball:

> As he that flings a *ball* to the ground, or to a wall, intends in that action, that that ball should returne back, so even now, when God does throw me down, it is the way that he hath chosen to returne me to himselfe. [3:193, 8:239]

The passage is a borderline case; the principle of literary decorum derived from books of ecclesiastical rhetoric does not account for it. Of course this is less a fault of the simile than of the theory. Every trope has multiple relationships to other figures in the sermon as well as to certain tropes outside the sermon, a fact that will be considered in later sections of this study. Here I want only to point to the tradition of the literary emblem.

There is a Spanish emblem that shows a hand coming from behind some clouds. The hand, now open, has just released a ball, which is pictured bouncing up and down and up again. The motto of the emblem reads, "Reges Deus habet quasi pilas." For the proud princes who need to be reminded that they are to God like balls, the *subscriptio* under the picture spells out the following warning:

> Divine power at play throws the ball from on high,
> It plummets down and rebounds, it rises and falls.
> You are lifted into the sky, prince, beware the steep heights.
> If you are a ball in the divine hands, you will be a toy.[63]

A prose commentary follows and quotes a number of similar pronouncements by philosophers and poets—notably Plautus's "The gods play with us as with balls"—which shows that the idea of man as a plaything for the gods has a respectable history and was quite popular with the ancients. The quotations are not particularly critical or even satirical, but they are meant to stress the *misera rerum humanarum conditio,* as the commentary has it, and the power of Fate, a theme with which Englishmen of the Renaissance were well acquainted through their "mirrors," histories, and chronicles. Because of its long history, the analogy between God and the ballplayer, then, does not present as striking and profane an anthropomorphism as it may at first appear to.[64] That Donne, moreover, puts the analogy to a different use is obvious and need hardly be stressed.

There may be some justification in calling such a figure somewhat homely, although as I have tried to show, it can be seen against the background of an old literary tradition, and thus was probably not inspired by Donne's outdoor activities.[65] It is true that one might be hard put to find a precedent for such metaphors as Donne's reference to "God's bed-chamber." And yet even this image is only seemingly anthropomorphic. The two instances of the metaphor occur in a context in which Donne adopts a perspective which is not his own. If dissimulation and meiosis, that is, making oneself small or seemingly adopting a lower and more limited perspective, are at the core of irony, then both passages can be called ironical: "Where is this *bill* of thy *Divorce?* Thou must not look for it in *Gods bed-chamber*, in his *unreveal'd Decrees* in heaven, but in his publique *Records*, his *Scriptures*" (7:89, 2:593). In his earlier sermon Donne had said: "I enquire not what God did in his bed-chamber, in his cabinet counsell, in his eternall decree" (2:323, 15:448). In both cases the implicit metaphor is a regal one: God is a king, and it is not unusual to speak of a king's most private deliberations and decisions as those of his bedchamber and cabinet council. The metaphors are used to show the unseemliness of the theological speculation of those guilty of a vice Donne never tires of chastising: the vice of curiosity.

# Decorum and Learning

The examples adduced so far have mainly shown, through the theory and practice of Donne's preaching, his awareness of decorum as a principle regulating metaphorical expression in terms of subject matter. The principle is based on the conviction that "language must waite upon matter, and *words* upon *things*" (10:112, 4:326). There is of course another type of relationship governing decorum, that between speaker and audience. As was apparent from some of the passages quoted in my introductory pages, even early books on preaching seldom omit the advice that the preacher should adapt his sermon to the comprehension of his audience. It goes without saying that such a recommendation, if followed, will affect the imagery of the sermon. In the case of Donne, the large number of "judicial" tropes—especially in the sermons he preached to the law students of Lincoln's Inn —has long been noticed. It is also easy to see that certain kinds of his tropes are especially tailored to please the merchants of the Virginian Plantation, to whom he preaches (Gosse pointed out the interesting fact that Donne had once hoped to hold an office with that company),[66] or to flatter the king. However, an analysis of ways in which Donne's sermons are determined by his respective audience will necessarily lead to a sociological study. One would have to examine in detail who was present and what were the theological and political issues of the day.[67] A treatment of such issues limited to Donne's imagery would be a very partial one, since more obvious references to current theological controversy and politics are contained in nonfigurative passages. Therefore, rather than isolating the consideration of Donne's audience, I would like to address myself to a special problem that crystallizes for Donne both the consideration of subject matter and the taking into account of the audience: the use of learning in preaching. The problem has some direct relevance for imagery, for tropes were from one point of view taken to be the fruit of a conscious endeavor for which the *ingenium* ("wit") of the preacher had been trained through rhetoric,[68] but they could also be viewed as receptacles of learned matter. I will attempt to clarify Donne's ideas about the "seemlines" of learning for preaching by examining his position concerning the following particular points: the value of the "studied" sermon as opposed to unpremeditated preaching, his attitude toward commonplaces in sermons, and finally his answer to the question whether "secular learning" has a place in the preaching of the word of God.

It is interesting to note that Hyperius condemns extempore preaching on account of indecorum. The word *unseemly*, which is used by the English translator in the 1577 edition of *The Practis of Preaching*, is synonymous with *indecorous*. "Truly," he says, "there is nothing more unseemely, nothing more perilous, then if a man presume to teach in the Church *ex tempore*, and without premeditation, or rather rashly without choice to powre out euery thing." [69] However, the writer's objection against preaching "without choise" is only partly motivated by an aesthetic reason. Hyperius leaves no doubt that the issue is also, if not primarily, a matter of ecclesiastical decorum, that is, of church discipline. He points out that in former times sermons were carefully written out so that if someone was accused of heresy, every particular point could be verified.

Similarly, Donne prefers the carefully prepared sermon for reasons of both form and content. Preparation affects the pleasing quality of the sermon, an element that Donne sometimes expresses through the notions of sweetness (echoing the *dulce* traditionally taken to complement the *utile*) and tenderness.[70] Particularly, sound figures "entender" and "mollify" (6:156, 7:215). In a passage in which he describes the effect of a successful sermon, he makes Augustine his ally for careful preparation:

> S. *Augustine* does not onely professe of himselfe, *Non praetermitto istos numeros clausularum*, That he studied at home, to make his language sweet, and harmonious, and acceptable to Gods people, but he beleeves also, that S. *Paul* himselfe, and all the Apostles, had a delight, and a complacency, and a holy melting of the bowels, when the congregation liked their preaching. [8:149, 5:704]

The issue for Donne, however, is also quite clearly a matter of church discipline. He sees a functional link between careful preparation and theological conformity. He expresses this view by using 1 Thessalonians 4:11 as an ingenious prop:

> When the *Apostle* says, *study* to be *quiet*, me thinks he intimates something towards this, that the lesse we *study* for our Sermons, the more danger is there to disquiet the auditory; extemporall, unpremeditated Sermons, that serve the popular eare, vent, for the most part, doctrines that disquiet the Church. *Study* for them, and they *will be quiet;* consider ancient and fundamentall doctrines, and this will quiet and settle the understanding, and the Conscience. [10:174, 7:564]

The theme of the long paragraph from which this is taken is in the margin indicated as "separatistae." It is of course addressed to the Puritans, and Donne goes on to hold up an instance of Calvin's respect for tradition. In spite of the rather tenuous scriptural link, the passage just quoted is more than a polemical aside; supported as it is both by his recurrent insistence on the "fundamentals" in religion and by the care with which he prepared his sermons, it expresses a deep conviction. The preparation, that is, the studies that go into the making of the sermon, and the public act of preaching by an authorized minister assure conformity and lend to the profession of the preacher the dignity of which Donne is always aware. As he applies Matthew 9:13 to preaching, he says that the word of Christ's calling the sinners

> implies a voice, as well as a Word; it is by the Word; but not by the Word read at home, though that be a pious exercise; nor by the word submitted to private interpretation; but *by the Word preached,* according to his Ordinance, and under the Great Seal, of his blessing upon his Ordinance. So that *preaching* is this *calling;* and therefore, as if Christ do appear in any man, in the power of a miracle, or in a private inspiration, yet he appears but in weakness, as in an infancy, till he speak, till he bring a man to the hearing of his voice, in a setled Church, and in the Ordinance of preaching. [7:157, 5:593]

This high and orthodox ideal of preaching cannot accept the extempore sermon. According to Donne, a sermon demands many days of thought and even many years of preparation and education under the guidance of those who are able and authorized to judge the fitness of a candidate's calling:

> Now, he that will teach, must have *learnt* before, many yeers before; And he that will preach, must have *thought* of it before, many days before. *Extemporall Ministers,* that resolve in a day what they will *be, Extemporall Preachers,* that resolve in a minute, what they will *say,* out-go Gods Spirit, and make too much hast. It was Christs way; He tooke first Disciples to learne, and then, out of them, he tooke *Apostles* to teach. . . . Though *your* first consideration be upon the *Calling,* yet *our* consideration must be for our *fitnesse* to that Calling. [6:104, 4:338]

When Donne talks of the "foolishness" of preaching, he does so with direct reference to First Corinthians 1 and 2, where Paul's "foolishness" is a higher form of wisdom.[71] Recasting Paul's exposition into his own terms Donne sees foolishness both in the subject matter of preaching—"to preach glory by adhering to an inglorious person" (i.e., Christ seen from a worldly perspective)—and in the manner of the first Christian sermons, since the Apostles were "heires to no reputation in the State, by being derived from great families, bred in no Universities, nor sought to for learning, persons not of the civilest education" (5:257, 13:454). Expanding a sentence of Paul's (1 Cor. 1:21), Donne explains that God chose to speak His new Word to man through ignorant, in the eyes of the world "foolish" people because earlier philosophers and wise men had failed to understand Him. Thus Donne sees the social and educational condition of the early preachers as an exception. The tone of his exposition suggests that he did indeed expect preachers of his own day to be educated in universities, to be chosen for their learning, and to be persons "of the civilest education."

I have already indicated how, according to Donne, such a

background, or preparation, would affect the style of the preacher. It could enable him to make his sermons harmonious, sweet, delightful, and acceptable. Now, as their titles sometimes indicate,[72] commonplace books were among the instruments designed to assist preachers in achieving just this result. They are compilations of famous sayings, tropes, "flowers of learning."

As one starts to examine Donne's attitude toward such repositories of learned matter, one is struck by what seems to be a discrepancy between his contempt for the "common placers" and his own practice of frequently using Latin quotations. However it appears that the practice of the "common placer" consists for Donne in reading excerpts and stringing them together, rather than reading original texts. Stating that in former times Christians had only an incomplete knowledge of the Bible, he says:

> Their case was somewhat like ours, at the beginning of the Reformation; when, because most of those men who laboured in that Reformation, came out of the Romane Church, and there had never read the body of the Fathers at large; but only such ragges and fragments of those Fathers, as were patcht together in their Decretat's, and Decretals, and other such Common placers, for their purpose . . . [6:56, 1:613]

Donne thus requires a preacher to read the original texts, but he certainly does not disparage the practice of collecting the fruits of one's reading under common headings with the intention of using them in one's own writings. Not only do Donne's sermons give evidence of the fact that he proceeded in this way himself,[73] but this was also a practice in which he and his audience were trained alike. He can remind his congregation, "Goe backe to our owne times, when you went to Schoole, or to the University; and remember but your owne, or your fellowes Themes, or Problemes, or Commonplaces" (8:238, 10:37). Although there is, of course, a great difference for Donne between a school exercise and the preaching of the word of God, this brief reference to a technique with which he could suppose his audience to be familiar[74] attests to a harmony between speaker and audience, and this harmony is a matter of decorum.

The use of specifically secular learning for preaching raises problems in which considerations of rhetorical decorum, which dictate that style be a function of subject matter and audience, overlap with considerations of what may be called ecclesiastical decorum, that is, theological beliefs concerning a hierarchy of branches of knowledge. As to the theological problem, it can be said in general terms that the Protestant emphasis on the word of Scripture had made the use and value of human learning problematical. Attitudes ranged from an outright rejection by the Independents[75] to a more or less qualified acceptance by conservative Anglicans.

In Ormerod's *Picture of a Puritane*, a copy of which bears Donne's autograph, one of the participants in the dialogue quotes the following passage from the work of a "Puritane":

> "My heart" (saith one of them, in a certaine Schismatical Booke that is very rife amongst our Puritans) "waxeth colde, and my flesh trembleth to heare you say, that a Preacher should confirme his matter out of the Fathers and humaine writers; doth preaching consist in quoting of Doctors, and alleadging of Poets and Philosophers? In what part of his commission hath a minister warrant to do so?" [76]

In his attempt to explain this rejection of learning, Ormerod first suggests polemically that such preachers are "like the Fox who despiseth Grapes, which he himself cannot reach" before indicating that they "contemne the writings of the Gentiles because the authors thereof were wicked, profane, and supersticious." Also leaning toward the conservative side, Thomas Adams says not less contentiously that "Arts have their use and humane learning is not to be despised . . . sottish *Enthusiastes* condemne all learning, all premeditation." [77] He pleads for the education of ministers, comparing them with medical doctors: "Spiritual Physitians (no lesse then the Sectaries of Nature) must have knowledge and Art. *Emperickes* endanger not more bodies, then ideotish Priests souls."

Such polemical passages derive their effect from overstatement and a rather vague conception of learning. When the problem is presented with a little more sophistication, a differentiation is made between the training essential to a preacher and certain disciplines that may assist him and to which he should at least have access. Thus Richard Barnard posits that "Theologus must be Philologus," but elsewhere only recommends that a minister should be furnished with books of all sorts: "First, for humanitie, of the severall Art's of Ethickes, Politickes, Oeconomicks, natural Philosophie, such as have written of Trees, Herbes, Beasts, of Husbandrie, Geographie." [78] He has no patience, however, with those who preach with an "intermixing of long sentences in strange languages not understood, differing from their natiue speech." [79]

It is useful to bear in mind the distinction between learning as the subject matter of the arts and sciences, and the skills derived from human learning, such as the methods of textual analysis and language training—a distinction that has helped to resolve some discrepancies in Milton's attitude toward the uses of human learning, a problem that continued to be discussed through most of the seventeenth century.[80] The controversy about extempore preaching and such a passage as that quoted from Barnard further suggest that on both of these levels it is not always a question of *how much* learning but a question of *when:* whether learning is to come into play only in the education of the clergy and in the preparation of the sermon, or whether it may show in the delivery. Thus William Perkins, less radical than the "enthusiasts," agrees that "the Minister must priuatly vse at libertie the artes, philosophie, and varietie of reading, whilest he is framing his sermon," but he makes it a rule that "he ought in publike to conceale all these from the people." [81] Since the power of God's word should be the center of the sermon, "*humane* wisedome must be concealed."

There can be little doubt that Donne imposed upon himself a

deliberate restraint in the use of non-Christian authors. It has long been noticed that in his sermons he shows no enthusiasm for the classics and that the only significant number of classical quotations is from the "moral man," Seneca.[82] John King, for instance, is more generous with allusions to classical learning. In one sermon he refers to Castor and Pollux, and urges the congregation to follow good counsel by saying, "Vlysses maie perswade, but *Diomedes* must through with it. There must be hands as well as heads." [83]

The overwhelming majority of Donne's quotations are from ecclesiastical sources. In a later chapter, on his fields of imagery, I will show, moreover, that elements of knowledge from profane spheres of learning such as geography, medicine, and law are an integral part of the tropes he finds in his sources and that figures derived from such tropes can consequently be called profane only with certain reservations. Here I will describe only Donne's theoretical solution to the problem of learning in preaching and point out how this solution relates to the principle of decorum.

To Donne, a deliberate show of learning is one of many manifestations of curiosity, a vice that in turn is a manifestation of pride and consists in not keeping to one's station. Ultimately, curiosity is a breach of decorum. Donne summarizes several kinds of unseemly interests by saying:

> All these ways men offend in curiosity. It is so in us, in Church-men, *si Iambos servemus, & metrorum silvam congerimus*, If we be over-vehemently affected or transported with Poetry, or other secular Learning. And therefore St. *Hierom* is reported himself to have been whipt by an Angel, who found him over-studious in some of *Cicero's* Books. This is curiosity in us. [4:143, 4:390]

The exemplum of Jerome's punishment, traditionally directed against all reading of non-Christian authors, has by Donne's manipulation lost its edge and is directed merely against excess in such reading.

Donne's final and most elaborate statement on the problem of secular learning can be found in an undated sermon that his editors assign to his later period. In words very similar to those used in the earlier sermon, ("over-vehemently" and "over-studious"), he rejects a practice of "overcharging" sermons "with too much learning" (10:149, 6:316). The overstatement is indicative of a strong revulsion against excesses and expresses his belief in a middle way in the matter of secular learning to go with the middle way that he, along with other Anglicans, advocated in theology. In his plea for the avoidance of excesses, he explicitly links style and doctrine. Talking of "two sorts of Excesses," he says that "one is, the mingling of too much *humane ornament*, and secular *learning* in *preaching* . . . The other is of mingling *humane Traditions*, as of things of equall value, and obligation, with the Commandements of God" (10:147, 6:246).

Throughout his discussion of the problem, "human ornament" is used in conjunction with "secular learning," so often that the two expressions become synonymous and he can use "ornament" to refer to learning (10:147, 6:252). The traditional language may suggest the view of style as a dressing or addition, sometimes expressed in the notion of color, paint, or flowers. Although this idea is not far removed from the basis even of the two central analogies by which Donne expresses his view concerning ornament, both comparisons point to a functional conception of ornament. In one simile he uses a gallery with paintings and furniture for comparison:

> If you furnish a *Gallery* with stuffe proper for a Gallery, with *Hangings* and *Chairs*, and *Couches*, and *Pictures*, it gives you all the conveniencies of a Gallery, walks and prospect, and ease; but if you pester it with improper and impertinent furniture, with *Beds*, and *Tables*, you lose the use, and the name of a *Gallery*, and you have made it a *Wardrobe;* so if your curiosity extort more then convenient ornament, in delivery of the word of God, you may have

a good . . . *Encomiastique,* but not so good a *Sermon.*
[10:147, 6:268]

The function of a thing is often declared by its name, a circumstance that Donne uses also in the other relevant passage. He
says: "In *sheep-pastures* you may plant fruit trees in the *hedge-
rowes;* but if you plant them all over, it is an *Orchard;* we may
transfer flowers of secular learning, into these exercises; but if
they consist of those, they are but *Themes,* and *Essays*" (10:148,
6:309). Donne thus allows the use of the flowers of secular
ornament, but only insofar as they serve to convey and "usher
the true word of life into your *understandings,* and *affections*
(for both those must necessarily be wrought upon)," and not
"more then may serve *ad vehiculum,* for a chariot for the word
of God to enter" (10:147, 6:262).

To some extent, the concept of the functional role of secular
ornament is an emphatic restatement of the doctrine of philosophy (including other disciplines) as the handmaid of theology,[84]
a doctrine often invoked by Catholics and conservative Anglicans
against Protestant polemic.[85] Donne's emphasis on the avoidance
of extremes in the issue, however, does not derive from Augustine, but is a corollary of the Anglican *via media* in theology.
The closest parallel in Augustine's *Christian Doctrine,* from
which Donne likes to derive his arguments, can be found in the
discussion of the moderate style, which, according to Augustine,
"should neither be left unornamented nor be ornamented inde-
cently." [86] But Augustine's moderate style is only midway between the grand and the subdued styles and otherwise acquires
no special virtue from its medial position. Donne makes one of
the styles *the* style and advocates it by a plea for decorum. His
plea, "onely avoid excesse" (10:148, 6:294), is a restatement of
the well-known Aristotelian concept of the mean between extremes as the criterion of all virtue.

The principle of decorum helps Donne define his position
regarding the issue of human learning in yet another way. In
accord with his functional view of ornament, he will of course

not allow himself to decide once and for all what kind of learning and how much is permissible. Comparing the times of the early Christians with his own, he notes that his contemporaries are generally more familiar with the names of David and Paul than with Seneca and Plutarch, and that hence his sermon should be different. Then, however, he makes the following interesting remark:

> I am far from forbidding secular ornament in divine *exercises*, especially in some *Auditories*, acquainted with such learnings. I have heard men preach against witty preaching; and doe it with as much wit, as they have; and against learned preaching, with as much learning, as they could compasse. [10:148, 6:283]

It is significant that in such a sensitive issue as the use of secular learning in the preaching of the word of God Donne ultimately relies on decorum as a principle regulating expression in terms of the audience.

# 3. Fields of Imagery

IN investigating the relative novelty and audacity of Donne's tropes I started from the assumption that every utterance is bound by multiple relations to the situation in which it occurs. Renaissance rhetoric to some extent dealt with this fact in the theory of decorum, in which a minimal number of types of situations were specified. A complete description of situations was hardly possible and would not have been of much help to the orator looking for a few handy rules. The few contemporary rules one finds concerning the use of metaphor were understood in the context of the general theory of decorum, although, more often than not, they referred to that theory only implicitly. The specific connection between the two parts of the trope, in modern theory called tenor and vehicle, was generally viewed in relation to its fittingness for the situation, for the purpose the orator had in mind. The connection varied, for instance, according to whether the speaker's intent was satirical or commendatory.

I have tried to show that the concept that the writers on pulpit oratory had in mind when they wrote about the distance between tenor and vehicle and warned against vehicles that were remote and farfetched was a hierarchical system, a tree, chain, or ladder. Often the distance between the things compared was conceived of in terms of their relative position on a scale of values. The tropes in Donne's sermons generally conform to this rule of decorous imagery, a rule that was, moreover, the major element of his critical theory of imagery. In the absence of an *Ars Praedicandi* by the Dean of Saint Paul's the evidence for this conclusion has to be derived from his sermons. It is not surprising that Donne's theoretical remarks always occurred on the occasion of tropes that he for some reason felt to be daring or not quite in harmony with the theory. The gist of these remarks, together with the rarity of images that would be imperfect according to the theory, make it seem likely that some such rules as those of decorum were applied deliberately or unconsciously by Donne when he prepared or delivered his sermons.

On the whole, the theory of imagery derived from Renaissance books on pulpit oratory—whose authors, like their secular counterparts, were so often content with listing the various tropes—is a rather rough instrument even when presented more systematically than it was in the original texts. Some important factors determining the relative novelty of a trope were not mentioned in this theory and cannot be accounted for in its terms even when the theory is given the most sympathetic reading. Renaissance theorists, unless, of course, they treated of such a special case as allegory, viewed only the single trope and tried to measure its fittingness for a certain speaking situation. They did not go beyond the single image to see how images stood in relation to each other. As far as the number of images is concerned, they contented themselves with the warning *ne quid nimis*—there should not be too many. With the modern interest in structures within speech and language, the relations between images can no longer be neglected. It is questionable, however, whether most of the modern attempts to group images have provided much insight into the functioning of figurative discourse. It seems, on the contrary, that some such attempts, when applied to Donne's imagery, have resulted in further confusion because they were founded on questionable assumptions about the nature of tropes.

Traditionally there have been three main approaches to imagery, which are described in Stephen Ullmann's brief methodology —one can approach it through the point of comparison, that is, the common ground between tenor and vehicle, or through the vehicles, or through the tenors.[1] Although it has been used to some advantage by Wells,[2] the first approach lends itself all too easily to subjective criticism and fruitless speculation. Moreover it has not even been shown that the use of metaphor is always primarily motivated by a *tertium comparationis* (point of similarity). According to the two remaining methods one will in the analysis of a metaphor such as *leprosy of sin*, for example, classify it with the various other sicknesses and medical terms used metaphorically for whatever purpose, or one will focus attention on the concept "sin" and study what other vehicles—*clouds, vapor*—are used to express it. The latter is more properly a study of subject matter,[3] the former is the approach of Spurgeon or, applied to Donne, of Rugoff. There is no question that Rugoff has broadened our knowledge about the range of references in Donne's works. If, before outlining my own approach, I look critically at this attempt, which presents the most rigorous and systematic application of views that in other studies are often only implicit, I do so not in a spirit of contention but in order to show that the adoption of certain assumptions about imagery had to lead to a cementing of the traditional verdict concerning Donne's "heterogeneous ideas . . . yoked by violence together."

A critic will concern himself primarily with vehicles if he believes that in tropes a writer's fancy is given free rein, that his vehicles reflect the driftings and soarings of unrestricted imagination.[4] By discovering and describing the patterns that result from this exercise of choice, the critic will hope to get a glimpse into the tides, drifts, and currents of a writer's imagination.[5] A critique of this approach must deal with two issues: the nature of psychological inferences to be made from tropes and, more importantly, the concept of figurative discourse on which the approach is based.

To exemplify the first complex of problems, I quote from such an analysis a comment interpreting data previously established: "If the little group of images from sports and games tells us anything, it is that Donne, by the time he had completed the major part of his writing, had lost most of his interest in such activities." [6] Lillian Herlands Hornstein has written a spirited critique of a method in which psychological inferences are drawn from the absence as well as from the presence of images of a certain kind. Although she takes issue mainly with Miss Spurgeon, her remarks apply to any such analysis.[7] She points out, for instance, that there is not a single fishing image in Izaak Walton's *Life of Donne*. If we had not his *Compleat Angler*, the method exemplified here would result in erroneous conclusions about Walton's interests and knowledge. In the same vein Stählin earlier remarked that Paul, "the maker of tent cloth," has no metaphor connected with his trade and only one ship metaphor.[8]

One may hold—and this seems to be Mrs. Hornstein's main point—that critics just went too far when they relied on negative as well as on affirmative evidence. Hence one might try to follow the same path and refine the method used by pioneers like Spurgeon and Rugoff. But the approach has also resulted in the view that an image is "an illumination of an idea by another not related to it in subject matter," [9] and even that Donne shared this conception, a view that ignores the fact that most of the vehicles in Donne's prose were already related through their history to the subject matter he was treating. The problem with such an approach is not just that it can lead to unwarranted psychological interpretation. The chief difficulty lies in its basic concept of imagery.

The studies under consideration arrive at their results by first grouping the figures of speech in a number of categories, for example, "Ideas of the Universe," "Medicine and Alchemy," "Religion and the Bible." This grouping rests on the separation of tenor and vehicle. The meaning parts, the tenors, are disregarded. This method is quite consistent with the axiom that tropes present the freewheeling fancy of an author. Little would be gained by replacing this axiom with a contrary one. The relation between image and subject is a matter of finer distinctions, as I hope to show in the following pages.

Ultimately, attempts at investigating imagery by arranging

vehicles according to topical spheres remain questionable because such spheres do not represent linguistic structures. At best they resemble a philosophical scheme,[10] but from the point of view of linguistic fact, the resulting arrangement is arbitrary.

The same criticism applies to the method by which such studies arrive at their individual spheres of imagery. There is no criterion by which Donne's exhortation "Be but wormes and no more, in your owne eyes" (8:142, 5:454) can be assigned to a particular sphere, since the vehicle *worm* can be assigned to at least two categories—with reference to Job's metaphor, to the one entitled "Bible," and also to the category "Animals." The fact that this metaphor is not an occasional borderline case but one among many hundreds of such tropes in Donne's writings seriously invalidates attempts at mapping out such spheres of imagery.

The recognition that it is impossible to reconstruct the inner biography of an author by describing the spheres of his imagery, as evidenced by the examples from Izaak Walton and Saint Paul, together with an awareness of the contradictions inherent in the method of establishing such spheres, has led at least one critic, Harald Weinrich, to discard such terms as *sea imagery*, and *medical imagery*, as artificial and inadmissible abstractions.[11] Weinrich's introduction of the concept of a "field" of imagery opens new and linguistically satisfying approaches to the problem of analyzing an author's figures of speech.

Weinrich rightly insists that a field is formed neither by a number of vehicles grouped together according to some scheme borrowed from the natural sciences or theology nor by a group of such vehicles as denote one tenor. Thus *sin* and *sickness* certainly represent spheres of meaning in a language, but separately they do not fall within the realm of metaphor. As he discusses the specific field of imagery in which words are "coins" and people "pay" with words, Weinrich writes:

It is only through the establishment of the field of imagery that one area of meaning becomes the image-supplying field, the other the image-receiving field. It would be an unacceptable and deceptive abstraction to isolate the image-supplying from the image-receiving field. Thus all the metaphors concerning matters of finance taken together amount to —nothing. Likewise if one takes together all the metaphors for the *Wortwesen* [i.e., for a certain idea] he gets nothing at all, at least no meaningful structure. As long as one does not keep in view both the image-supplying and the image-receiving fields, he is not speaking of metaphor at all.[12]

It is therefore imperative to keep in view the two areas of meaning that are the constituents of a field of imagery—the area of the tenor and that of the vehicle. No matter what its particular terms are, a trope is considered to be a part of such a field as long as it spells out a version of the basic analogy constituting the field.

# Sin as Sickness

In the third sermon of the Simpson-Potter chronological edition, Donne calls grace the "physick of the soul" and urges the listener to make it his daily diet:

> That's the true, the proper Physick of the soul, it is the only means to recover thee. But yet, wert thou not better to make this grace thy diet, then thy physick? Wert thou not better to nourish thy soul with this grace all the way, then to hope to purge thy soul with it at last? This, as a Diet, the Apostle prescribes thee, *Whether you eat or drink, do all to the glory of God.* [1:196, 3:480]

Should "diet" and "physick" in this text be derived from the words quoted from Paul, who, according to Donne, "prescribes" a regimen? In the First Epistle to the Corinthians (10:28, 31)

Paul advised only that Christians should not take part in any meal if they know that the food has been offered as a sacrifice to idols; whatever they do should be to the glory of God. Donne, then, takes Paul's sentence out of context and extends its meaning, an operation quite in keeping with his customary way of using quotations from Scripture. The quotation is used as proof for an argument and is not itself the source of the metaphors. When he uses the words *physick*, *purge*, and *diet*, Donne moves within a field of imagery in which he sees sin as sickness.

The field has its main support in the words of Christ, spoken when he was criticized for having his meal with sinners: "The whole need not the physician, but the sick do." [13] The analogy between sin and sickness was developed further by the church fathers. Donne quotes Basil for the metaphor: *"Lachrymae sudor animi male sani;* Sin is my sicknesse, the blood of Christ is my Bezar, teares is the sweat that that produceth" (4:339, 13:565). He also notes how "elegantly" Tertullian says "that *Esay* presents Christ, *Praedicatorem, & Medicatorem,* as a Preacher and as a Physitian" (5:347, 17:347). He further quotes Tertullian's concise statement *si dolorem, ipse medicus* and paraphrases it as "Lay downe all thy diseases there, and he shall heale thee" (9:272, 11:831). Joan Webber draws attention to Chrysostom, who likes to speak of the Word as medicine.[14]

Yet Augustine appears to have woven the densest net of analogies in this field of imagery. One can safely assume that Donne not only was familiar with his elaborations but that he was particularly impressed by them, since he quotes one in an early sermon:

> He prepared and he prescribed this physick for man, when he was upon earth; *etiam cum occideretur medicus erat,* then when he died, he became our physitian; *medici sanguinem fundunt, ille de ipso sanguine medicamenta facit:* other Physitians draw our blood, He makes physick of blood, and of his own blood. [1:313, 9:458]

In passage after passage Augustine compared God to a physician and noted similarities and differences. He urged his listeners to trust in God as their physician because His purpose is not to please the patient but only to heal him: "For the sick person asks much of the physician, but the physician does not give it to him. He does not hear him for his will but for his health. Therefore make God your physician." [15] A physician's medicine, Augustine explained elsewhere, is meant to heal and not to punish. When he burns out a patient's wounds he will not listen to his cries.[16] Who can know what part is diseased, he asked in a very similar passage, but he who cuts through the wound with a knife? The yelling of the patient does not make the surgeon retract his hand: "He cuts while the patient is crying." [17]

The concept of sin in terms of sickness also helped Augustine to point out the foolishness of hiding sin. "That patient was perverse . . . who showed to the doctor the parts of his body that were whole and covered his wounds." Only God covers our wounds, he argued, and He will not hear us if we hide them. The doctor covers and heals, for he covers with plaster. Under his bandage the wound heals, whereas under the patient's covering it is only hidden.[18]

At this point Augustine turned the analogy into a figure of difference: "From whom do you hide it? From Him who knows everything." [19] From here it was only one step to a further expansion of this field of imagery in which God was presented as the omniscient physician. The theme of "homo medicus fallax, Deus medicus certus" would also appear in Donne. Augustine pointed out in detail how a patient will deliver himself into the hands of human doctors even though he is aware of their limited knowledge: he knows they did not make man, and yet he will let them bind him, or will remain unbound, and have them burn his wounds and amputate his limbs.[20] Whereas this trust may lead to his death, man's confidence in the Divine Physician is never betrayed, for He knows with what medication to cure man.[21]

Augustine's fondness for medical metaphor has not gone unnoticed, and a few articles on his use of medicine have helped to put his accomplishment in the right perspective. Jean Courtès remarks that "the sicknesses he mentions are rarely clearly defined; we seldom find any which do not have an immediate spiritual analogue":[22] the eye diseases and blindness of the Jews, pagans, and heretics, the madness of the persecutors, the tumors and gangrene to be operated on. Courtès notes that Augustine was interested in medicine not in its own right but only insofar as it could be used rhetorically in preaching to people accustomed to reasoning by analogy. Rudolf Arbesmann has pursued the subject a little further. Using a method similar to mine he looked for the significance of Augustine's medical imagery and found that it points to the central concept of *Christus medicus* and particularly to *Christus medicus humilis*, the humble Physician.[23] Arbesmann stresses that medical imagery in Augustine has above all a homiletic function, since "even a cursory examination of the texts reveals that, except in rather a small number of cases, the figure of *Christus medicus* is confined to the sermons."[24]

This minimal sketch of a history of the field may serve as a foil against which Donne's elaborations can be delineated. We may now examine his presentation of spiritual disease, of therapy, and finally of spiritual doctors.

If Augustine used the word *putria* to describe the diseased parts that the Divine Surgeon is to remove, Donne was in many cases more specific. He asserted that as there is a "bodily leprosie," so there is a "spirituall" one (9:208, 8:708), which he elsewhere likened to a "scurff" (3:223, 9:636). Envy was for him "the cancer at the heart" (3:66, 1:206), and just as the physician "must consider excrements, so we must consider sin, the leprosie, the pestilence, the ordure of the soule" (10:123, 5:160).

In these examples the two areas of meaning that in combination constitute the field, sin and sickness, are fairly distinct; in content as well as in form the tropes resemble those of the church fathers. Occasionally, however, and particularly when he had set up a convenient context through similar analogies, Donne fused both areas into one image, into a submerged metaphor. Thus, assuming the role of Everyman, he could call his sin "my leprosie":

> How many heare Sermons, and receive Sacraments, and when they returne, returne to their vomit? *Domine Tu*, Lord, except the power of thy Spirit make thine Ordinance effectuall upon me, even this thy Jordan will leave me in my leprosie. [5:305, 15:352]

The identification of sin and sickness, here purely metaphorical, takes on a somewhat different meaning in a few passages that suggest Donne's agreement with the biblical view that there was some kind of causal relation between sin and sickness. Whether this was simply a theological and academic point for Donne, to whom the Fall of Man was of course a reality, or whether he deeply believed that sin was the actual cause of sickness is hard to determine. John King was more specific on this point when he said that "*Sinne*, the sicknesse of the soule, is the reall and radicall cause of all bodily sicknesse." [25] In the sermon in which Donne dwelt on the idea, it seems that he used it just to impress on his listeners the importance of *sanitas spiritualis* —this is the key phrase that appears in the margin—and that he wanted to point out a hierarchy in which spiritual and bodily disease differ in importance: "What ease were it . . . to be delivered of Cramps, and Coliques, and Convulsions in my joynts and sinewes, and suffer in my soule all these?" (10:80, 2:545).

Spiritual "cramps, coliques, and convulsions" were only one part of the wide gamut of manifestations of spiritual sickness. In a sermon on Psalm 51:7, "Purge me with hyssope, and I shall be cleane; wash me, and I shall be whiter than snow," Donne made use of the traditional idea of the location of the emotions in various parts of the body:

> Except, I say, the Fathers take Pride in so large a sense as that they would not prescribe Hyssop to purge *Davids* lungs, for his disease lay not properly there; They must have

purged his liver, the seate of blood, the seat of concupis-
cence; They must have purged his whole substance, for the
distemper was gone over all. And to this rectifying of his
blood . . . had *David* relation in this place. [5:309, 15:471]

The preacher explained that under the Old Law, blood was sprin-
kled on people by means of an instrument made from a plant
called hyssop. The blood David looked for to cure him from the
distemper of his blood, the disease of his sins, was the blood of
Christ. Since all generations are subject to the disease of sin, the
disease might be called hereditary:

> The causes in the wounds of the soule, are intrinsique . . .
> are hereditary . . . for the wounds were as soone as we
> were, and sooner; Here was a new soule, but an old sore; a
> yong childe, but an inveterate disease. [5:348, 17:391]

Melancholy, the fashionable sickness of the epoch, also appeared in the same field. Images using terms like *distemper*, and
designations of a sinner as "a vessell of peccant humors" (5:298,
15:73), rested of course on the theory of the humors, body fluids
that in a healthy person were supposed to be both unpolluted
and in proper proportion. According to orthodox opinion based
on the authority of Galen, a predominance of black bile led to
a distemper, the disease of melancholy. The writers of medical
compendia wrestled with the problem of harmonizing this view
of melancholy as disease with another tradition in which, according to view expressed in the (pseudo-) Aristotelian *Prob-
lemata* and some remarks by Plato, melancholy was seen as the
necessary condition of genius.[26] In our context this fact is of
interest only insofar as it may help to explain the number and
variety of atrabilious diseases with which the Elizabethans were
familiar: since such prestigious authorities as Aristotle and Galen
could not be wrong, the contradictions had to be explained by
introducing distinctions and subdistinctions. "Natural melancholy," a sickness arising from the predominance of black bile
among the humors, was distinguished from a particularly grievous

disease thought to result from the "adustion," or drying up, of any of the natural humors,[27] and this distinction was complemented by the division of melancholy into that of the head, of the hypochondries, and of the whole body, of which the last species was considered the most serious. Donne referred to therapy for this particularly harmful disease when he said "As melancholy in the body is the hardest humour to be purged, so is the melancholy in the soule, the distrust of thy salvation too" (3:302, 14:394). Of the special varieties of head melancholy, he invoked "lycanthropy," [28] which also appeared in the title of a book of his library. One of the most common cures for the excess of this peccant humor and for its "burnt" variety was the purge,[29] which lent itself easily to metaphorical use:

> The proper use and working of *purging Physick,* is, not that that Medicine pierces into those parts of the Body, where the peccant humour lies, and from which parts, Nature, of her selfe, is not able to expell it: the substance of the Medicine does not goe thither, but the Physick lies still, and draws those peccant humours together; and being then so come to an unsupportable Masse, and burden, Nature her selfe, and their owne waight expels them out. Now, that which *Nature* does in a naturall body, *Grace* does in a regenerate soule, for *Grace* is the *nature* and the *life* of a regenerate man. [6:198, 9:446]

In spite of the wealth of references to the theory of the humors in Donne's imagery I must refrain from discussing the question of whether he believed in the orthodox theory or in the Paracelsian.[30] However it is interesting to note in the context of this study that Donne apparently never mentioned that "other" melancholy, which Marston calls the "nursing mother of fair wisdom's lore, Ingenious Melancholy," [31] best known to us through its parody in the character of Don Quixote. The omission shows how closely imagery interacts with subject matter: Donne's sermons were about man's condition in this world, about sin, and the ways to remedy it. Therefore there could be a place for melancholy only as a disease.

It has already been observed that the terms designating remedies were often elaborations of the same field of imagery. Everything that had the effect of counteracting the disease of sin in
this field of imagery necessarily became "physick." What was
misfortune in human terms could be interpreted as a sign of
God's providence, as part of God's therapy by which he cured
man and for which he had to be thanked (4:82, 2:696) as much
as for such other remedies as his means of grace, particularly the
sacraments. The Book of Psalms was an "Oyntment powred out
upon all sorts of sores, A Searcloth that souples all bruises, A
Balme that searches all wounds" (7:51, 1:8). Even grief might
serve this function: "It is proper and peculiar physick for that
disease, for sinne" (3:341, 16:320). Affliction might in some cases
have a cathartic function: "Affliction is my Physick; that purges,
that cleanses me" (6:237, 11:538); yet if it sometimes served as
a remedy, it did not always do so. It is not a universal remedy,
Donne says with Chrysostom, "Water for sore eyes, will not
cure the tooth-ach, sorrow and sadnesse which is prescribed for
sinne, will not cure, should not be applyed to the other infirmi-
ties" (3:341, 16:323). In the poets and the classical writers one
may find some "receipts," we are told, yet for "cordials" one will
have to look in the Scriptures:

> If any distresses in my *fortune* and *estate,* in my *body,* and
> in my *health,* oppresse mee, I may finde some *receits,* some
> *Medicines,* some words of consolation, in a *Seneca,* in a *Plu-
> tarch,* in a *Petrarch:* But I proceed in a safer way, and deale
> upon better *Cordials,* if I make *David,* and the other *Prophets*
> of *God,* my *Physitians,* and see what they prescribe me, in
> the *Scriptures.* [8:74, 2:401]

Marriage in particular, as Donne pointed out throughout his
ministry, is a remedy, since it preserves from sin:

> Let him then that takes his wife in this first and lowest
> sense, *In medicinam,* but as his Physick, yet make her his
> cordiall Physick, take her to his heart, and fill his heart with
> her, let her dwell there, and dwell there alone, and so they

will be mutuall Antidotes and Preservatives to one another against all forein tentations. [3:244, 11:123]

The preacher talked with special insistence of the means of grace. He deplored the sinner who did not make use of Christ's death as "antidote" or "plaister" (3:163, 6:252). Such metaphor must be seen embedded in a long tradition of Christian rhetoric. In his *Premiere Sepmaine*, for instance, Du Bartas, who stands in the same tradition, portrayed God holding a piece of plaster in his hand.[32] "Beautiful" and "poetic" or not, these images are but slight elaborations of Augustine's divine plaster analogy quoted earlier: "Deus tegat vulnera; noli tu. Nam si tu tegere volueris erubescens, medicus non curabit. . . . emplastro enim tegit."[33] Quite similarly Donne called the sacraments "cooling julips" and "warming cordials" (3:163, 6:258). Whereas "morall and civill counsailes" were but "drugs of the earth" (5:349, 17:411), Donne saw the sacraments as medicinal "dry figs," which, when boiled in water or milk, gave a sweet liquid then used as a gargle:[34] "The medicinall preaching of the Word, medicinall Sacraments, medicinall Absolution, are such dry figs as God hath preserved in his Church for all our diseases" (5:349, 17:421). From "cooling julips" and "dry figs" preserved in the Church, it is not so far to spiritual "syrups and liquors":

This then is the soules *Panacaea*, The *Pharmacum Catholicum*, the *Medicina omnimorbia*, The physick that cures all, the sufficient Grace, the seasonable mercy of God, in the merits of Christ Jesus, and in the love of the Holy Ghost. This is the physick; but then, there are *Vehicula medicinae*, certaine syrups, and liquors, to convey the physick; water, and wine in the Sacraments . . . [5:349, 17:428]

It would be not only stretching the point but also misplacing the emphasis to deduce from such a passage that Donne was especially attracted to the subject of the alchemists' quest for a panacea, also known as the quintessence, or the *elixir vitae*.[35] Donne was explicating an old analogy and giving his metaphors a new and professional look. The panacea, however, already had a firm place in the field of imagery under consideration. Thus, in a sermon with the programmatic title "Physicke from Heaven," which purported to explicate this basic analogy, Thomas Adams indicated the possible source of the idea of the *remedium omnium morborum*:

> Panace is an hearbe, whereof *Plinie* thus testifieth. *Panace, ipso nomine, omnium morborum remedia promittit.* The very name of it, promisseth remedie to all sicknesses. It is but a Weede to our *Balsame;* which is a tree, a tree of life. . . . It is a Phisitians Shop of *Antidotes*, against the poisons of heresies, and the plague of iniquities.[36]

That the spiritual panacea was part of a preacher's traditional store of images is also borne out by Cawdrey's *Treasurie of Similies*, where the word appears in the same field of imagery: "As the hearbe *Panax*, or *Panace*, hath in it a remedie against all diseases: So is the death of Christ, against all sinne, sufficient and effectuall."[37]

The quotation from Adams points to a similar figurative use of the word *balm*, or *balsamum*. In Donne's sermons scholars have seen two clear references to the *balsamum naturale*, which according to Paracelsus was contained in every living body and worked as an antidote for all poisons.[38] The importance of such references, however, has been overstated and their rhetorical purpose overlooked. Donne's references to medicine are obvious enough; sometimes they are even introduced by a "Now the physitians say . . ." It has not been sufficiently emphasized, however, that in his sermons medical lore is as a rule presented in figurative speech or by way of analogy. In this case the use of the Paracelsian medical theory blends perfectly with the traditional use of the word *balm* in the field of imagery in which sin is seen as sickness. Deriving from Jeremiah's question, "Is there no balm in Gilead; is there no physician there?"[39] the spiritual balm had been preached in sermons and sung in hymns.[40] Thomas Adams had Jeremiah's words in mind when he said that "the

*Prophets* are allegorically called Physicians, as the *word* is *Balme*," and when he called the Scriptures "the *intrinsique Balme*." [41] When Donne called the Book of Psalms a "balm" he was thinking in terms of the Song of Songs also: the book is "*Oleum effusum*, (as the Spouse speaks of the name of Christ), an Oyntment powred out upon all sorts of sores, A Searcloth that souples all bruises, A Balme that searches all wounds" (7:51, 1:7).[42] Elsewhere he moved from the natural *balsamum* of the physicians straight to the "perfume" of the soul, "*Nardum suam*, her Spikenard, as the Spouse sayes" (5:348, 17:357). However, he also seemed to have in mind Jeremiah's "balm of Gilead" when he called the Church a "hospital" and said that Christ "hath stored it with the true balme of *Palestine*, with his bloud" (5:125, 5:443).

Not only have critics overlooked the multiple ties by which Donne's metaphorical use of therapeutical methods was bound to tradition, but their preoccupation with his "interests" has sometimes led them to misinterpretations. Donne's reference to God as an apothecary who makes treacles from the poison of vipers has been linked with a certain tenet of Paracelsus (that each disease is caused by a bad essence that must be purged chemically), and has been called "probably the most fantastic analogy to issue from this source [i.e., Paracelsus]." [43] The opposition of "triacle" to "poison" resembles so many similar pairs common in homiletic literature—for instance, Donne's "rheubarbe" versus "ratsbane" (5:285, 14:630) or his "sweet" versus "bitter" (6:166, 7:607),[44] which goes back to the traditional *mel* versus *fel* ("honey" versus "gall")—that it would be surprising if Donne had actually invented it under the influence of Paracelsian theory. The same figure was in fact listed in Cawdrey's *Treasurie*, which is a pretty safe indication that it was old: "As the Physition in making his Triacle, occupieth Serpents and Adders, and such like poyson, to drive out one poyson with another; Euen so God in afflicting and correcting of vs, occupieth and vseth the diuel and wicked people, but yet all do vs good withall." [45] As it was used by Donne, the old simile was a pointed formulation of the idea expressed in the tropes quoted earlier in which even affliction appeared as a remedy, a "bitter pill," as Thomas Adams put it,[46] administered by the Divine Physician.

Because of the nature of this field of imagery, the diversity of agents, that is, of spiritual doctors, was not so wide as the range of remedies. In the first place, if sin was sickness,[47] everyone had to be his own spiritual doctor: "We must . . . anatomize our soule . . . and find every sinnewe, and fiber, every lineament and ligament of this body of sinne" (2:159, 6:549). Even more than this, the preacher's profession was to "dissect" and to "anatomize" (2:85, 2:471), and his words were "medicinall herbs" (4:164, 6:25). But, although the individual was called upon to be his own doctor and, as in the case of David, could be exceptionally successful in being "his owne sprituall Physitian" (8:213, 8:760), his ability could be taken only as limited and delegated power, for the greatest doctor was God, whose "corrections" had to be taken as "medicine" (2:125, 4:227), and who still had the same "receipts" and "antidotes" he had had in Egypt (3:152, 5:660). Donne expressly refers to Augustine's statement that Christ by his death became our "physician." But Christ is a physician with a difference: "Other Physitians draw our blood, He makes physick of blood, and of his own blood" (1:313, 9:461); therefore "Christ is truly both, both the Physitian and the Physick" (1:312, 9:412). This physician's therapy is radical but effective:

> You see Christs method in his physique; It determines not in a preparative, that does but stirre the humours . . . Christs physique determines not in a blood-letting, no not in cutting off the gangren'd part, for it is not onely *Cut off*, and *pull out*, but *Cast away*. [3:179, 7:310]

This is Donne's version of Augustine's "homo medicus fallax, Deus medicus certus." Finally—and here one has, if not the source of the field, at least its main support—Donne quotes the words of Christ that were referred to earlier: "*The whole need not a Physician*, but the sick doe" (2:93, 2:800).

This field has been presented in such detail for two reasons. First, the analysis shows that specialized and fashionable medical terms (*dissect, anatomize, melancholy, dry and peccant humours,* etc.) only, as it were, occupy free positions in a field of imagery that is already well established in Christian tradition. Second, it provides a basis for questioning the validity of certain psychological conclusions that have been drawn about Donne from his use of a large number of medical terms.

Concerning the first point it has become obvious that Donne was occasionally very close to Augustine in his use of analogies. The Surgeon who cuts off the "gangren'd part" is comparable to Augustine's Physician, "who knows by what surgery, by what cauterization he will cure you." [48] Consider a longer analogy, which takes on the proportions of an epic simile:

> As the body of man, and consequently health, is best understood, and best advanced by Dissections, and Anatomies, when the hand and knife of the Surgeon hath passed upon every part of the body, and laid it open: so when the hand and sword of God hath pierced our soul, we are brought to a better knowledge of our selves, then any prosperity would have raised us to. [9:256, 11:226]

The hand and knife of the Surgeon who amputates the "gangren'd part" or, as in this case, lays it open, may be compared with "the hand of the doctor who cuts skillfully" and "works the knife through decaying tissue." [49] Indeed, the terms used are sometimes almost identical. Just as for Donne, the Divine Physician's "corrosives are better then others fomentations" (5:306, 15:370), so Augustine's *Deus medicus* "came not only to foment, but to amputate and to cauterize." [50] Such similarities are pointed out here not to suggest that Donne's tropes were necessarily borrowed from Augustine, although there can be little doubt that some of them actually were. The point is that once a field of imagery that has at its center an important metaphor is taken over, it will "by itself," as it were, generate new and similar images.

The analysis also has some consequences for the psychological inferences that have been made and that can be made from the presence of such imagery. The function of an allusion in its context needs to be considered before its personal importance for Donne can be accurately assessed. Donne's and Herbert's medical preferences have been contrasted as follows: "Syrup of rhubarb is the favorite of Donne, whereas Herbert likes the more gentle effects of a distillation of white and damask roses"; for which contrast the explanation is given that "Donne being of a more explosive temperament advocates the use of more potent herbs than Herbert."[51] As far as I know Donne did not advocate the use of any herbs in his writings, though he sometimes referred to them by way of analogy. As for Herbert, the reference appears to be to his chapter on "The Parson's Completeness" in *The Priest to the Temple*, where he urged the poor parson to "make the garden the shop," to grow herbs for use as, for instance, laxatives, rather than buy drugs from the apothecary.[52] Herbert's subject matter here is so different from Donne's in the latter's usually figurative use of drugs and herbs that the inference as to the difference of taste and temperament between the two writers, so pleasantly set forth, is hardly well founded.

In drawing psychological conclusions one must distinguish between figurative and nonfigurative discourse. The mere presence of such words as *anatomy*, *antidote*, *dissect*, *fever*, *gangrene*, *physick*, *plaster*, and *purge*, and other medical imagery does not justify the conclusion that Donne took a special interest in medicine as a science.[53] I have tried to show that in the field of imagery in which sin is seen as sickness, words like *gangrene*, *plaster*, *fever*, have their figurative predecessors in Augustine's *putria*, *emplastrum*, *febris*.[54]

It is often very difficult to determine whether Donne was drawing an analogy from contemporary medical theory or developing a metaphor he had found in homiletic literature or in the Bible. But such a distinction is not very fruitful since in so many cases he did both. It *is* important to notice what his primary purpose was when he used a medical term or theory. To support the view that Donne was preoccupied with medicine the following passage has been quoted: "*Non sanitas*, there is no health in *any*, so universall is sickness; nor at *any time* in any, so universall; and so universall too, as that *not in any part* of any man, at any time."[55] The passage is seen as related to the medical concept of a universal *neutra constitio* or medium state between health and sickness, a concept which, though seldom discussed in Donne's time, received some mention in Fernelius, the favorite medical authority of Herbert. Now it is of course quite possible and even likely that Donne was using some such source. But valuable as a study of Donne's knowledge of medicine may be, it has to be recognized that he drew upon learned medical authorities only for elaboration. In the passage in question Donne was obviously paraphrasing and expanding on Psalm 38:3 (37:3 in the Vulgate), in which sin was seen together with sickness: "Non est sanitas in carne mea a facie irae tuae: non est pax ossibus meis a facie peccatorum meorum." Donne was in complete agreement with Augustine, who wrote in his discourse on the same psalm:

> That very remembrance of the Sabbath, and the nonpossession of it at present, prevents me from rejoicing at present, and causes me to acknowledge that there is neither health in my very flesh, nor should it be called so when I compare this sort of soundness to that soundness, which I am to possess in the everlasting rest; where this corruptible shall put on incorruption, and this mortal shall put on immortality, and see that in comparison with that soundness this present kind is but sickness.[56]

There can be little doubt that Donne had read Augustine's exposition of this psalm very carefully.[57] In a similar passage in the same sermon, a marginal reference identifies the following quotation as being from Augustine: "and so *non sanitas*, there is no Health . . . there is *never* any soundness in us: for *semper deficimus*" (2:80, 2:314).

These critical remarks do not preclude the possibility of drawing psychological conclusions from figurative discourse. An instance like the following, in which Donne renders the neutral *solvere* of 1 John 4:3 as the medical *dissect,* can be revealing: "and for matter of beleefe, he that beleeves not all, *solvit Iesum,* as S. *Iohn* speakes, he takes Jesus in peeces, and after the Jews have crucified him, he dissects him, and makes him an Anatomy" (8:146, 5:584). But I am advocating an interpretation that takes into account the peculiar nature of figurative discourse and gives priority to the rhetorical intent.

Once the long-standing existence of a field of imagery has been demonstrated, one can describe how Donne developed various possibilities latent within it. Terms like *dissect* and *anatomize* added a dimension of professional precision. The word *melancolia* does not occur in the Vulgate, and Augustine seems not to have used it, certainly not in the field of imagery under consideration. But even for melancholy, the "dry" and "cold" disease, the ground had been prepared by Augustine's figurative use of the oppositions hot and cold, dry and moist:

> As the human physician, attending to a wound of the body, sometimes applies contraries, as hot to cold, or dry to moist, or something else of this kind . . . , in the same way the Wisdom of God in healing man applied Himself to his cure, being Himself healer and medicine both in one. Because man had fallen through pride, He applied humility to cure him.[58]

Donne rarely appealed to any specialized knowledge. That the knowledge he drew on was commonplace at the time is borne out, for instance, by the plays of the epoch; after all, the people who watched Hamlet were, as Levin Schücking has shown,[59] able to identify him immediately as a melancholic. Seventeenth-century authors like Timothy Bright and Robert Burton compiled and popularized medical knowledge that earlier had been available only in Latin. Books on surgery, moreover, had been fairly popular from the beginning; they were among the first scientific books to be written in the vernacular, since they addressed themselves to the barber.[60] When, as he did occasionally, Donne worked out a detailed analogy, he was so explicit that it was impossible to miss the point.[61]

Donne's relative originality, then, consists in this development and expansion of a field. He had a particularly strong urge to present certain religious truths in the terms he thought congenial to his age. It was not an urge to explore the "intrinsic agonies of his own viscera," but an urge to communicate. If the structural approach to his imagery is taken, one finds little to sustain the view that "in the sermons, where Donne is unhampered by the requirements of rhyme and meter, he unwinds his medical knowledge to the delight of the hypochondriacs of his parish." [62]

Aside from the nature of the tropes with which he furnished this sin-sickness field, the mere fact that he supplied it with so many may be a basis for interpretation. It might tentatively be said that sin seen as sickness expresses for Donne the "humane condition" (3:341, 16:225). At the same time this conception reflects the age-old Christian effort to find a satisfactory theodicy. Sickness can imply the idea of a possible cure, suffering itself becomes medicine, new strength is derived from the means of grace that the Church administers on behalf of *Christus medicus*. It would be a distorting abstraction—that much has become apparent—to separate "sickness imagery" from "therapy imagery." Augustine had already insisted that the rhetoric of one calls for the rhetoric of the other: "All this in the human heart, as it were, teems with the worms of human corruption. We have exaggerated the disease, let us also praise the Physician." [63]

Mülhaupt has observed that Calvin stressed the roughness by which the Physician makes the patient see and confess. The author goes so far as to say that in Calvin the concept of the Physician was entirely removed from the range of problems in which it was traditionally used in the language of the Church, that is, justification, or the experience of grace.[64] Donne's *medicus* was a loving God: "God would not give him [man] his physick, God would not study his cure, if he cared not for him" (7:70, 1:711). His office was to heal, not to punish:

But after God hath remitted the sin, the after-afflictions
are but from a Physitian, not from an executioner, and intended to keepe us in our station, and not to throw us lower;
So that they are neither properly satisfactions, nor punishments. [8:215, 8:833]

In terms of Augustine's dialectics of *iudex* and *medicus*[65] Donne
clearly put the emphasis on the side of the physician. In a different context Ruth Wallerstein expresses well this side of Donne's
preaching: "Donne's emphasis on love, upon consolation, is most
characteristically his own, his tenderest note of awareness of the
troubled spirits in the first and second quarters of the seventeenth
century of the very men who sat below his pulpit." [66] The recognition of the elaborateness of this field of imagery can be a
necessary complement to earlier studies that have stressed the
"otherness" of Donne's God.[67] The vindication of God's ways
with men was expressed almost schematically in the threefold
relation of disease (sin), physick (suffering), and restorative
(grace) when Donne prayed: "Give us our *Cordials* now, and
our *Restoratives*, for thy physick hath evacuated all the peccant
humour, and all our naturall strength" (2:54, 1:199).

# Life as a Journey

Donne used some striking analogies drawn from voyages and
the sea that have not gone unnoticed. Like his tropes invoking
medicine, Donne's marine imagery has sometimes been taken
to show that he turned to secular areas when trying to illustrate
points of religion.[68] Such an observation, however, is not only
of little consequence if Donne's use of tropes is viewed in isola-
tion, but it may also be misleading if it is meant to imply that
the secular and the spiritual ever have been or ever can be
neatly separated. There have also been attempts to explain the
metaphorical use of contrary winds, storms, and shipwrecks in

terms of Donne's own maritime experience—even a particular storm has been pointed out.[69] In the following few pages I will try to show that Donne's maritime imagery is linked with the central concept of life as a journey and to clarify its relation to that concept.

The field of imagery in which life is seen as a journey is deeply rooted in Judaeo-Christian tradition. Of course the representation of time in terms of space is not only a literary phenomenon but is inherent in nearly all Indo-European languages.[70] What characterizes the Judaeo-Christian concept of life as a journey, however, is its point of destination.

The concept of man as a *viator* has its main support in several New Testament epistles. By *status viatoris* theologians mean man's state of being on the way.[71] The complimentary term is *status comprehensoris*. He who has apprehended, grasped, or reached is no longer *viator* but *comprehensor*, a word that theology has taken from Philippians 3:13-14: "Brethren, I count not myself to have apprehended [*comprehendisse*]: but this one thing I do, forgetting those things which are behind, and reaching forth unto those things which are before, I press toward the mark for the prize of the high calling of God in Christ Jesus." The dialectics of here and there, of earthly dwelling and real home as used in 2 Corinthians 5:6 are also relevant. The field of imagery under consideration has its strongest support, however, in the "strangers and pilgrims" (*peregrini et hospites*) of other New Testament epistles,[72] as is shown by many passages in the church fathers in which these words are quoted and elaborated.[73]

To Augustine this world was like a wayside inn (*stabulum viatoris*) where travelers arrive and move on:

> Nor are the things among which we are created created for us since we have been recreated in Him. These things should be for necessity's use, not for love's affection: they should be like the traveler's inn, not like the possessor's prize. Refresh yourself and move on. You are traveling, think to

whom you have come, for so great is He who has come to you. In leaving this life you make room for the next comer. This is the condition of an inn: You go so that another may come.[74]

It is possible that Donne had this passage in mind when he played on what is the possible etymology of the word *inmate* (as *inn* plus *mate*). He makes the *viator* a personified Righteousness, homeless and transient in this life, but at home in the new Jerusalem toward which we look.

> *We looke for new Heavens, and new Earth:* in which, that which is not at all to be had here, or is but an obscure *In-mate*, a short *Sojourner*, a transitory *Passenger* in this World, that is, *Righteousnesse*, shall not only *Bee*, but *Dwell* for ever. [8:64, 2:41]

With Jacob (Gen. 47:9), Donne elsewhere says that life is a pilgrimage (3:287, 13:490) and continues, "Here we are but *Viatores*, Passengers, way-faring men" (3:287, 13:499). In the next sentence he turns the old topos to effective use when he argues: "This life is but the high-way, and thou canst not build thy hopes here." From a spiritual perspective, if the Christian wayfarer is aware of Christ's guidance, life may not be a "high-way" but "a royall progresse" (2:299, 14:462)—that is, an "onward march" or "state procession." This latter elaboration of the field may have been suggested to Donne by a passage in which Bernard called the path of our pilgrimage a *via regia*.[75] Further, if life is conceived in terms of a progression in space, then "this, where we are now, is the suburb of the great City, the porch of the triumphant Church" (3:288, 13:524), and Donne could urge the Christian to "rise early" in order not to be obliged to "ride" too hastily (4:283, 11:2). That the elaboration of this field was no accident but may be taken to reflect a concept that was dear to Donne is borne out by the fact that he was ready to quarrel with the Vulgate over the translation of Exodus 17:1:

Whatsoever moved Saint *Ierome* to call the journies of the
*Israelites,* in the *wildernes,* Mansions, the *word* (the word
is *Nasang*) signifies but a *journey,* but a peregrination. Even
the *Israel of God* hath no mansions; but journies, pilgrimages
in this life. By that measure did *Iacob* measure his life to
*Pharaoh, The daies of the years of my pilgrimage.* [10:234,
11:152]

A journey implies not only limitation in time but also labori-
ousness and danger (2:266, 12:603; 3:111, 3:743). It is these aspects of life that in Donne's sermons were most often expressed
in terms of a sea voyage. Allen has devoted a brief pioneering
article to Donne's use of the ship metaphor, in which he traces
the metaphor in its Christian form to Augustine, who "equates
the sea with the life of men," and goes on to examine Donne's
metaphorical uses of the word *ship.*[76] To continue the inves-
tigation on a broader basis, I will consider the idea of man's
spiritual navigation as an expansion of the biblical life-pilgrimage
field. That such metaphors actually do belong together is indicated
by the fact that they seemed to the preacher easily exchange-
able, as in a passage in which Donne paraphrased a "spiritual
navigation" metaphor of Cyprian—a usage showing, incidentally,
that the basic analogy existed long before Augustine's metaphor:

*Ad nostros navigamus, & ventos contrarios optamus,* we
pretend to be sayling homewards, and yet we desire to have
the winde against us; we are travelling to the heavenly
Jerusalem and yet we are loath to come thither. [3:203,
8:600]

This approach can be further substantiated by a passage from
a sermon of Augustine in which he calls man a *peregrinus* and
this life an *iter,* and thereupon launches into the imagery of a
spiritual sea journey:

Yet in all that which the Lord did, he instructs us as to
the nature of our life here. In this world there is not a
man who is not a stranger; though not all desire to return

to their own country. Now by this very journey we are exposed to waves and tempests; but we must at least be in the ship. For if there are dangers in the ship, outside there is certain destruction. For whatever strength of arm he may have who swims in the open sea, some time he is carried away and sunk, overpowered by the greatness of its waves. Therefore we must be in the ship, that is, in the wood, that we may be able to cross the sea. Now this wood in which our weakness is carried is the Cross of the Lord, by which we are signed, and delivered from the dangerous tempest of this world. We are exposed to the violence of the waves; but he who helps us is God.[77]

This lengthy passage shows Augustine first indicating the central metaphor and then expanding the field of imagery. Although Augustine's sea imagery has been examined in detail,[78] the connection with the life-journey or life-pilgrimage metaphor has not been clearly stated. Likewise in Donne's writings the various metaphorical uses of the word *sea* have been studied,[79] but the connection between the *mundus-mare* theme and the spiritual journey has gone unnoticed. It is possible that this link was the main reason for Donne's interest in the *mundus-mare* theme: "All these wayes the world is a Sea, but especially it is a Sea in this respect, that the Sea is no place of habitation, but a passage to our habitations" (2:307, 14:724).

The idea of the transitoriness of this life, which is explicitly or implicitly stated in nearly all Christian metaphors spelling out the basic analogy of this field of imagery, was well expressed by Donne in a passage in which he varied the *mundus-mare* theme by introducing a geographical name:

So then, in this our *Voyage* through this *Sea*, which is truly a *Mediterranean Sea*, a *Sea* betwixt two *Lands*, the *Land* of *Possession*, which wee have, and the *Land* of *Promise* which wee expect, this *Old*, and that *new Earth*, that our dayes may be the *better* in this land which the *Lord* our *God* hath given us, and the *surer* in that *Land* which the *Lord* our *God* will give us, In this *Sea-voyage* bee these our *Land-markes*, by which we shall steere our whole course. [8:64, 2:46]

In this expansion of the field, the perils of life become rocks: "How many . . . have struck upon a Rock, even at full Sea, and perished there" (4:320, 12:643). Man and man's soul are seen as a ship: "Neither can rich men comfort themselves in it, that though they be subject to more storms then other men, yet they have better ground tackling, they are better able to ride it out then other men" (3:54, 1:265). Paul is seen as a seaworthy freighter (argosie) (3:240, 10:543). Spiritual navigation demands a right estimate of one's own resources (4:329, 13:177), for the soul will be shipwrecked on her voyage if she does not carry the right ballast (1:205, 3:800; 2:346, 11:423; 2:249, 11:506); only the right freight assures a rich return (7:440, 18:220). Such metaphors are certainly no evidence that Donne particularly feared the perils of the sea, since they belong to an established field of imagery and therefore were to some extent suggested by the subject matter.[80]

Further, if life is seen as a journey or voyage, much will depend on its direction, "For, let the winde be as high as it will, so I sayle before the winde, Let the trouble of my soule be as great as it will, so it direct me upon God, and I have calme enough" (6:59, 1:750). Donne here furnished the field with more specialized nautical terms: "points of the compass," "North and South," spiritual "landmarks." [81] Although the core of such metaphors can be found to some extent in early Christian writings, the precise and specialized terms that express this spiritual orientation were more properly Donne's own expansion. In general the spiritual navigation of the early Christians was simply described as directed toward the East, the rising sun.[82] But, even in this case, Donne's achievement is not so easily defined. Thomas Adams's "spiritual navigator," for instance, was threatened by rocks, storms, seasickness, and sirens on his course, which led past Scylla "in the *Sicilian* sea" and past Charybdis, "a place of dangerous swallowes," to the "Cape of *Bona Speranza*." [83] As is indicated by the mixture of the legendary with the real in some of these tropes, Adams's voyage was more obviously moralized than Donne's. There are, however, passages in Adams not unlike Donne's: "There be *Straites* in the *sea* of this *world:* those of Magellan or Giberaltare are less dangerous. The hard exigents of hatred, obloquie, exile, penurie, misery: difficult *Straites,* which all *sea*-faring *Christians* must passe by to the Hauen of blisse." [84]

Finally, the destination was even more important than the art of navigation, for the pilgrimage derived its value from its goal —the heavenly Jerusalem:

> As he that travails weary, and late towards a great City, is glad when he comes to a place of execution, becaus he knows that is neer the town; so when thou comest to the gate of death, be glad of that, for it is but one step from that to thy *Jerusalem.* [2:266, 12:603]

A comparison with a very similar passage from Ochino, some of whose sermons Donne had in his library, may show how closely Donne's traveling metaphor was linked with the idea of the right destination. Ochino wrote: "So that as a feeble and unarmed straunger, who trauayleth alone thorough a thick and darke woode, full of most cruell wilde beastes and theeues, if he doth but perceiue a bough wagge, he trembleth for feare." [85] Whereas Ochino was elaborating a simile for the condition of being without the armor of faith, Donne's traveling metaphor has a wider significance: it represents Everyman on the way to his destination.

If one compares Donne's passage with Cyprian's "Ad nostros navigamus, et ventos contrarios optamus," one may be tempted to take it for a more poetic attempt to express a devout man's complex and even contradictory feelings toward the approach of death: joy mingled with terror. Yet the context makes it clear that Donne wanted to stress joy alone. The vehicle *place of execution* was chosen for its connotations of terror, but the terror is negated in the joyful arrival at the city itself, so that it functions only as an intensifier of the traveler's joy. The field in which life was seen as a pilgrimage seemed to exert something like a compelling influence; within its radius death, almost by necessity, became a place—the last station before the heavenly Jerusalem.

In this connection, it is not stretching the point too far or reading too much into the following passage to note in it the way Donne fits into this field of imagery a figure borrowed from Augustine:

> *Amor est pondus animae; sicut gravitas, Corporis;* As the weight of my body makes that steady, so this love of Pureness is the weight and the ballast of my soul; and this weight stays the palpitation, the variation, the deviation of the heart upon other objects; which variation frustrates all endeavors to cure it.
>
> The *love* of this pureness is both the *ballast* and the *frait* to carry thee steadily and richly too, through all storms and tempests, spiritual and temporal in this life, to the everlasting Jerusalem. [1:204, 3:794]

Augustine spoke of a spiritual ballast that would steady the soul; Donne places it in the context of the "spiritual journey" metaphor by emphasizing its usefulness in helping the traveler toward his destination, the heavenly Jerusalem.[86]

If such tropes occupied an important place in Donne's metaphorical universe, this is not to say, of course, that he saw life exclusively in terms of a journey or voyage. In her study of Donne's archetypal images of roundness, Mary Ellen Williams has discussed his imagery of the crown, egg, sphere, coin, and womb, and stressed the importance of the circle for Donne's representation of life:

> One idea that Donne never tires of is that man's life, from womb to grave, is a circle. He refers, for example to man's fear of death, as being loath to make up his circle and

return to the earth (IV, 51-52). The circle in the context of man, symbolizes his beginning and prophesies his end. As such, it is a symbol of mortality rather than of immortality.[87]

Her remarks can serve as a welcome reminder that certain fields of imagery (and in the terms of this study "life as a circle" might perhaps be called one) are somehow related to archetypes. Definition of this relation lies outside the scope of my study, which may, however, help to elucidate one little problem. In the last sentence quoted above, the writer notes that the circle, which often, and in agreement with the emblematic tradition, stands for eternity, is here a symbol of mortality. Donne's concept of the cyclical nature of life has a biblical basis. For centuries Christians had heard on Ash Wednesday the words of Genesis 3:19: "Pulvis es, et in pulverem reverteres." To see Donne against the background of this tradition is not to diminish his life-circle figures but to see them as what they are: elaborations of concepts suggested in the Old Testament.

The importance of the life-pilgrimage concept for Donne can also be recognized from the fact that almost all his other travel metaphors fit into this field. His poetry is much more varied, because there he has another important field of imagery, the "ship of love." Again this is not to deny that there are, even in his sermons, other metaphors using the same vehicles. Nautical metaphors belong to the stock traditionally used by poets and orators when setting out to make a speech or to write a poem and when concluding their exercise. Thus Virgil speaks of "setting sails" (*vela dare*) when he begins his *Georgics*.[88] Similarly, Jerome sets the sails of interpretation, which are then blown by the Holy Ghost.[89]

Donne takes up the device, which is one of the topics of the exordium, and elaborates it by using his favorite geographical terms: "I cannot hope to make all this voyage to day. To day we shall consider onely our longitude, our East, and West; and our North and South at another tyde, and another gale" (9:50, 1:130). When, at the beginning of another sermon, he resorts to the old device, he does so only after having filled the navigation metaphor with new meaning. Characteristically he sees the navigation to which he compares his exegesis as a pilgrimage to the heavenly Jerusalem. The first part of the text on which he preaches—words promising forgiveness of all sins—becomes an inexhaustible sea, the sea of Christ's blood. The analogy between the sea and Christ's blood has been called a striking one.[90] The fact that Donne's analogy grows out of a variety of traditional elements may dampen some of the astonishment but not one's admiration for the passage. Its opening sentence exemplifies his inextricable fusion of rhetorical device, traditional field of imagery, and personal vision:

> As when a Merchant hath a faire and large, a deep and open Sea, into that Harbour to which hee is bound with his Merchandize, it were an impertinent thing for him, to sound, and search for lands, and rocks, and clifts, which threaten irreparable shipwrack; so we being bound to the heavenly City, the new Jerusalem, by the spacious and bottomelesse Sea, the blood of Christ Jesus, having that large Sea opened unto us, in the beginning of this Text, *All manner of sin, and blasphemy shall be forgiven unto men,* It may seeme an impertinent diversion, to turne into that little Creek, nay upon that desperate, and irrecoverable rock, *The blasphemy against the Holy Ghost shall not be forgiven to men.* [5:77, 3:1]

# The Book of the World

It is a favorite cliché in the popular view of history, says E. R. Curtius, that men of the Renaissance shook off the dust of yellowed parchments and turned instead to reading the book of nature or the book of the world. Yet, as he shows, this metaphor

also comes down from the Middle Ages.[91] M. A. Rugoff noticed in Donne's sermons a number of images that seemed "to
issue directly from a sense of books as books," but he did not
want to deal with them, for "the whole group was so heterogeneous that any attempt at generalizations or deductions would
have been hazardous." [92] The concept of the book of the creatures in Donne's sermons has received some attention from Joan
Webber,[93] who sees it, along with his grammatical figures and
occasional use of emblems, hieroglyphs, and images based on
rhetorical terms as evidence for Donne's "literary approach to
the world" and therefore as supporting her general thesis that
Donne "is describing the world in terms of art." [94] Her attempt
to see relations between metaphors that had been thought heterogeneous constitutes a major advance. However, since I can see
no meaningful way in which one could delimit and describe a
group of "bookish tropes," I will use the method outlined
earlier and keep in view both the image-supplying and the image-
receiving sides of the metaphors.

It might seem that the Renaissance had some right to claim
tropes based on the processes of printing as its own. But even
here novelty is rarely absolute. Donne's printing metaphors express relations that potentially exist in an old field. They are so
well integrated into existing metaphorical fields that they can
almost be said to derive from the language of the Bible and of
the church fathers.

According to Curtius, the concept of the world, or nature, as
a book originated in pulpit eloquence. Later it became a favorite
concept of orthodox asceticism and mysticism.[95] Curtius reports
that from the twelfth century, philosophy too used book metaphors. For Hugo of St. Victor, both the creation and the God-
Man are books of God.[96] Hugh of Filieto constructs a minor
system of theology out of corresponding "books": one was written in Paradise, another in the desert, the third in the Temple,
and a fourth one has been written from all eternity. The idea of
the authorship of these books is important: God wrote the first
in the human heart, Moses the second on tablets, Christ the

third on earth, and divine Providence the fourth in history.[97] Curtius also points out that comparisons with books frequently occur in Bonaventura's *Breviloquium*, but notes that "the simile of the book is not logically confined to a single function and a single significance but rather serves to illustrate very various facts."[98] I will try to show that in Donne most of the book metaphors have a clearly definable function: they belong to one field of imagery and their use is governed by one overriding intention.

Curtius quotes a passage from Luis de Granada's *Simbolo de la fé*, which I bring in here because it shows clearly the didactic character that distinguishes tropes belonging to this field and that marks Donne's metaphors.

> What else will be all the beautiful and accomplished creatures of this world but like broken and illuminated letters which declare the excellence and the wisdom of their author? . . . And so . . . you put before us this wonderful book of the whole universe in order that we read, as from living letters, the excellence of the Creator.[99]

None of the texts adduced by Curtius speaks of such a multitude of books as does a passage from one of Donne's sermons of 1622. God here becomes a *polígrafo* who has surrounded man with an infinite library in which he can read Him:

> All other authors we distinguish by *tomes*, by *parts*, by *volumes*; but who knowes the volumes of this Author; how many volumes of Spheares involve one another, how many tomes of Gods Creatures there are? Hast thou not room, hast thou not money, hast thou not understanding, hast thou not leasure, for great volumes, for the *bookes of heaven*, (for the *Mathematiques*) nor for the books of *Courts*, (the *Politiques*) take but the *Georgiques*, the consideration of the *Earth*, a farme. . . . Goe lower; every *worme* in the grave . . . is an abridgement of all . . . a *worme*, a *weed*,

thy *selfe*, thy *pulse*, thy *thought*, are all testimonies, that *All*, this *All*, and all the parts thereof, are *Opus*, a *work made*, and *opus ejus*, *his work*, made by *God*. [4:167, 6:148]

Some parts of the quotation are reminiscent of Proverbs 6:6: "Go to the ant, thou sluggard; consider her ways, and be wise." Moreover, the idea of the heavens as a book had been familiar since the Middle Ages.[100] But what is more important to notice here is the preacher's deliberation in methodically working out analogies in a familiar field, which thus becomes a tool of his rhetoric. Moreover, he elaborates the field of imagery in a specific way. Here it is not the familiar ants or some other exemplary creatures that are books, and the books are not manuals for learning or industry or some other faculty or virtue: they are books only in the sense that they point to an author. Thus even the worm in the grave becomes an argument for God's authorship. The book of nature does not teach specific behavior, it teaches God:

Here God shewes this inconsiderate man, his book of creatures, which he may run and reade; that is, he may go forward in his vocation, and yet see that every creature calls him to a consideration of God. Every Ant that he sees, askes him, Where had I this providence, and industry? Every flowre that he sees, asks him, Where had I this beauty, this fragrancy, this medicinall vertue in me? Every creature calls him to consider, what great things God hath done in little subjects. [9:236, 10:168]

The "book of the world" tropes took various forms, but Donne's usual purpose in such tropes was simply to point to an *artifex*, to God. In a paragraph the topic of which is given in the margin as "*opera*," Donne based his argument on the wide range of meaning of the word *works*, which signifies concrete things as well as literary creations (8:121, 4:450). Works argue the existence of an author. One can read something about God in his works, for every creature bears the *vestigia Dei*, "traces of God." Even when Donne spread, as it were, a text over the whole world, he was just fashioning a cliché to the same purpose:

> and by that Text which we have read to you here, and by that Text which we have left at home, our house and family, and by that Text which we have brought hither, our selves, and by that Text which we finde here, where we stand, and sit, and kneel upon the bodies of some of our dead friends or neighbors, he gives to us, he repeats to us, a full, a various, a multiform, a manifold Catechism. [6:351, 18:65]

When Joan Webber says that such tropes narrow the gulf between art and life, and are evidence of a "literary view of the world," [101] it seems to me that she goes beyond what can be demonstrated from Donne's use of a traditional analogy to make a traditional point. It is questionable whether tropes that are so characteristic of the genre indicate any such predilection. As my brief sketch of the concept of the book of the world has shown, one of its purposes, often its prime purpose in early homiletic literature, was theologically didactic; it was much later that the idea of the world as God's book was secularized, a process that Curtius has well described. Donne, in his sermons, shaped his book-world figures to fulfill the specific didactic purpose that motivated their first users. The world was called a text because a text had to be interpreted until the meaning its author encoded in it had been recovered. It is consistent with the didactic purpose governing Donne's use of metaphors in this field of imagery that he presented the world as "a multiform, a manifold Catechism," a large book in which every creature is a "leaf":

> Outward and visible means of knowing God, God hath given to all Nations in the book of Creatures, from the first leaf of that book, the firmament above, to the last leaf, the Mines under our feet. [2:253, 12:95]

From the world as a manifold catechism it was only a small step to the world as God's library, consisting of a variety of his books: "When God gives me accesse into his *Library,* leave to consider his proceedings with man, I find the first book of Gods making to be the *Book of Life*" (7:353, 14:165). In the passage that follows, Donne moves swiftly from book to book, pointing out degrees of their certainty. The book of life, which is the one John speaks of in Revelation 20:12, is supplemented by another book of life in the Church, "the Testimony of our Election here" (7:354, 14:184). Of course these expressions do not belong to the field of imagery under discussion, since their tenor is different, and they are to be interpreted as books of the names of the living, as in the Psalms.[102] The use of this expression in the Bible, however, supports the world-library metaphor.

The idea of the existence of two "books" that supplement each other, the Bible and the book of creatures, came down from the Middle Ages.[103] Donne worked it out in great detail:

> There is an elder booke in the World then the Scriptures;
> It is not well said, in the World, for it is the World it selfe,
> the whole booke of Creatures; And indeed the Scriptures are
> but a paraphrase, but a comment, but an illustration of that
> booke of Creatures. [3:264, 12:284]

This field of imagery also lent itself to the expression of differences in size and the idea of the smaller contained in the larger, a favorite idea with Donne, of which the microcosm-macrocosm idea is the best-known formulation: "The world is a great Volume, and man the Index of that Booke; Even in the Body of man, you may turne to the whole world; This body is an Illustration of all Nature" (7:272, 10:543). Most of these metaphors at the same time argued God's authorship: "Gods abridgement of the whole world was man. Reabridge man into his least volume, *in pura naturalia,* as he is but meer man, and so he hath the Image of God in his soul" (9:83, 2:563).

Donne was unusual in so stressing the topos of the book of creatures as continually to imply that man is a book within a book.[104] In this elaboration of the field, Donne may have been influenced by Paracelsus, in whose thought, as Curtius has noted,[105] book metaphors had important functions. In Paracelsus's *Labyrinthus medicorum errantium*, for example, each chapter takes its title and subject from a specific "book," and there are as many as eleven, such as the book of the firmament, the book of the elements, the book of experience. The primary metaphorical function of the book in this treatise is to image the interrelatedness Paracelsus sees between his various topics. In the fourth chapter, which treats of man as a microcosm, he writes: "This is the proper book, from which anatomy has to be derived, that man should know how to compare the substance, proportions, etc. of the elements with those of the microcosm [man]. Not that it is enough to look at the human body as it is dissected. . . . This kind of seeing is just the way a peasant looks at a Psalter; he only sees the letters. That does not get him very far." [106] The concept of the body as a book and, according to the setup of the treatise, a book within other books, appears here in conjunction with the microcosm-macrocosm idea.

In spite of the similarity, however, the comparison between the Paracelsian book metaphors and those of Donne brings out an important difference: in Paracelsus the concept of the book of nature is secularized. The firmament is a book but it is a *buch der arznei*,[107] a "book of medicine," not a catechism. The astrologer "reads" it by joining the stars together (*zusammenkuppeln*). It is true that God is referred to as the first book[108] and that Paracelsus also sometimes refers to Him in expounding some of the other "books"; but this reference is only meant as confirmation of their authority. Paracelsus used the concept of the book of nature to argue for the observation of nature as an authority equal or superior to the books of medical theory transmitted through tradition.

The contrast with Paracelsus points up the specific purpose for which Donne used most of the metaphors of this field—to point to the divine Author. Another indication is the fact that they were to him easily interchangeable with metaphors from a field that will later be discussed in detail, the *speculum* metaphors. The frequent use of *speculum* in titles of medieval books may have facilitated this interchange, but the similarity of function of the two analogies in homiletic literature was a still more important cause of it. Bernard wrote in a sermon:

> The Apostle says: "His invisible attributes have been visible, ever since the world began, to the eye of reason, in the things he has made" [Rom. 1:20]. The visible world is like a public book tied to a chain (as the custom is) and in which whoever cares to can read the wisdom of God. One day heaven will be folded like a book in which no-one will have to read any more because "they shall be taught by God." And the creatures of the world as well as those in heaven will see God face to face, not as in a glass, darkly; and they will see the wisdom of God in itself. In the meantime, however, the human soul needs the creation as a vehicle by which it may be lifted to a knowledge of the Creator.[109]

Donne switched easily from the mirror to the book because both are used as *vehicula* to gain knowledge of God. The two analogies were so close in homiletic tradition[110] that Donne could telescope them together to form a mixed metaphor: "Our *medium*, our *glasse*, is the Booke of Creatures, and our light, by which we see him, is the light of Naturall Reason" (8:220, 9:44). Later he said once more in the same sermon: "The whole frame of nature is the Theatre, the whole Volume of creatures is the glasse" (8:224, 9:196).

The metaphor *book of the world* does not occur in the Bible, but it has already been suggested in passing that the analogy is supported, and was felt by its users to be supported, by such passages as Romans 1:19–20, the *Vade ad formicam* of Proverbs 6:6, Revelation 5:1, with its description of the *liber vitae*, and

Ezekiel 4:1. If the world is conceived of as a book, then it becomes man's duty to decipher the letters of God's textbook. Donne's frequent use of the verb *to print*, which may sometimes seem a mere mannerism, has here its justification. The metaphor occupies an important position in the field in which the world is deciphered as God's writing. The "book of the world" and "book of creatures" concept quite naturally generated vehicles of printing and imprinting:

> Take it [divine guidance to belief] first, at the first, and weakest kinde of proofe, at the book of creatures . . . And then, continue this first way of knowledge, to the last, and powerfullest proofe of all, which is the power of miracles, not this weak beginning, not this powerfull end, not this *Alpha* of Creatures, not this *Omega* of miracles, can imprint in us that knowledge, which is our saving knowledge. [6:133, 6:58]

In Donne's sermons *to imprint* became a term signifying particularly the transmission of any kind of information from God to man. God "imprints" divine terror in man's heart (4:184, 7:173; 4:169, 6:215), humility and apprehension (5:347, 17:325), or joy (5:291, 14:873) and holiness (7:323, 12:856). He "imprinted" knowledge about the existence of certain degrees in crimes (7:407, 16:515). The word also turned up in a mixed metaphor, which is proof that its figurative strength had faded.[111] Possibly the frequent use of the word *imprimere*, which in Latin was used figuratively so often that it had lost most of its concrete meaning,[112] influenced Donne's choice of words. It is significant, however, that the three times Donne quoted Augustine's words, "Natura cujusque rei est quam indidit Deus," his translation rendered the verb as "imprint" (2:148, 6:174; 3:344, 16:444; 5:363, 17:915). He chose the same word again when he paraphrased a passage from Jerome in which God is once again the agent (7:106, 3:459). Every trope of this kind served Donne to remind his audience that the world is created and has an Author.

Important as was the concept of the book of nature in Donne's sermon, the preacher was aware of the limits of its persuasiveness:

> We consider two other wayes of imprinting the knowledge
> of God in man; first in a darke and weake way, the way
> of Nature, and the book of Creatures; and secondly, in that
> powerfull way, the way of Miracles. [6:142, 6:387]

Perhaps Donne so often chose this "darke and weake way" because he preached before people placed squarely in the middle of this life. Bernard addressed himself to clerics devoted to a life of abstinence and contemplation, whereas Donne spoke to men in business and politics. He may have considered the "weak way" the most effective method of initiating his congregation into the life of the spirit.

In general, then, Donne's figures in this field point to the "outward and visible means of knowing God" (2:253, 12:95). Some of the passages quoted have further shown that the emphasis could shift to man as the "least volume." If the *liber mundi Dei* concept was not argued but firmly assumed, it could be used to prove the dignity of man who, as an extension of that analogy, is a "picture" in that book:

> *Mundi moles liber est*, This whole world is one Booke; And
> is it not a barbarous thing, when all the whole booke be-
> sides remains intire, to deface that leafe in which the Authors
> picture, the Image of God is expressed, as it is in man?
> [9:373, 17:73]

The idea of man as "image of God," here argued from a word by Basil, was most often linked by Donne with a kind of "printing" much older than Gutenberg's, that is, with sealing. Some of Donne's printing metaphors grew quite naturally out of analogies with sealing that were as old as the Bible and the first Christian homiletic writings.[113] I will attempt to describe the metaphorical use of the process of sealing as I map out a field of imagery in which the sacraments are spoken of as seals.

# The Seal of the Sacrament

In the previous section I was able to account for some of Donne's vehicles referring to printing, but others, especially those using the idea of imprinting, apparently did not stem from the concept of the world as a book. Moreover, a large number of vehicles invoke the process of sealing. Donne's use of such metaphors may be elucidated if it is compared with patristic tradition, in which the sacraments, and particularly baptism, were called seals. I will describe the extent of this field of imagery and then show that within it Donne put particular emphasis on a certain complex of images in which the mark of the seal is thought of as representing God's image; finally, a study of a number of images in which the seal of the sacrament is a "surety" or pledge for Redemption will bring us to the large field of imagery in which Salvation is spoken of in terms of a purchase.

The noun *seal* and the verb *to seal* are frequent in both the Old and the New Testaments. The best-known occurrence is in the Book of Revelation, where the book with seven seals is mentioned.[114] A document is certified by seals, which bear a mark stamped into them. Sealing a document was usually done to protect it from curious eyes and also to prove its authenticity. Wilhelm Michaelis has shown that the element of protection, that is, assurance of integrity until the time of breaking the seal, lent itself to the metaphorical expression of the idea of safe preservation and protection until the eschatological revelation.[115] In this sense men bear the "seal of the living God,"[116] a mark that shows them to be his property and to be under his protection. In the Book of Revelation hand and forehead are mentioned as the location of such signs. The followers of the beast bear its mark on the right hand or on the forehead,[117] the followers of the lamb are "sealed" on the forehead. The question of what the "seal of the living God" was thought to look like is in the province of the biblical scholar and need not detain us here.[118]

Donne and the commentators with whom he sympathized moved freely from passage to passage in the Old and the New Testament, and there was little doubt in their minds that the taw of Ezekiel 9:4 was shaped like a cross and thus pointed forward to the cross on which Jesus died. To them it was also the mark by which the followers of the Lamb were sealed.

Confronted with what G. W. H. Lampe calls "the confusion of much patristic teaching on the sacramental bestowal of the gift of the Spirit," [119] I can only be very tentative in my attempt to provide some background for Donne's tropes. From Lampe's study it appears that the word *seal* was frequently used in reference to baptism. Baptism was said to confer a seal, and sometimes was even equated with it.[120] There is a striking passage in Chrysostom where he exhorts his congregation to bewail the lot of those who died "without illumination, without the seal." [121]

The Latin word used in this passage is *signaculum;* other words used with roughly the same meaning in patristic writings are *sigillum, character,* and *tessara.* Cyril said, "where God sees a clear conscience He confers His wholesome and admirable seal." [122] He had in mind a *sigillum militare,* with which a soldier was customarily branded on the hand.[123] Shortly before this passage Cyril called baptism a "mysticum signaculum" and compared it to the brand given a sheep as a mark of possession.[124] Such a mark, also produced by sealing or stamping, was often called a *character.* Metaphors and comparisons that present baptism as a *character dominicus* or *character militaris* were frequent in the writings of the church fathers; they occurred, for instance, in Basil, in Nazianzen,[125] and particularly in Augustine, who wrote: "You are the sheep of Christ and bear the mark [seal? stamp?] of the Lord, received in the Sacrament." [126] It is true that Augustine also expressed the idea that the stamp or mark needs preservation: "Thus the error of the sheep has to be corrected so that the mark of the Redeemer be not corrupted in it," [127] an idea that I will study in the context of the *imago Dei* concept; however, the main drift of his metaphors using the *character dominicus* was to point out the irreversible nature of baptism. God's ownership is lasting: he claims the baptized by the same right the herdsman invokes when he claims the animal he once branded. When Augustine wanted to express the idea that this claim overrules even the will of the baptized, that baptism remains valid even in spite of his will, the comparison of the *character militaris* easily suggested itself. For the military badge, uniform, or tattoo-mark, which Cyril and other writers called *sigillum*, constituted a hold upon the soldier, signifying the obligation of his calling and even proclaiming him to all the world as a deserter should he try to escape his obligations.[128] The comparisons with the stamp, mark, or letter are important in Augustine's thinking and had a great impact on the tradition deriving from him. A modern scholar, whose interest is theological, writes: "It is through the two images of the *character militaris* and *character dominicus* that Augustine's doctrine of baptism has become so epoch-making." [129]

According to Augustine, the *character* received in baptism is a distinguishing mark by which a person is incorporated into the Body of Christ, the Church. This concept of baptism not only was a part of Donne's theological creed but was so fundamental to his symbolic world that it influenced, for example, his response to differing interpretations of Ezekiel 9:4 (where in the Vulgate the letter *Tau* is mentioned) and in turn generated new images:

> When he [God] heares . . . these sighs of thy soule, then he puts thy name also into that List, which he gave to his Messenger . . . *Signabis signum super frontibus virorum suspirantium & gementium*, Upon all their fore-heads, that sigh and groane, imprint my mark; Which is ordinarily conceived by the Ancients to have been the letter *Tau;* of which though *Calvin* assigne a usefull, and a convenient reason, that they were marked with this letter *Tau*, which is the last letter of the Hebrew Alphabet, in signe, that though they were in estimation of the world, the most abject, and

the outcasts thereof, yet God set his mark upon them, with a purpose to raise them; yet S. *Hierome,* and the Ancients for the most part assigne that for the reason, why they were marked with that letter, because that letter had the forme of the Crosse. [8:197, 8:189]

The use of the sign of the cross in the rites of the Church, or the use of any sign for that matter, was of course a matter of controversy in reformed ritual. To forestall any criticism Donne makes a comment on the use of that sign in the early Church, insisting that it was not used "to drive away devils." Then he continues:

> And as we in our Baptisme have that Crosse imprinted upon us, not as a part of the Sacrament, or any piece of that armour, which we put on of spirituall strength, but as a protestation, whose Souldiers wee became: so God imprinted upon them, that sighed, and mourned, that *Tau,* that letter, which had the forme of the Crosse, that it might be an evidence, that all their crosses shall be swallowed in his Crosse, their sighs in his sighs, and their agonies in his. [8:198, 8:212]

The *character* given in baptism is not only a distinguishing sign with eschatological relevance, but it is also, according to Augustine, important within history, since its effect is protective. Baptism is baptism into the kingdom of Christ, where the devil regains power only to the extent that the individual grants it to him. In the changes and vacillations of man's beliefs and emotions the imprint remains, keeping open the way to penitence, to the return to active service in Christ's kingdom.[130] The protective and safeguarding element of baptism was stressed in Thomas Aquinas's definition, in which it was again presented as a seal: "Therefore baptism is not a mere washing, but it is rather a regeneration, *et sigillum, et custodia.*" He then referred, apparently with approval, to Damascene, who "set down two things as relating to the *character,* namely *seal* and *safeguarding;* inasmuch as the character which is called a seal, so far as itself is concerned, safeguards the soul in good." [131]

For Donne it was Augustine who expressed most effectively man's restlessness before, as well as his security after, baptism. Donne was particularly impressed with that part of Augustine's report of his conversion dealing with the spiritual insight he gained by reading the Psalms and with the spiritual upheaval into which he was thrust when the prayer of his household was heard and he was delivered from his pain. These events led up to Augustine's baptism. It is interesting to note that where Augustine's language remained conceptual, Donne, in his paraphrase, introduces sealing metaphors:

> *Insinuati sunt mihi in profundo nutus tui*, In that halfe dark-nesse, in that twi-light I discerned thine eye to be upon me; *Et gaudens in fide, laudavi nomen tuum*, And this, says he, created a kinde of faith, a confidence in me, and this induced an inward joy, and that produced a praising of thy good-nesse, *Sed ea fides securum me non esse sinebat*, But all this did not imprint, and establish that security, that assurance which I found as soon as I came to the outward seales, and marks, and testimonies of thine inseparable presence with me, in thy Baptisme, and other Ordinances. [5:74, 2:578]

The words of Augustine are from the fourth chapter of the ninth book of his *Confessions*. Donne's sealing metaphors, so congenial to Augustine's thought, were used here to express the conceptual content with which they were usually associated. The content of Augustine's account, his inner struggle leading up to the long-deferred baptism, suggested to Donne the familiar field of imagery as a natural means of expression.

In the sense of safeguards and distinguishing marks, not only baptism but also the sacrament of communion and the other rites and ceremonies were "seals" for Donne. Somewhat polemically he extended the idea of baptism as a "tessera" to communion: "As Baptisme is *Tessera Christianorum*, (I know a Christian from a Turke by that Sacrament) so this Sacrament is *Tessera ortho-*

*doxorum* (I know a Protestant from a Papist by this Sacrament)" (5:263, 13:657). Elsewhere he applied the word *seal* to confirmation without any special theological or rhetorical significance.[132]

In the field in which the sacraments are spoken of as seals, however, there is a group of images that have some such significance. Quite a number of them refer to more technical aspects of sealing than those discussed so far. They took their inspiration from certain metaphors of the church fathers, which were in turn variously supported by such different biblical passages as Genesis 1:27, where man is said to be created in God's image, the Song of Solomon 8:6 and Ezekiel 28:12, which mention "seals" and "sealing," Matthew 22:20, where Christ's question concerning the image represented on the coin is reported, and even, as I hope to show, John 6:27, which is about the Son of man, whom God the Father "sealed." Most of these metaphors are used to express the thought that by virtue of his divine creation man bears the imprint of the image of God, which after its partial loss in the Fall, needs to be restamped.

I will not attempt what a specialist like Lampe has refrained from doing, that is, to sketch the outlines of so vast and complicated a subject as the doctrine of the *imago Dei*. Instead I will concentrate on the metaphorical expression of the doctrine of sacramental sealing.

In terms of stamping and sealing, the history of Salvation can be represented by three steps. First, in his creation in God's image, man received a seal that was impressed upon him by the divine Logos, who is also an image of God but represents him in exact likeness. Second, through the Fall the divine image in man was defaced, and it became necessary therefore to restamp the image. The possibility of restamping was opened by the Incarnation of the archetypal Logos. Thus raised to participation in the divine nature, man may receive the renewal of the image.

One might object that this scheme, though it presents sealing imagery, has little to do with the field of imagery in which the sacraments are seals. This objection can of course only be removed by going to the texts.

It was often understood and sometimes expressed by the Fathers that the image of God impressed on man at his creation is the same "seal of the Spirit," the presence and activity of the Holy Spirit, of which Paul speaks.[133] Theologically speaking, the equation of the image with the indwelling Spirit motivated the identification of the restitution of the image with baptism.[134] The link was expressed by Cyril of Alexandria, who, after quoting Genesis 1:27, interpreted the inbreathing of the breath of life to mean that man was "sealed through the Spirit in the image of God." [135] Donne states that man has the image of God; he "hath the Image of the Father, the Image of the Sonne, the Image of the holy Ghost in Nature; and all these also in Grace; and all in Glory too. How all these are in all, I cannot hope to handle particularly" (9:81, 1:497). The preacher judiciously refrains from elaborating this point too precisely, and it is not necessary to hunt for an expressly stated theological link between the two concepts of the image of God and the seal of the Spirit, for by Donne's time they had been closely joined by tradition. This is borne out by Cornelius à Lapide, whose commentary Donne often consulted, in his explication of Colossians 3:10 ("secundum imaginem ejus qui creavit illum"): "For as God created man in Genesis according to His image, so Christ reshaped man, who was fallen and lost, in baptism by His death and created him once more, as it were, according to God's image and His own." [136]

However, the most conclusive argument to meet the objection noted above is the fact that the concept of baptism as a seal fits so well into the history of Salvation just outlined in terms of sealing that the seal of baptism was early felt to be linked with the *imago Dei* concept. Lampe, who addresses himelf to the theological question, is nevertheless aware of the role of metaphor as a force contributing to the combination of the two ideas:

As we might expect, although this conception of the seal has no immediate connection with Baptism, the idea of the indwelling Spirit is so closely related to that of the seal of the image that the thought of Baptism as the medium by which the Spirit is received is never very far from the minds of those who employ the conception of the seal of the image in their theology.[137]

The restoration of God's image in man was expressed in various ways and particularly by the Greek Fathers.[138] Athanasius says that if in a painting someone's image has been blotted out by some dirt, it can only be restored in the presence of the person whose picture it is. Therefore, the Son, who is the image of the Father, came to us to restore man to His image.[139] Cyril calls Christ a "signaculum perfectum Dei et Patris" with reference to John 6:27, "ponam quasi signaculum." He explains that Christ has this perfect likeness to the Father, who by Christ seals us to himself.[140] Elsewhere Cyril says that God seals the saints with the Spirit and in an elaborate simile relates this fact directly to the sealing of the Son by the Father.[141] When Donne exhorted his congregation to "see" God in the seal of the sacrament, he also had in mind a model-image relation between the Father and the Son: "See him in that seal, which is the Copy of him, as he is of his Father, see him in the Sacrament" (4:130, 3:1502).

Thomas Aquinas pointed out that the concept of Christ as the Father's seal may fail to express Christ's consubstantiality.[142] With reference to Aquinas, Donne took up a similar distinction in order to impress on his congregation the degree of man's participation in the divine nature: "that God may be in us, *Non tanquam in denario*, not as the King is in a peece of coine, or a medall, but *tanquam in filio*, as he is in his sonne, in whom the same nature both humane, and Royall doth reside" (5:158, 7:259). But Thomas elsewhere joined the voices of tradition and used an elaborate sealing metaphor to express the dignity and grace conferred upon man by Christ's assumption of human nature.[143]

Donne was particularly impressed by the way Cyril expressed the restoration of the divine image through the Incarnation of its archetype, and in the context of a discussion of the divine image he says:

But this Image is in our soule, as our soule is the wax, and this Image the seale. The Comparison is Saint *Cyrills*, and he addes well, that no seale but that, which printed the wax at first, can fit that wax, and fill that impression after. No Image, but the Image of God can fit our soule. Every other seale is too narrow, too shallow for it. [9:80, 2:434]

Cyril's comparison provides the key for a long and somewhat mechanical variation on the theme of congruence and fittingness:

The magistrate is sealed with the Lion; the woolfe will not fit that seale: the Magistrate hath a power in his hands, but not oppression. Princes are sealed with the Crown; The Miter will not fit that seale. . . . All men, Prince, and People; Clergy, and Magistrate, are sealed with the Image of God, with the profession of a conformity to him: and worldly seales will not answer that, nor fill up that seale. [9:80, 2:439]

Examples strung together in this fashion tend to lead the attention in various directions, although they all have the same logical base. Some of them present a minor political program. But Donne eventually comes back to the comparison of "pictures" as he continues:

We should wonder to see a Mother in the midst of many sweet Children passing her time in making babies and puppets for her own delight. We should wonder to see a man, whose Chambers and Galleries were full of curious masterpeeces, thrust in a Village Fair to looke upon sixpenny pictures, and three farthing prints. We have all the Image of God at home, and we all make babies, fancies of honour, in our ambitions. The master-peece is our own, in our own bosome. [9:80, 2:453]

Even the "three farthing prints" in this passage, which has surprised some readers by its homeliness,[144] are part of the system of seals and pictures that Donne builds up in this sermon on the creation of man "in God's image."

The idea of the seal of the image, it should be pointed out, was often conveyed by the Fathers through the simile of a coin stamped with the emperor's image. As a coin bears Caesar's image so the believer has engraved upon him the seal or stamp of the Spirit or the inscription of the name of God.[145] Augustine wrote:

> Regain, therefore, the likeness to God which you lost through your sins. For as the image of the emperor on the coin is one thing and his image in his son another: for there are different kinds of images; but the image of the emperor is engraved in the coin in one way, in the son in another, and in solid gold even in a different way: so you too are a coin of God; and even better since you are God's coin with reason and life, so that you know whose image you bear and according to whose image you are made: For the coin is not aware of bearing the emperor's image.[146]

I have already mentioned Donne's use of Thomas's distinction *tanquam in denario* versus *tanquam in filio* (5:158, 7:259). Elsewhere he refers to the story of the tribute money, where a reference to the divine image may originally have been intended by Jesus:[147] "Now much of the strength of the assurance, consists in the person, whose seale it is; and therefore as Christ did, we aske next, *Cujus inscriptio*, whose Image, whose inscription is upon his seale, who gives this assurance?" (5:104, 4:311). Developing a figure taken from Basil he exhorts his listeners to hold the divine inscription in esteem and to prevent it from being "defaced" and "demolished":

> *Numismatis inscriptiones inspicitis, & non Christi in fratre,* thou takest a pleasure, to look upon the figures, and Images of Kings in their severall coyns, and thou despisest thine own Image in thy poore brother, and Gods Image in thy ruinous, and defaced soule. [5:203, 10:198]

In the field of imagery in which the sacraments are seals and man is stamped and restamped with the image of God, man's duty can be shown in several ways, particularly by reference to his willingness to receive the stamp and his care in preserving the image of the seal. According to Cyril, the Holy Spirit, who proceeds from God the Father, is stamped into the hearts of those who take him upon themselves as a picture is pressed into wax.[148] Donne derives this moral of obedience even from John 6:27, where Christ is said to be sealed by the Father:

> To insist upon a word of the fittest signification, *Him hath God the Father sealed.* Now, *Sigillum imprimitur in Materia diversa:* A Seal graven in gold or stone, does not print in stone or gold: in Wax it will, and it will in Clay; for this Seal in which God hath manifested himself, we consider it not, as it is printed in the same metal, in the eternal Son of God: but as God hath sealed himself in Clay, in the humane Nature; but yet in Wax too, in a person ductile, pliant, obedient to his will. [4:124, 3:1284]

Donne is less concerned with the sealing of Christ by the Father than with the sealing of man. When he speaks of the former, as in this passage, he makes it clear that he does not mean Christ's begetting before all ages, but His sealing in the Incarnation, which is really a sealing of human nature. In his commentary, Cornelius à Lapide had distinguished three senses in which John 6:27 could be taken. The sealing of the Son by the Father could be an anointing. Or, according to some authorities, such as Hilary, it could mean that Christ received the seal of the Father not in his divine but in his human nature, thus becoming endowed with the divine nature of the Word; Hilary had said, "a seal is normally pressed into a different material [*sigillum solet imprimi in materia diversa*], which is then said to be sealed; thus human nature is sealed by the divine nature of the Son." [149] Finally, the verse from the Gospel could mean that God manifested or confirmed that Jesus was his Son. Cornelius concluded: "This sense is simpler and plainer but the second is more solid and sublime." [150] In his similes Donne enthusiastically supports Hilary's reading, although he concedes that the Father sealed Christ first in begetting his divine nature, a sealing that defies the metaphor, since

Father and eternal Son must be of the same "metal," or consubstantial. His concern is to show how the divine stamp is received in man. For this purpose he uses Hilary's explanation and another sealing metaphor from the Psalms.[151] The sealing of Christ, interpreted as a sealing of his human nature, is here applied to "us":

> And there [in a person ductile, pliant, and obedient to His will], *Signatum super nos Lumen vultus tui*, says *David*, *The light of thy countenance*, that is, the image of thy self, *is sealed;* that is, derived, imprinted, upon us, that is, upon our nature, our flesh. [4:124, 3:1291]

The imagery under consideration lends itself to another and to Donne very important moral and didactic purpose. It was noted earlier that Cyril's simile of an imprint that can be filled again only by the seal that stamped it provided Donne with a key for a whole string of examples built on the idea of matching, or fitting. I found his procedure there somewhat mechanical, but it seems that the mechanical or, possibly, systematic quality of his imagery has not yet received proper attention. A system of imprints produced by seals lends itself to comparison. The history of man—Creation, Fall, Incarnation, baptism, confirmation, and communion—is represented in terms of states of one picture. The symmetry within that system results from the belief that the sacrament of communion restores the image after the effects of actual sin, as baptism does after original sin. The effects of grace become visible, and at the same time man's obligation to preserve that image is emphasized.

In Donne's sermons the systematic character of his imagery is a corollary of his didactic intent. This is particularly obvious in the following passage:

> These two seales then hath God set upon us all, his *Image* in our soules, at our *making*, his *Image*, that is his *Sonne*, upon our bodies and soules, in his *incarnation;* And both these seales he hath set upon us, then when neither we our selves, nor any body else knew of it: He sets another seale upon

us, when, though *we* know not of it, yet the *world*, the *congregation* does, in the Sacrament of *Baptisme*, when the seale of his *Crosse*, is a testimony, not that Christ was *borne*, (as the former seale was) but that also he *dyed* for us; there we receive that seale upon the *forehead*, that we should conforme our selves to him, who is so sealed to us. And after all these seales, he offers us another, and another seale, *Set me as a seale upon thy heart, and as a seale upon thine arme*, says Christ to all us, in the person of the spouse; in the *Heart*, by a constant *faith*, in the *Arme*, by *declaratory works*. [6:160, 7:357]

The eschatological relevance of the seal will need some special attention later. Here I would like to stress Donne's insistence on man's duty to conform himself to God by esteeming and preserving his seal.

A similar insistence on a series of seals and the injunction to preserve the image of God represented in them can be found in Bernard's works and in writings traditionally connected with his name. Thus the author of the treatise *De charitate* explains that the Creator by his grace stamped (*significavit*) man with his image. Is not man obliged, he asks, to conform himself to Him? He continues:

> Love the seal and the image that you bear within you; and in order that the form of your Creator appear more clearly in you, conform yourself by charity and faith to Him who is charity . . . Your divine Lover asked you to do so with the prophetic words: "Set me as a seal upon your heart, as a seal upon your arm;" which means, place me as a reminder in your heart and in your arm, that is, in thought and deed, so that after putting off the image of the earthly man you bear the image of the heavenly man, whose attention the signs of divine love cannot escape. Set me upon your heart as a seal of faith, as the example of love. Before his prevarication the apostate angel had in himself this seal, for Ezekiel says to him: "Thou sealest up the sun, full of wisdom, and perfect in

beauty." At his creation, the angel was in fact united to God by such a conformity that he was rather the seal [i.e., the instrument] of the likeness than the likeness or the stamp. By means of a seal one produces the likeness in figure which in the seal is contained in essence: and such likeness is in man. The angel, however, being of a very subtle nature, completely and only spiritual, was united to God by a greater likeness. As for ourselves, imprisoned and left in a dwelling of earth, it is charity that raises us to the dignity of the angels. And though our body by its corruption drags down our soul and though our earthly preoccupations debase our thoughts, lost on too many things, the new commandment to love God restores us, deformed as we are by sin, to the image of God.[152]

In vision and in hortatory technique this passage is close to the last one quoted from Donne, a fact that is not sufficiently explained in terms of common sources. Moreover some almost verbatim resemblances between them, for instance, in the paraphrase of the verse from the Song of Solomon, make it seem likely that Donne was familiar with it. As I will show, Bernard had formulated most clearly the difference between the concepts of the *imago Dei* and of the *similitudo Dei*. It is of course the idea of resemblance that lends the dynamic character to metaphor in this field.

In her notes on Donne, Ruth Wallerstein wrote that Bernard's sentence "imago Dei uri potest in gehenna, non exuri" was "the one single phrase which Donne cites most often in his sermons." [153] Although this statement may be exaggerated, Donne's preoccupation with the phrase is real. Its true significance can be understood only if, rather than taking the phrase too narrowly as expressing "the indestructibility of the will," it is viewed in relation to the field of imagery in which the sacraments are "seals."

Bernard used it in his first sermon on the Annunciation. He insisted there that the divine image is not sewn but stamped on man. Then he stated that man was made in the image but also in the likeness of God; the image is free will, the likeness his virtues. He explained that this likeness can be lost, but the image remains, for "If the image will be susceptible to burning in hell, it will not be consumed; it will burn but will not be destroyed." [154] He further pointed out that the image is always with the soul wherever the soul moves. This, however, is not the case with likeness, which dwells only in a virtuous soul; for through the effects of sin, the soul is badly mutilated and comes to resemble, rather, a beast without reason (*anima iumentis insipientis similata*).

Donne does not say that the indestructible image of God is specifically free will; he identifies it—quite traditionally—as the rational soul of man: Reason and Will. Thus the concept is kept wide enough to be linked with the sealing metaphor:

> Properly this Image is in Nature; in the naturall reason, and other faculties of the immortall Soule of man. For, thereupon doth Saint *Bernard* say, *Imago Dei uri potest in Gehenna, non exuri:* Till the soule be burnt to ashes, to nothing, (which cannot be done . . .) the Image of God cannot be burnt out of that soule. For it is radically, primarily, in the very soule it selfe. And whether that soule be infused into the Elect, or into the Reprobate, that Image is in that soule, and as far, as he hath a soule by nature, he hath the Image of God by Nature in it. [9:81, 2:478]

Many Protestants—notably Calvin[155]—refused to make any distinction between the "image" and "likeness" referred to in Genesis. Donne, however, follows Bernard rather closely. He keeps Bernard's distinction between indestructible image and mutable likeness, but finds more comprehensive metaphors that juxtapose the two in an edifying relationship: "But then the seale is deeper cut, or harder pressed, or better preserved in some, then in others, and in some other considerations, then meerly naturall."

The observation may be important enough to deserve some further illustration. In the same sermon from which a passage presenting Incarnation and baptism as a restamping was adduced earlier, Donne says:

First, God sealed us, in imprinting his *Image* in our soules, and in the powers thereof, at our *creation;* and so, every man hath this seale, and he hath it, as soone as he hath a soule: The *wax,* the *matter,* is in his *conception;* the *seale,* the forme, is in his quickning, in his *inanimation;* as, in *Adam,* the waxe was that *red earth,* which he was made of, the *seale* was that *soule,* that *breath* of *life,* which God breathed into him. Where the Organs of the body are so indisposed, as that this soule cannot exercise her faculties, in that man, (as in *naturall Idiots,* or otherwise) there, there is a *curtaine* drawn over this Image, but yet there this Image is, the Image of God, is in the most *naturall Idiot,* as well as in the wisest of men: worldly men draw *other pictures* over this picture, other images over this image: The *wanton* man may paint *beauty,* the *ambitious* may paint *honour,* the *covetous wealth,* and so deface this image, but yet there this image is, and even *in hell* it selfe it will be, in him that goes down into hell: *uri potest in gehenna, non exuri,* sayes St. *Bernard.* [6:158, 7:312]

The ideas of the permanency of the seal and the mutability of likeness are again linked and expressed in terms of sustained metaphors. The drawing of "other pictures over this picture" is in a sense an explication of the traditional idea of "defacing" or "deforming." [156] The combination of the ideas of a lasting *imago* and changing *similitudo* is expressed most schematically in the "curtaine drawn over the Image." Bernard's phrase "Imago Dei uri potest in Gehenna, non exuri" was for Donne more than a proof text for the importance of free will. One may conjecture that it captured his imagination because it fit into the larger field of imagery in which the sacraments were seen as stamps applied and reapplied to bring out the contours of the original image, and because he could develop from it simple and effective models to illustrate the effects of sin while appealing to the love of God rather than to fear.

There is yet another sense in which the sacraments are seals.

This sense is somewhat related to the concept of the *character dominicus*, but here the emphasis is placed not upon man's duty to the Lord but on the Lord's promise to fulfill his pledge. In modern studies of imagery such metaphors, which often point out the eschatological relevance of the sacraments and relate them to covenant theology, usually come under the rubric "legal imagery." Calvin very often referred to the sacraments as seals, and usually in this sense. Occasionally he managed to express both duty and promise in such a metaphor, as when he said in one of his sermons that the seal, by which the Holy Spirit imprints in us obedience and fear of God, is the seal and mark of Election.[157]

Imagery of this kind is derived from such passages as Paul's words to the Ephesians: "Grieve not the holy Spirit of God, whereby you are sealed unto the day of redemption."[158] Cornelius à Lapide explains: "By the Holy Ghost you are signed and as it were sealed as witnesses, not like cattle in the flesh, as the Jews are sealed with the sign of circumcision, but in the soul as sons of the promise."[159]

The relation of circumcision to baptism was part of traditional baptismal typology. As a token of the covenant with God, circumcision played a part in the Old Testament similar to that of baptism in the New.[160] Donne expressed the idea in terms of a typology of seals:

> When my reason tells me that the *Seale* of that Covenant, *Circumcision* is gone, (I am not circumcised, and therefore might doubt) my reason tells me too, that in the Scriptures, there is a *new Seale, Baptisme.* [5:103, 4:243]

Sealing for Donne is a way of expressing the evidence for and confirmation of a prior fact. Thus for him the Scriptures have their seal in the sacraments (5:127, 5:510), and preaching is sealed in applying them (7:112, 3:660). Communion in particular is the "seale of reconciliation" (5:84, 3:274), as the receiving of this sacrament is "a sealing of my Pardon" (5:318, 16:22). Donne clarifies two injunctions that Scripture gives with only the coordinate "and" as a connective by imposing on them the logical relation expressed by the sealing metaphor: "God hath given his Commission under seale, *Preach and Baptize;* God lookes for a returne of this Commission, under seale too; *Believe, and bring forth fruits worthy of beliefe*" (5:264, 13:692).

The sacraments are a ratification of the covenant renewed by the Incarnation. Christ's death itself is a seal, a confirmation of the pact renewed in his Incarnation:

> It was then his Deed; and it was his gift; it was his *Deed of gift:* and it hath all the formalities and circumstances that belong to that; for here is a *seale* in his blood. [5:122, 5:335]

In the sacraments, Donne says in the same sermon, man is "presently sealed to the possession of that part of Christs purchase, for which he gave himselfe" (5:129, 5:590).

The use of the word *seal* in the context of legal terms is not unusual in homiletic literature. The idea of Christ's death on the cross as a final ratification, a seal of Redemption, can be illustrated by a number of medieval texts. An example is the following passage from *De charitate:*

> After He had produced various witnesses, laws, oracles, prophets, signs, and finally even his own blood, he obtained the sentence of your deliverance. The formula of this sentence has been written on the head of the crucified and confirmed at the moment when compassion and truth, peace and justice met. Finally a seal has been applied, that is the wound of his side, which Christ keeps showing to the Father to appease Him and to pay for our Redemption.[161]

Donne's use, then, of *sealing* in the sense of a legal confirmation in spiritual contexts was far from extraordinary. Moreover, his use of such metaphors was often quite casual. Where he did revivify the faded metaphor, he did so in the context of Salvation as a purchase, a large field of imagery that was traditionally fraught with legal terms.

# Salvation as a Purchase

"In *Adam* we were sold in *grosse;* in our selves we are sold by *retail*" (2:115, 3:755). Even such trade metaphors as this have to be seen in connection with biblical usage. The "Holy Ghost's metaphors" are Donne's avowed examples:

> To pursue then the *Holy Ghosts* two *Metaphors*, of *selling away* and *putting away*, First, *venditi estis*, sayes our *Prophet* to the *Iewes*, and to *all, Behold, you are sold;* and so they were; sold *thrice over;* sold by *Adam* first; sold by *themselves* every day; and at last, sold by *God*. [7:77, 2:146]

Becoming subjected to sin is described as selling oneself to evil.[162] In the same field of imagery, the divine act of Salvation is considered as a purchase that nullifies the first sale according to the promise: "Ye shall be redeemed without money." [163]

Such metaphors are so old that the primary job in analyzing Donne's use of them must be to compare his versions with earlier ones; the category of contemporary commerce and trade would be of only secondary importance as a source for certain elaborations. Metaphors presenting the concept of Salvation in terms of an exchange of goods, or barter, and in terms of a purchase abound in the Fathers and in liturgical texts.[164] Some of the expressions they use are *sacrum commercium, commercium emptionis,* and *redemptio*.

Augustine used the term *commercium* to mean sometimes a barter, sometimes a purchase; both present the act of Salvation, but from slightly different perspectives.[165] The first idea may be said to stress more the positive aspect of Salvation, that is, the bestowing of life on man; the second, the negative aspect, that is, redemption from foreign domination. Christ appears as a heavenly merchant (*negotiator caelestis*) who, in the former perspective, effects an exchange of wares in the world by taking on human nature and giving in exchange what is divine, that is, life, according to John 10:10. In the other perspective the heavenly merchant is not a trader but a "buyer" (*emptor*), who pays the price of His blood in order to ransom mankind.[166]

In Augustine's theology of the divine barter, Christ died that "compensation be made for a certain heavenly merchandise so that man would not see death." [167] His death is given in exchange for that "merchandise," eternal life. In the same sermon Augustine stresses the idea that Christ could effect this *commercium* only because of his double nature as God and man: "Since He therefore was God and man and wanted us to live of what is His, so He died of what is ours. For He did not have what He was to die of; and we did not have what we were to live of." [168] The entire passage serves to underline the disparity between the items exchanged: "What an exchange! What did He give and what did He receive?" [169]

In a related context Jean Rivière has argued against taking Augustine's passages about buying and selling too literally, and rightly insisted that "commercial similes by themselves have no doctrinal significance." [170] This opinion can be paraphrased by saying that vehicles alone cannot be the basis for theological argument. It would seem, moreover, that the most elaborate passages of this kind very often show in fact how unbusinesslike the divine *commercium* is. Thus Augustine once specifically referred to the ancient practice of commerce (*commercia antiqua*) as having consisted in the exchange of goods. Man bartered the things he had for those he needed. The amount of goods given or received in the bargain depended on the value of the merchandise, so that one gave much lead for a little silver: "However, no one gives his life to receive death." [171]

Donne used the idea of *commercium* in the sense of an exchange of goods only once, when elaborating a figure borrowed from Bernard:

So he [God] hath sealed the bodies of all mankind to his glory, by pre-assuming the body of Christ to that glory. For by that there is now *Commercium inter Coelum & terram:*

there is a Trade driven, a Staple established betweene Heaven and earth; *Ibi caro nostra, hic Spiritus ejus;* Thither have we sent our flesh, and hither hath he sent his Spirit. [4:62, 1:621]

Donne does not develop the Augustinian idea of Salvation as a divine *commercium* in the sense of an exchange, or *commutatio.* Instead of the *commercia antiqua,* which apparently required an explanation even in Augustine's time, Donne develops the idea of Salvation as *commercium emptionis,* or redemption.

This concept presents Christ as a *negotiator caelestis* who pays a price, often not specified, in order to buy man. Augustine usually developed this idea when he defended the universality of Salvation against the Donatists[172] and wanted to show that Christ gave his blood for all mankind. Augustine's use of the word *emere* ("to buy") echoes similar passages in Paul,[173] as in this passage from an exposition on the Psalms:

See the transaction of our purchase. Christ hangs on the wood; see the price at which He bought, and so you will see what He bought. He is about to buy something: you do not know what it is. See, see the price and you will see the thing. He shed His own blood; with His own blood He bought; He bought with the blood of the immaculate Lamb, He bought with the blood of His only-begotten Son. What was bought with the blood of the only-begotten Son of God? Look still what the price was. The prophet said long before it took place: "They pierced my hands and my feet, they counted all my bones." I see Christ, a large price: "All the borders of the earth shall remember themselves, and be turned unto the Lord." In one and the same Psalm I see the purchaser and the purchase! The purchaser is Christ: the price, His blood: the purchase, the world.[174]

Augustine speaks in quite similar terms of the deliverance of the individual soul. Christ's redemptive action is a *commercium,* in the sense of a buying back, or ransoming:

For your life has been redeemed from corruption: rest secure now: the contract of good faith has been entered upon; no man deceives, no man circumvents, no man oppresses, your Redeemer. He has made a bargain, he has already paid the price, He has poured forth His blood.[175]

The wealth of the Divine Merchant was often referred to by the Fathers. Bernard, developing a figure from Augustine, goes so far as to represent the Christ child as a sack which will be torn open in the Passion and from which will flow forth our ransom money.[176]

Donne likens Christ's wealth to the Wise Men's possessions and finally to the exchequer's treasure:

He came to us then, as the Wisemen came to him, with treasure, and gifts, and gold, and incense, and myrrhe; As having an ambition upon the soules of men, he came with that abundant treasure to purchase us. And as to them who live upon the Kings Pension, it is some comfort to heare that the Exchequer is full, that the Kings moneyes are come in: so is it to us, to know that there is enough in Gods hands, paid by his Son, for the discharge of all our debts. [5:372, 18:294]

Donne likes to quote Acts 20:28: "*God hath purchased his Church, with his owne blood, sayes S. Paul*" (3:294, 14:96), and 1 Corinthians 6:20: "*Ye are bought with a price sayes the Apostle*" (1:162, 1:395). Though man has to contribute to the new buying, his will alone, as Donne puts it, does not pay "one penny towards this purchase" (1:293, 8:303). If someone receives from God more than other people his obligation increases. Donne pictures this process in terms of an economic change: "The market changes, as the plenty of money changes" (2:286, 13:605). In his *Ninety-Six Sermons*, the first sermon, Lancelot Andrewes indicates the possible source of this analogy: "Further, we are to understand this: That *to whom much is given*, of them will much be required; and (as *Gregoris* well saith) *Cum crescant dona, crescunt et rationes donorum*, As the gifts grow, so grow the accompts too."[177]

Paul's sentence, which reappears in many variations[178]—in several sermons it even takes the particularly emphasized final posi-tion[179]—is, together with 1 Corinthians 6:20, in the center of a field that Donne furnishes not only with commercial but with specifically legal terms. God, he tells us, sends us the Holy Ghost as "Guardian Curator" to release us from the old contract (1:163, 1:447). He gives us a "Quietus est"; that is, he discharges us from the debts we incurred through our sins (1:163, 1:453) and finally sends us to a new "market," "the Magazine of his graces, his Church" (1:167, 1:594). Donne insists that Christ, who "bought us with himselfe, his blood, his life, is not dead *intestate*, but hath left his Will and Testament" (7:121, 4:126).

To understand the use of the word *emere* in 1 Corinthians 6:20 and 7:23 it is essential to realize that Christians are considered not as freemen but as the property of Christ. Expositors of Paul's words have traditionally taken these passages to refer to the practice of buying and selling slaves, an interpretation that has recently been contested.[180] The problem of biblical usage can be left to the specialist. In any case some of Augustine's expres-sions, such as "Ecce possessio Domini mei. Ius lego . . ." in the exposition from which I quoted earlier,[181] suggest that he thought along such lines. The idea of Christ's possession of man is of course closely connected with that of Satan's dominion over man, which Christ's dominion replaces. On the basis of scriptural passages dealing with Satan's tyranny over man,[182] some of the Fathers had developed the idea that by Adam's sin Satan had gained legal sovereignty over man. Some of the early writers, in-cluding Gregory of Nyssa, Basil, and Ambrose, went so far as to say that in order to release man from his bondage the price of Christ's purchase was paid to Satan, into whose power Adam had sold himself.[183] It is often hard to determine how literally such passages should be taken. Jean Rivière, who because of his life-long work on the subject has been called "théologue de la Rédemption," understands this idea as part of a "more or less rhetorical soteriology"[184] and stresses its metaphorical nature.

It may be significant that Donne, who so often echoed patristic metaphor, leaves out this ambiguous element of early redemptive theology. In his metaphorical thinking, what Christ has paid is "in Gods hands," as he says in the passage quoted above (5:372, 18:300). He does not hesitate, however, to present the Fall, in agreement with his sources, as the outcome of a negotiation between Adam and the Devil. In his translation of a Latin quotation he even omits the *ut ita dicam* by which Cassianus had tried to attenuate the metaphor of Adam's *commercium*:

> Now, how are we sold to sin? By *Adam?* That's true; *Ejus praevaricatione, & ut ita dicam, Negotiatione, damnoso, & fraudolento commercio venditi sumus:* Wee were all sold under hand, fraudulently sold, and sold under foot, cheaply sold by *Adam.* [2:115, 3:744]

Elsewhere he illustrates the idea of Adam's sellout in these terms:

> How and how justly do we cry out against a Man, that hath sold a *Towne,* or sold an *Army.* And *Adam* sold the *World.* He sold *Abraham,* and *Isaac* and *Jacob,* and all the *Patriarchs,* and all the *Prophets.* [7:78, 2:180]

Donne's hortatory purpose often makes him point out the consequence for the individual soul of Adam's "sale": man "forfeited his interest and state in heaven by *Adams* sin" (1:303, 9:93), and by his consent to do evil man ratifies Adam's heinous bargain (2:115, 3:749). Donne feels, however, that the analogy between sale and sin is not perfect, for, paradoxically, "we sell our selves and grow the farther in debt, by being sold" (1:157, 1:220). The analogy holds insofar as man is not immediately "discharged" as soon as he realizes that his "bargain" was a bad one (2:116, 3:770).

The quotations above point up what may be, if not a peculiarity, at least a somewhat divergent tendency of Donne's elaboration of this field of imagery. According to the Fathers, Adam's sin was often the submission by sale to Satan's tyrannous rule. Men come to be held as prisoners (*captivi*).[185] They are prisoners of the Devil and serve demons.[186] Accordingly, Christ's redeeming action is presented as the deliverance of slaves.[187] Now it is true

that Donne occasionally echoes the traditional view that by con-
senting to sin men become its "slaves" (2:115, 3:738); he has a
tendency, however, to present what with the Fathers was often
a bondage to Satan as a financial bond. Augustine's *possessio* and
*ius* become a financial obligation, man's "sale" to sin a contracting
of debts. Adam's sin consisted above all in his prodigality, he
spent everything (1:162, 1:428). This is why Donne can say that
"we sell our selves and grow the farther in debt by being sold,"
and why man is not "discharged of his bargain of being sold
under sin, as soon as hee sees that he hath made an ill bargain"
(2:116, 3:770).

The nature of the metaphorical field in which the Fall is seen
naturally influences the terms used to represent Salvation through
Christ. In spite of Rivière's insistence on the metaphorical character of the concept of Christ's purchase, it is possible that the
symmetry expressed in the idea of *commercium*, of sale and purchase, by the early Fathers was not merely the result of consistent metaphorical thinking. Originally, at least, the symmetry
had to do with the concept, so popular in patristic theology, of
*recirculatio*, the idea that a previous state is restored in the same
way in which it has been lost.[188] The idea was supported by
Paul's parallel between Adam and Christ,[189] and was most clearly
expressed by Ambrose:

> One must remember the manner in which the first Adam
> was driven out of Paradise into the desert in order to under-
> stand the manner in which the second Adam returned from
> the desert to Paradise. See how the first decisions are resolved
> by their own knots and how the divine benefices are restored
> in their own traces. From virgin soil Adam, Christ from the
> Virgin; the former made in the image of God, the latter the
> image of God . . . death by the tree, life by the cross.[190]

Although there is no evidence that Donne shared the patristic
view of a recirculation or recapitulation, the symmetry had been
operative in the metaphorical expression of Fall and Salvation for
too long not to influence Donne's expression of these concepts. It

is not surprising, then, that the Dean of Saint Paul's, who so often presents Adam's sin as a financial obligation, speaks of Salvation as a discharge of that obligation. Christ is the divine merchant who accomplishes man's Redemption by paying all man's debts. In the following passage this idea is combined with the concept of the recirculation, here expressed by a similarity in kind between debt and discharge:

> Not disputing therefore, what other wayes God might have taken for our redemption, but giving him all possible thanks for that way which his goodnesse hath chosen, by the way of satisfying his justice, (for, howsoever I would be glad to be discharged of my debts any way, yet certainly, I should think my selfe more beholden to that man, who would be content to pay my debt for me, then to him that should entreat my creditor to forgive me my debt) for this work, to make Christ able to pay this debt, there was something to be added to him. First, he must pay it in such money as was lent; in the nature and flesh of man; for man had sinned, and man must pay. [4:288, 11:171]

Donne assures his congregation elsewhere that no one can have "a better *pay-master*" than Christ (4:189, 7:356). In a passage already quoted he likens Christ's wealth to the treasure of the Wise Men, who came loaded with gold and precious gifts, and refers to the comfort a pensioner derives from the knowledge that the king's exchequer is well provided with funds (5:372, 18:294). He prays with the Psalmist, paraphrasing him in monetary terms:

> Therefore I have also another Prayer in the same Psalme, *Spiritu principali confirma me*, Sustaine me, uphold me with thy free spirit, thy large, thy munificent spirit: for thy ordinary graces will not defray me, nor carry me through this valley of tentations; not thy single money, but thy Talents; not as thou art thine owne Almoner, but thine owne Treasurer. [5:358, 17:726]

To explain the nature of Christ's *commercium*, of His "bargain of Redemption," Donne often refers to financial transactions. In the following passage Christ is compared to someone entering upon a bond to relieve someone else from his debts:

> But yet, Beloved, Christ hath not made so improvident a bargaine, as to give so great a rate, himselfe, for a Church, so farre in reversion, as till the day of Judgement: That he should enter into bonds for this payment, from all eternity, even in the *eternal decree* between the Father, and him, that he should really pay this price, his precious bloud, for his Church, *one thousand six hundred years* agoe, and he should receive no glory by this Church till the next world: Here was a long lease. [5:126, 5:493]

Donne carries the analogy even further. If Christ pays our debts, he also helps us not to relapse into the old sin of prodigality by sending us the Holy Ghost as tutor. The preacher compares the Holy Ghost to a guardian or curator who will "reverse all contracts and bargains" a minor has made and "hinder him from making new contracts": "This blessed Spirit of consolation . . . seals to our consciences a *Quietus est,* a discharge of all former spiritual debts, he cancells all them, he nails them to the cross of Christ" (1:163, 1:451).

The last part of this quotation indicates that such "prosaic" metaphors are not so extraneous to the matter of a sermon as they may seem, for it links the legal metaphors with the words of Paul (Col. 2:14), who assured the Colossians that Christ blotted out "the handwriting of ordinances that was against us, which was contrary to us, and took it out of the way, nailing it to his cross." There can be no doubt that even in his many metaphors referring to the "debt" contracted by Adam and discharged in the Passion Donne could to some extent follow the example of the Bible and of the church fathers. This is not to belittle the influence such a learned and relatively homogeneous audience as that at Lincoln's Inn may have had on his sermons; the knowledge of legal terms that he could assume his congregation to have certainly influenced his choice of metaphor. It cannot be over-looked, however, that legal terms have a firm place in early Christian homiletics and in the Roman liturgy.

One of many sources is Paul's letter to the Colossians just quoted, which mentions a *chirographum*, a "handwriting," or signature expressing the obligation of a debtor. The Latin *chiro-graphum* also means "bond" or "security." According to Augus-tine, it is by signing such a contract that man, through his consent to sin, sells himself into the bondage of Satan.[191] The "signature under sin" thus becomes synonymous with the document of the contract.[192] The *chirographum peccatorum* is proof that we are held in bail; it is *cautio contra nos*, as Augustine puts it, that is, a security, bond, or warranty.[193] Through it man "forfeited his interest and state in heaven" (1:303, 9:93). It is this contract that is conceived to have been nailed to the cross and voided in the Passion.

Another important source of metaphor in Christian literature is the legal term *pignus* (also *arrhabo*), which is used in the Vul-gate in connection with Redemption. Paul represents the Holy Spirit to the Ephesians as "the earnest [*pignus*] of our inheritance until the redemption of the purchased possession."[194] *Pignus* as used in legal language, as E. Hegemann-Springer has shown, has a clearly definable meaning. It is a pledge in the sense of a *Faustpfand;* that is, it indicates a definite right to full possession, whereas the mortgage-holder's contract (*hypotheca*) contains only a possibility of future possession.[195] The expression fits perfectly into the field of imagery under consideration, as Herz recognizes in his study of the concept of the *sacrum commer-cium*.[196]

Donne's fondness for the church fathers as models even for his legal imagery suggests that we should push the analysis a little further, although, because of the complexity of the subject, we will be on less firm ground. In the earliest Christian writings *pignus* appears in close connection with the concept of *fides* (faith), and this relationship has recently been stressed in studies of early Christian language.[197] Herz has shown that in Augustine *pignus* does not express a legal relationship (*Rechtsverhältnis*).[198] To read it merely as a technical term of legal and business language would obscure the fact that it is applied to something that is not yet an accomplishment, but a future possession—our salvation. Christ's death, which we have as a pledge (*tenemus pignum mortem Christi*),[199] is our title, our assurance of receiving the life of Christ, and it strengthens our faith in the fulfillment of all God's promises. "The divine merchandise, life," Herz summarizes Augustine, "is granted us now in the sacrament, but is also the future possession of Salvation. The *sacrum commercium* is both present and future, an event in the history of salvation that must be tested in faith."[200] Herz and Dürig observe that in early Christian literature *pignus* and *commercium* are raised from the level of profane legal terminology to a sphere of sacred usage. Although Donne was of course familiar with Calvin's more legalistic theology of Salvation, the closeness of Donne's imagery to that of the church fathers may serve as a warning not to interpret his clothing the history of Salvation in legal terms as necessarily legalistic or even mercantile thinking.[201]

Besides *pignus*, the Vulgate also uses the word *arrhabo*.[202] In Genesis the Authorized Version translates it as "pledge"; it can mean, more specifically, a deposit or, as Donne says, the "earnest-money." In the following passage he develops a figure from Jerome:

> *Vt ex arrabone aestimetur haereditas;* That by the proportion of the earnest, we might value the whole bargaine: For what a bargaine would we presume that man to have, that would give 20000 *l.* for earnest? what is the Joy of heaven hereafter, if the earnest of it here, be the Seale of the holy Ghost?
> [10:226, 10:507]

For Donne and for Jerome, from whom he takes his inspiration, *arrhabo* was identical with the *pignus haereditatis nostrae*, as the Holy Ghost is called in the Epistle to the Ephesians. Donne's analogy, loosely presented as a question, argues the greatness of the joy to be expected in the afterlife. His use of a sum of money for illustration does not make the relation between the joy in this life and the joy to be expected any more legalistic or mercantile than it is in Paul, for this relation is grounded on faith. Donne has made this very clear in the previous paragraph, where he chose Abraham, the archetype of the man of faith, as an example of a man in whom joy was not destroyed but sanctified through the expectation of the joy of the next world.

In a sermon preached at Whitehall in 1620, Donne says:

> To them, who have temporall blessings without spirituall, they are but uselesse blessings, . . . they shall not purchase a minutes peace of conscience here, nor a minutes refreshing to the soule hereafter. . . . But when a man hath a good title to Heaven, then these are good evidences: for, *Godlinesse hath a promise of the life to come, and of the life that now is;* and if we spend any thing in maintenance of that title, give, or lose any thing for his glory and making sure this salvation, *We shall inherit everlasting life,* sayes the best surety in the world; but we shall not stay so long for our bill of charge, we shall have *A hundred fold in this life.* [3:79, 2:221]

The "surety" in this passage is of course Christ. In the field of imagery in which Adam's sin is a "sale" formulated in a contract that Satan holds up to man as a *cautio*,[203] Salvation can be represented as a purchase set down in a new contract, a *contractus bonae fidei,* as Augustine says in a passage already quoted.[204] It is a new "contract, and bargaine, of acceptation by the Father, that *Pactum salis*" (5:135, 6:185), Donne says with reference to Numbers 18:19, and Christ is its "surety." The "surety" takes it upon himself to pay our "debts": "Consider our debts to God, to be our sins, and so we dare not come to a reckoning with him, but we discharge our selves intirely upon our surety, our Saviour Christ Jesus" (4:304, 12:28). The idea of Christ as a surety is not so unusual in homiletic literature. In Cawdrey's handbook it is worked out in an elaborate simile.[205] Donne presents the metaphor as a hypothesis: "Consider . . ." Later in the same sermon he rules out any doubt that he is speaking figuratively when he points to what in terms of human economics is a paradox: "This is a circumstance, nay, an essentiall difference peculiar to our debts to God, that we doe not pay them, except we contract more; we grow best out of debt, by growing farther in debt" (4:309, 12:228).

Occasionally it could in fact be called his method to show that Salvation is a bargain and not a bargain, and thus to make his congregation aware of the fact that he is speaking a special idiom, a language raised from the profane level and adapted to the expression of the profoundest mysteries of religion. Thus, developing a figure quoted from Bernard, he refers to the divine purchase as "simony": *"Ecclesiam quaesivit, et acquisivit,* Hee desired a Church, and he purchased a Church; but by a blessed way of Simony; *Adde medium acquisitionis, Sanguine acquisivit, He purchased a Church with his own blood"* (7:232, 8:613). Apparently the preacher was so pleased with this elaboration that, in a later sermon, he sharpened it to form a pointed oxymoron: "The holy Ghost is so ours, as that we, we in Christ, Christ in our nature merited the holy Ghost, purchased the holy Ghost, bought the holy Ghost; Which is a sanctified simony" (7:441, 18:254).

If in the language of the Church, as authors like Dürig and Herz insist, legal terms are raised from the profane sphere to a higher one, the reason is that by frequent metaphorical use based on one and the same analogy and in the same context, the vehicular sphere and the conceptual, in this case the religious, sphere become automatically associated. Constant use of such terms in the same field of imagery may in fact blunt their metaphorical character: they become theological terms. *Redemption* is a case in point. The fading of the metaphor is noticeable as early as in Augustine's time. Jean Rivière has observed that Augustine used *redimere, emere, comparare,* without distinction.[206] I hope to have shown that Donne, like the preachers he imitated, revivified the old metaphor by devising new analogies, by taking in, as it were, new aspects of the secular realm and linking them to the venerable concept. A sermon in Latin would often accomplish this more smoothly than one in the vernacular, since the theological terms, which were originally devised in Latin, would be more transparent. In this respect Donne was from the start at a disadvantage. He tried to obviate the difficulty by quoting and paraphrasing. Thus his "own" imagery seems one step further removed from the central theological concept, to which, however, it is linked by many ties. The point may be illustrated by another example.

In what may be called a *figura etymologica*, which brings to light the original meaning of *redemption*, Donne quotes Jerome,[207] referring also to Paul's words:

> S. *Hierome* saies, *Gentes non Redimuntur, sed emuntur:* The Gentiles, saies hee, are not properly Christs, by way of Redeeming, but by an absolute purchase: To which purpose those words are also applied, which the Apostle saies to the Corinthians, *Ye are bought with a price.* [6:344, 17:489]

It is true that what was said earlier about the liturgical use of *pignus*—that by being used in connection with *fides* it had shed some of its legalistic connotations—cannot be said of the word *mortgage*, which Donne now proceeds to use figuratively. At any rate he deems it necessary to draw support from Jerome. It is only after referring to his *Gentes non Redimuntur, sed emuntur* and to the passage from the First Epistle to the Corinthians (6:20) that he embarks on more elaborate figures:

> S. *Hieroms* meaning therein, is, that if we compare the Jews and the Gentiles, . . . the Jews were but as in a mortgage, for they had beene Gods peculiar people before; But the Gentiles were as the devils inheritance, for God had never claimed them, nor owned them for his. [6:344, 17:493]

The examination of an extensive field of imagery in which Salvation is seen as a purchase keeps one from artificially isolating such spheres as commerce and law. Because of the large number of such metaphors the temptation to misinterpret the material is great. They do not necessarily reflect Donne's special interests, nor are they adequately characterized as "homely." [208] It has been said that profane things used as they are by Donne to illustrate some profound truth of religion give us a shock of surprise, and that a suggestion of profanity arises when the things coupled are sacred and secular.[209] This conception of metaphysical metaphor has been too rigorously applied. In some respects it is no more helpful than the Renaissance attention to a "distance" between tenor and vehicle in a supposed hierarchy of being. Both views ignore the fact that the two things coupled together cease to be two things and become a third, which then stands in relation to similar metaphors. Salvation can be called a profound truth of religion; however, Donne can clothe it in mercantile and financial terms without disharmony because there is a metaphorical field of redemption.

In his poetry Donne can in fact step even "lower." The following metaphor has been called, with some justice, "a peak in his [Donne's] juxtaposition of the holy and the worldly":[210]

And as a robb'd man, which by search doth finde
His stolne stuffe sold, must lose or buy it againe:
The Sonne of glory came downe, and was slaine,
Us whom he had made, and Satan stolne, to unbinde.[211]

It may be that, as Helen Gardner supposes in her note to this poem, the original version had "steede" instead of "stuffe," a reading that is supported by one of the manuscripts and that, moreover, gives a more apt analogy if contemporary legal practice is taken into account. Salvation would then be presented in terms of a horse trade. However, it is not necessary to build on speculation: "stolne stuffe" is "low" enough. And yet in this case as in those discussed above one can hardly speak of dissonance or profanation of the divine, because Donne moves within a traditional field of imagery. Donne may, as he so often does, especially before his listeners at Lincoln's Inn, clothe the history of Salvation in the legal terms with which they are familiar, but his frame of reference, whether in his sermons or in his poetry, is always the central biblical metaphor of Salvation as a purchase.

That Donne used such metaphors for their rhetorical effectiveness can be inferred from his admiration for the biblical images of Redemption:

As *Christ* in his *Parable* comprehends all excuses, and all backwardnesses in the following of him, in those two, *Marriage* and *Purchasing*, (for one had bought the Land and stocke, and another had married a Wife) So *God* expresses his love to Man, in these two too, Hee hath married us, he hath bought us; that so he might take in all dispositions, and worke upon Uxorious Men, men soupled and entendred with Matrimoniall love, and upon worldly men, men kneaded and plaistred with earthly love. [7:91, 2:670]

Such metaphors, then, are codes through which God spells out his love to different minds. The preacher may hope to reach his listeners, whom he here dichotomizes, in the same manner.

Before I give some brief attention to the other field of imagery referred to in this passage, divine marriage, I want to examine in some detail the important concept of spiritual vision.

# The Eyes of the Soul

"Eyes of the soul" is here considered as the central metaphor of a field of imagery in which the act of understanding is represented in terms of visual perception. The "angle" [212] of such images may often be smaller than the angle of images in other fields, but it is not my intention to start from an arbitrary distinction between "dead" metaphor (as when we say "I see" to indicate that we have understood something), commonplace metaphor, and original coining. An analysis that would begin with such distinctions in order then to eliminate the dead and faded imagery would disregard the organic nature of figurative discourse, in which the faded is constantly revivified and the novel supported by the old. In any case such distinctions cannot be made at the beginning, although they may eventually evolve. In fact, in most instances visual perception and spiritual vision are clearly distinct. Incidentally, the difference was for Donne theologically relevant; even after the transfiguration of our body, he tells us, we will not be able really to see God, for the perception referred to in 1 John 3:2 relates only to the eyes of the soul:

> but the eyes of our soul, shal be so enlightned, as that they shal see God *Sicuti est*. . . . Now the *sight* of God in this text, is the *knowledge* of God, to *see* God, is but to *know*, that there is a God. [4:168, 6:187]

The mirror metaphor of the First Epistle to the Corinthians ("we see through a glass, darkly") had great influence on this field of imagery. The reader of patristic literature soon recognizes the intimate connection between the *oculus mentis* (or *oculus animae*) metaphor and Paul's words, which seem to have given it its special status. His words stimulated the exegetes to coin new metaphors of spiritual sight, and such metaphors tended to be supported by a quotation from the epistle. The passage reads in the Vulgate: "Videmus nunc per speculum in aenigmate: tunc autem facie ad faciem. Nunc cognosco ex parte: tunc autem cognoscam sicut cognitus sum." [213] Augustine referred to the passage in his explanation of the Psalms: "They had eyes, have not we? Yes, we too have the eyes of the heart: but as yet we see through faith, not by sight. When will it be by sight? When shall we, as the Apostle says, see him 'face to face?'" [214] In another place, which might have been in Donne's mind when he wrote the passage quoted above, Augustine insisted on the special nature of this vision, thus giving the whole passage a figurative turn: "Glory to our Lord . . . because his first truth veiled in flesh came to us and healed through His flesh the interior eye of our heart, in order that thereafter we may be able to see It face to face." [215] In his comment on Paul's words, Rhabanus Maurus referred to Pope Gregory's variation of the image.[216] According to Gregory, the apostle's sight is obstructed as by smoke or thick fog (*caligo*).

The field of imagery was particularly elaborated by the mystics. Bernard liked to point out the analogy between the *oculus corporeus* and the *oculus interior*. Quite naturally he used the verb *caligare* to express the idea that, just as one's eyesight may be dimmed even after the piece of straw that caused the irritation has been removed, so inner vision can be impaired through the aftereffects of sin.[217]

Sometimes the analogy between the two kinds of vision allowed Bernard to make some fine distinctions, as when he explained that God in his goodness sometimes removes the cloud that hides him from us: then we may "see" even though, as long as we are on our pilgrimage, we cannot see *proprie* but only as through a mist (*caligo*).[218] Elsewhere he constructed out of a few elements a regular system that was meant to take care of all possibilities of faulty spiritual vision. He said there that as there are two requirements for a good eye, love of the good and knowledge of the truth, so there are two vices that pervert it, blindness and distortion. Now between the two virtues of the *oculus interior*, which consist in not deceiving and not being deceived (*nec fallere, nec falli*),[219] and its two vices, which consist in permitting just these things to happen, there are two more possibilities: the *oculus interior* may be deceived by ignorance of the truth, yet because of love of the good refuse its consent to the deception; or worse, while not being deceived about the truth, yet it may fail to love good rather than evil.[220] The description of this truly medieval system of spiritual vision was followed by some examples in which the basic analogy of the field of imagery was further explicated.[221]

The use of the field allowed Bernard to speak effectively about purifying man's spiritual vision. One of his passages culminates in the sentence: "These are the two things that purify the eye of the heart: prayer and confession." [222] Treating of impaired spiritual vision in his *Sermo de conversione ad clericos*, he naturally also quotes the mirror passage from the First Epistle to the Corinthians. The quotation is preceded by this passage:

> How detestable is the defect that robs us of such a vision [of God]; and how abominable the negligence of not purifying the eye of the soul. For as our corporeal vision is sometimes hampered by an inner humor or by some dust which falls into it from outside, so our spiritual vision is troubled sometimes by the pleasures of the flesh and sometimes by worldly dissipation and ambition.[223]

As a background for Donne's figures it is interesting to note that quite specialized optical imagery had its traditional place in the explanation of Paul's metaphor. Tommaso de Vio, bishop of Gaeta, whom Donne usually refers to as Cajetan, gave two readings of the speculum metaphor:

> But to see *per speculum* can be understood in two ways: either we see in a glass the images resulting from people, trees, etc. or we see through eye glasses. And it is proven by both ways that we see *per speculum* in a divine mystery: for we see God not in Himself but in His likenesses which are His creatures: And the knowledge we gain of God and of the heavenly kingdom by looking at these likenesses is not clear but obscure. Only very darkly, incompletely, through images as if through dark glasses do we see what belongs to God and His heavenly realm.[224]

Cajetan's reading was a matter of controversy, as is evidenced by Estius's comment printed in the *Biblia maxima versionum:*

> Cajetan believes that *per speculum videre* can be understood as to mean the manner in which we see through optical glasses called spectacles; but that is not likely. For such are used to see more clearly; and therefore this simile or metaphor would not serve its purpose.[225]

Nicholas of Lyra develops a whole system of corresponding kinds of vision.[226] There is first the kind of natural perception by which something is immediately perceived by the senses, as when light enters the eye and is perceived. Secondly, something may be perceived not by its presence "but through a representation received in the sensory apparatus, derived, however, directly from the sensible object, as color is perceived." The third kind of perception is also through a representation or image, but this time an image derived indirectly from the sensible object. This is the way something is seen in a mirror. Parallel to these kinds of perception there exist, according to Lyra, three types of cognition by which God can be seen: one *per essentiam*, of which God alone is capable, another by similitude directly derived from God, a form of cognition especially fitting for the angels, and a third, *quasi in speculo*, by which man is led through the creatures as through a mirror to a cognition of God.

Donne was aware of the controversy about Paul's *speculum* metaphor, which fascinated him so much that he chose it as a text to preach on. In a sermon on 1 Corinthians 13:12, he says:

> But how doe we see in a glasse? Truly, that is not easily determined. The old Writers in the Optiques said, That when we see a thing in a glasse, we see not the thing itselfe, but a representation onely; All the later men say, we doe see the thing it selfe, but not by direct, but by reflected beames. . . . This may well consist with both, That as that which we see in a glasse, assures us, that such a thing there is, (for we cannot see a dreame in a glasse, nor a fancy, nor a Chimera) so this sight of God, which our Apostle sayes we have *in a glasse*, is enough to assure us, that a God there is. [8:222, 9:129]

Cornelius à Lapide, whose commentaries Donne often consulted, says that a glass does in fact show the thing itself, however, not by direct but by reflected rays, and therefore "not properly or distinctly, but as from afar, obscurely and confusedly." [227] To the examples used to explain this idea—the eyeglass (*perspicilla senum, speculum oculare*) and a "green glass" used to support weak eyes while reading—he adds a dark shop window that conceals the wares as much as it shows them.

Donne takes up the field of imagery in which insight is presented as sight and elaborates it in two directions: first, our vision can be obstructed in the sense that we perceive something only indirectly, that is, we see only a reflection or our vision is clouded (Cajetan speaks in this context of *aliquid medium offuscans*) [228] or, second, spiritual vision may be concentrated, an idea that will be expressed in terms of mirrors and lenses.

In the first case Donne closely follows traditional lines. Sometimes he just paraphrases the Vulgate: "We see God *per speculum* . . . by reflection, upon a glasse" (3:111, 3:731), where the Authorized Version has "through a glasse darkly." As the creatures were to Lyra the *speculum* in which to behold God, so Donne explains that to see God *sicut manifestetur* is to begin "to see him, *Sicuti est*, As he is, in his Essence" (4:73, 2:378). In the sermon, mentioned earlier, on 1 Corinthians 13:12, cognition of God is often spoken of in terms of the optical process of reflection. In the English rendering of Paul's words, which he once varies with the *in speculo* of the Second Epistle to the Corinthians,[229] Donne alternates freely between "in a glasse" and "through a glasse" thus leaving himself scope for a variety of tropes of spiritual sight.

> This glasse is better then the water; The Water gives crookednesse, and false dimensions to things that it shewes; as we see by an Oare when we row a Boat, and as the Poet describes a wry and distorted face, *Qui faciem sub aqua Phoebe natantis habes*, That he looked like a man that swomme under water. But in the glasse, which the Apostle intends, we may see God directly, that is, see directly that there is a God. [8:223, 9:139]

In this sermon Donne chooses to disagree with Cyril's interpretation of Paul's phrase, "*Videmus quasi in fumo*, sayes he, we see God as in a smoak" (8:223, 9:146). Yet he often echoes such traditional elaborations of the field as Bernard's, mentioned above, or Cyril's, who elsewhere spoke of those who are "obscured by murky darkness." [230] The body, the flesh, obstructs man's vision like a cloud, "All other men, by occasion of this flesh, have darke *clouds*" (3:354, 17:235); in particular, original sin veils and paralyzes the understanding because man has "*within him*, a darke vapor of *originall sinne*, and the cloud of *humane flesh without him*" (3:355, 17:265). It is likewise original sin that—also as a cloud of passion (3:277, 13:100)—prevents the eye of the soul from adequately perceiving dimensions (2:118, 3:863), it "ever smoakes up, and creates a soote in the soule" (3:355, 17:280).

Such metaphors, which make sin visible by showing how it obstructs spiritual vision, are almost timeless in homiletic literature, yet they were still felt to be interesting enough to be included in Robert Cawdrey's *Treasurie of Similies*. The sinner's vision is there said to be obscured by "filthy mysts and stinking vapors." [231] As to a difference between Donne's and Cawdrey's tropes in this field of imagery it may tentatively be said that Cawdrey's are fairly gross, with adjectives calling forth an emotional appeal, whereas Donne's figures tend to rely more on the diminution of light that results from interposing a medium. This is true even of a passage like the following, which is part of a longer paragraph on the "terror of God" and not quite free from what T. S. Eliot has called Donne's "cheap effects":

When I look upon God, as I am bid to doe in this Text, in those terrible Judgements, which he hath executed upon some men, and see that there is nothing between mee and the same Judgement . . . I am not able of my selfe to dye that glasse, that spectacle, thorow which I looke upon this God, in what colour I will; whether this glasse shall be black, through my despaire, and so I shall see God in the cloud of my sinnes, or red in the blood of Christ Jesus, and I shall see God in a Bath of the blood of his Sonne . . . I of my selfe cannot tell. [8:123, 4:482]

Although the basis of such metaphors is topical, some concentration is noticeable when one compares them with an elaborate and labored simile from Cawdrey:

As wee looking through a Glasse, be it blue or yellow, or

of any other colour, all the things wee see, seeme to us to
be of the colour of the glasse, through which we did behold
them: So God also, beholding and looking upon us in his
Sonne, we seeme to him to be of his colour, (notwithstanding
our manifold Imperfections and wants) and we have the
appearance and brightness of his innocence and righteous-
nesse, which causeth, that in seeing, and touching us, he
thinketh, he seeth and toucheth his owne naturall Sonne.[232]

By their nature, the images in which Donne represents a focusing of spiritual vision make use of more precisely optical processes. Rather than appealing to a moral sense of light and color
(as do to some extent "clouds of flesh," "vapors of sin," and
so on), they address themselves to a sense of quantity and size,
and are a means of conveying rapid diminutions and sudden
changes of proportion. They occur even in passages of theological
argument:

> *Saint Augustine* hath seen Christ in the flesh one thousand
> two hundred yeares; in Christs glorifyed flesh; but, it is with
> the eyes of his understanding, and in his soul. Our flesh,
> even in the Resurrection, cannot be a spectacle, a perspective
> glasse to our soul. [3:112, 3:774]

"Multiplying glass" and "spectacle" were Donne's favorite terms
for expressing a concentration of spiritual vision: "He [God]
seeth all the way, and at *thy last gaspe,* he will make thee see
too, through the multiplying Glasse, the Spectacle of *Desperation*"
(4:150, 5:175). As in this case, Donne often used the metaphor
to express the extreme intensity of terror in spiritual vision just
before death. Thus he asks elsewhere: ". . . and will he forgive
that over-quick sight, when I shall see my sins through Satans
multiplying glasse of desperation, when I shall thinke them
greater then his mercy, upon my death-bed?" (5:81, 3:163). The
distortion of spiritual vision at the approach of death is presented
as a deceptive blowing-up of the objects seen, "when in that
multiplying glasse of *Despaire,* which he shall present, every

sinfull *thought* shall have the proportion of an Act, and every *Act*, of a *Habite*" (7:413, 16:745).

The processes of focusing, multiplying, and coloring spiritual vision summarize what in the first chapter was observed to be one of Donne's main intents when forming tropes, to adjust and readjust proportions and scales of values. Any trope, even mere description, can accomplish this aim, yet the representation of such changes of spiritual perspective in terms of optical processes, so frequent in Donne's sermons, is the most concrete expression of the design he has on his congregation. Although such tropes often deal with man's extremity, their appeal to a sense of perspective and proportion removes them at least one step from mere evocation of the horror of death. By their "intellectual" nature they even help to balance scenes of horror:

> 'Tis the *end* that qualifies all; and what kinde of man I shall be at my end, upon my *death-bed*, what trembling hands, and what lost legs, what deafe eares, and what gummy eyes, I shall have then, I know; and the nearer I come to that disposition, in my life, (the more *mortified* I am) the better I am disposed to see this object, future glory. God made the Sun, and Moon, and Stars, glorious lights for man to see by; but mans infirmity requires *spectacles;* and affliction does that office. [4:171, 6:301]

The difference in kinds of vision that can tentatively be described in terms of "understanding" versus "imagination" has little to do with the distinction between images using and not using color. If the following trope making use of color is different from the medieval *caligo* metaphor in that Donne insists on the optical process, it is even more different from later writers' use of "colored" images (as, for instance Marvell or Burns) to represent more complete emotional attitudes and processes: "But that man, who through his owne *red glasse*, can see Christ, in that colour too, through his own miseries, can see Christ Jesus in his blood, . . . this man . . . beholds God" (4:174, 6:426). Red is not only the color of the martyrs, the color of human sacrifice, but it is also, as Donne never tires of explaining, the name of Adam,[233] who was formed from red clay. Spiritual vision is made concrete by the same optical process in Donne's injunction: "Through that *Spectacle*, the bloud of thy *Saviour*, looke upon that *Bill*, and thou shalt see, that that *Bill* was nayld to the *Crosse* when he was naylde . . ." (7:91, 2:661); and again one can observe that in spite of references to blood and to nails, the intellectual precision with which the analogy is presented keeps the image from working on a merely emotional level.

In a number of cases Donne's use of *theatrum mundi* metaphors is an explication of the larger field of imagery in which understanding is presented in terms of perception. This may be a puzzling statement, since Weinrich, the only theorist on the subject, conceived of the field of imagery as a unit and did not investigate either substructures or the interrelation of such fields. It stands to reason, however, that the fields of imagery do not lie neatly one beside the other like the compartments of an egg carton; they occasionally overlap. If, as in the present case, one observes in an individual writer that the majority of the images of one field (*theatrum mundi*) are used in such a way that they fit into another field (spiritual vision) so as to become part of the substructure of the larger field, this individual usage deserves some attention.

In a section entitled "Theatrical Metaphors," E. R. Curtius has written a brief history of the *theatrum mundi* topos.[234] Starting with Plato, he traces the world-stage metaphor through classical and medieval writers. He finds that among writers as early as the Cynics, the comparison of the world to a stage was a much-used cliché. Augustine writes: "Here on earth it is as if children should say to their parents: Come! think of departing hence; we too would play our comedy! For nought but a comedy of the race of man is all this life, which leads from temptation to temptation." [235] An entire chapter in *Policraticus*, Shakespeare's *As You Like It*, Cervantes's *Don Quixote*—they all vary the basic analogy of the *theatrum mundi*. Most such elaborations of this field of imagery have in common a theme of pretense, illusion, and disillusionment. Donne used the metaphor at least once in this sense in his sermons. Talking about sincerity in prayer he says:

> Nor is it those transitory and interlocutory prayers, which out of custome and fashion we make, and still proceed in our sin; when we pretend to speake to God, but like Comedians upon a stage, turne over our shoulder, and whisper to the Devill. [9:325, 14:422]

In another passage Donne refers to the acclaim or disapproval an actor may get for his performance:

> He that relyes upon his *Plaudo domi,* Though the world hisse, I give my selfe a Plaudite at home, I have him at my Table, and her in my bed, whom I would have, and I care not for rumor; he that rests in such a Plaudite, prepares for a Tragedy, a Tragedy in the Amphitheater, the double Theater, this world, and the next too. [9:309, 13:478]

This variation is in line with many traditional *theatrum mundi* metaphors in which the world was conceived of as a place where action, determined by its end, is particularly significant. Neither of the passages quoted belongs to the field of imagery in which understanding was presented in terms of perception, nor do any of those adduced by Curtius in his brief study of theatrical metaphor.

In Donne the nine occurrences of the *theatrum mundi* analogy that do fall within the field of spiritual vision all come within one sermon. Significantly it is the sermon on 1 Corinthians 13:12. One paragraph, the theme of which is indicated by the marginal note "Theatrum, mundus" (8:223, 9:152), closes with the sentence: "Whether we be in the darknesse of ignorance, or darknesse of the works of darknesse, or darknesse of oppression of spirit in sadnesse, The world is the Theatre that represents God, and every where every man may, nay must see him" (8:224, 9:171). The theme, varied many times throughout the sermon, can be called *mundus theatrum Dei:* "By the light of Nature, in the Theatre of the World, by the Medium of Creatures, we see God . . ." (8:228, 9:345). In the other seven occurrences this "medium" is specified as a "glasse," or mirror (vol. 8, no. 9, lines 44, 177, 197, 234, 260, 429, 633).

This, then, is the special shape Donne gave to his *theatrum mundi* metaphors. Illusion, pleasure, or any of the other points of comparison that traditionally motivated images in this field were not used. The tropes are firmly incorporated into the field of spiritual vision. In such figures the theater is not primarily a place where a play is staged; the relevant fact about it is that it is a place which allows for concentrated vision:

> For our sight of God here, our Theatre, the place where we sit and see him, is the whole world, the whole house and frame of nature, and our *medium*, our *glasse*, is the Booke of Creatures, and our light, by which we see him, is the light of Naturall Reason. [8:220, 9:42]

The text of the sermon is the passage from First Corinthians that was, as we have seen, a primary source of spiritual vision images. This subject matter, along with the general importance the field of spiritual vision had for Donne, is sufficient to explain how that field has here drawn a related one into its compass. However, the seeming inconsistency of these passages in which theatergoers apparently are not watching plays but peering into "lookingglasses" (8:225, 9:178) requires an additional note.

In spite of the fact that these figures might be labeled "optical imagery," they apparently do not appeal to the visual imagination. A visual representation of their metaphorical content is not required; rather, immediate abstraction is called for. It can be said that their inspiration is more philological than visual. Donne does not expressly link them with Paul's stage metaphor,[236] but nevertheless the incorporation of the *theatrum mundi* field into that of spiritual vision is apparently facilitated by the phonetic and semantic similarity between *speculum* and *spectaculum*—"spectacle." Apart from its most common meaning of "show," or "display," which is intended by Paul, *spectacle* of course means a lens, a device for assisting defective eyesight, a meaning for which the *OED* quotes from Donne's sermons, "I thank him . . . that assists me with a Spectacle when my sight grows old," another reference incidentally, to spiritual sight. But *spectacle* also had the meaning, now obsolete, of "a window or mirror," [237] in which sense the word is synonymous with the Latin *speculum*. The fact that *spectacle* had this wide meaning, ranging from the eyeglass to the stage, overlapping at one point with the meaning of *speculum*, facilitated or even prompted Donne's metaphorical usage.

In the field in which understanding is presented as perception, the complement to the "glass" of creatures, a metaphor often used in conjunction with the *theatrum mundi* idea, is the "glass" of the Scriptures. In one of his later sermons Donne distinguishes several ways of apprehending God, all expressed in terms of spiritual vision and in this context calls the Scriptures the clearest glass that man possesses:

> The blindest man that is, hath the face of God so turned towards him, as that he may be seen by him; even the *nat-urall man* hath so; for, therefore does the Apostle make him inexcusable, if in the visible worke, he doe not see the *invisible* God. But all sight of God, is by the benefit of a *law;* the naturall man sees him by a law written in his *heart, the Jew,* by a law given by *Moses,* the Christian, in a clearer glasse, for, his law is the *Gospell.* [10:108, 4:177]

The concept of the mirror, or glass, of Scripture, which is suggested in James 1:22-25, had been used by Augustine, who had called the Scriptures *serenissimum speculum,* the clearest mirror, in which everyone may behold himself and see the greatness of his sin.[238] According to him, God gave man the Bible as a glass in which those who are of a clean heart will see Him;[239] especially God's commandments are to be inspected like a glass.[240]

For Donne's contemporaries the notion of the Law or Scriptures as a glass must have been quite commonplace. In Cawdrey's *Treasurie* several similes are constructed on it.[241] But Cawdrey shows at the same time how a clever rhetorician can give a fresh luster to an old analogy by pointing out new resemblances.

With this tradition in mind, a tradition that has been more suggested than sketched out here, one will hardly be satisfied with such rubrics as "optical images" or "domestic images." Donne's tropes are often both, and they are sometimes more. Donne may simply repeat an old cliché, or he may take an old analogy and develop it more or less elaborately in the manner of Cawdrey by pointing out more similarities. Donne's law-glass metaphor in the passage quoted above is one of the clichés. In his best passages he may find a new formula just transparent enough to allow the listener to link it with its ancestors, that is, to integrate it into a field of imagery, but at the same time concentrated and precise enough to have the luster of novelty. This may be true of the following passage:

> These [events], because God hath represented them, in so clear, and so true a glass as his word, we in a manner see them. Things in other stories we do but hear; things in the Scriptures we see: The Scriptures are as a room wainscotted with looking-glass, we see all at once. [3:56, 1:350]

The metaphor "glass of the word," which Donne uses and develops so effectively in this passage, is interesting in another respect. This metaphor, in which sight is preferred to hearing, may be the key to the question provoked by consideration of the extent and density of the field of imagery in which insight is presented in terms of sight—that is, the question of the significance of this density and the reason for Donne's fondness for such metaphor.

It is well known that light is widely used metaphorically in both the Old and the New Testament. Many studies have been devoted to the subject.[242] Moreover, the symbolism of light may come closest to being universal; one might be hard put to point to a culture in which light does not have some significance or to a work of literature from which some "light" metaphors may not be culled.[243] The special significance of this field of imagery

for Donne's metaphorical universe is shown in some of his theoretical statements on the subject of light.

With reference to the multiple meanings of metaphors based
on typology, Donne notes that the use of *light* in the Bible is
more limited:

> In all the Scriptures, in which the word *Light* is very often
> metaphorically applyed, it is never applyed in an ill sence.
> Christ is called a *Lyon;* but there is an ill Lyon too, that
> *seeks whom he may devour.* Christ is the serpent that was
> exalted; but there is an ill serpent, that did devour us all at
> once. But Christ is the light of the world, and no ill thing
> is call'd light. Light was Gods signature, by which he set
> his hand to the Creation: and therefore, as Princes signe
> above the Letter, and not below, God made light first; in
> that first Creature he declared his presence, his Majesty;
> the more, in that he *commanded light out of darkness.* [4:103,
> 3:503]

Not only is light "never applyed in an ill sence" but, according
to Donne, its meaning in the Bible when used metaphorically
can be more clearly defined:

> Light is never, (to my remembrance) found in any place
> of the Scripture, where it must necessarily signifie the light
> of nature, *naturall reason;* but wheresoever it is transferred
> from the naturall to a figurative sense, it takes a higher sig-
> nification then *that;* either it signifies *Essentiall* light, Christ
> Jesus, . . . or it signifies the *supernaturall light* of *Faith* and
> *Grace.* [3:352, 17:167]

The two passages are quoted here to show Donne's critical interest in the topic; their significance for his exegetical practice
will be studied in the next chapter. As an exegete, Donne constantly finds in the Old and New Testaments metaphors of light
that demand a spiritual reading. It would not be precise to say,
however, that his emphasis on the sense of sight derives directly
from the Bible as a whole. For, first, it is Donne who chooses the

passages he wants to preach on, and his choice of texts indicates a preference for passages containing metaphors or words that denote sight, allowing for metaphorical development. Second, the role and importance of light metaphor is not the same in all the writings included in the Bible. Donne turns to it with a certain set of preferences.

The position that a field of imagery based on such a concept as "eyes of the soul" has in someone's metaphorical universe is apparently dependent on the relative importance he gives to the various senses. For orientation in the world and as a means to understand his existence, man also uses the faculty of hearing. Scholars have observed that there are cultures in which hearing takes precedence over seeing, a fact that will naturally be reflected in the kind of light metaphors they use.[244] It is a well-known fact that in the Old Testament tradition special power is attributed to the spoken word. Franz-J. Leenhardt writes: "For the Hebrew, the word is not *logos*, it is *praxis*. It is commandment, efficacy." [245]

The creation is the effect of God's utterance. The God of the prophets, Leenhardt explains, is a God who speaks because he directs history. This high conception of the spoken word is also shown by the importance the biblical narrators attribute to reports of vocation; they illustrate how God creates a personality as man listens to the interior voice addressed to him.[246] For the Hebrew, therefore, man's relation with God culminates in an exchange of words, in dialogue. It is man's nature to hear, to listen, and to be able to answer; as Leenhardt puts it: "Pour l' hébreu, l' homme est essentiellement un être capable de répondre, un être *responsable*." [247]

"The sight," says Donne in a paragraph the title of which is given in the margin as *visio*, "is so much the Noblest of all the senses, as that it is all the senses" (8:221, 9:61). These words show an emphasis on the faculty of seeing that is not found in the Old Testament. Christian tradition owes this emphasis to Greek philosophy.[248] Plato had asked, "Have you ever observed how much the greatest expenditure the creator of the senses has lavished on the faculty of seeing and being seen?" and then had affirmed that "neither vision itself nor its vehicle, which we call the eye, is identical with the sun . . . but it is, I think, the most sunlike of all the instruments of sense."[249] The Greek tradition helped to shift the emphasis in Christian thinking from the faculty of hearing to the faculty of seeing. Donne emphatically agrees with Augustine when he says:

> As the reasonable soul of man, when it enters, becomes all the soul of man, and he hath no longer a vegetative, and a sensitive soul, but all is that one reasonable soul; so, sayes S. *Augustine* (and he exemplifies it, by severall pregnant places of Scripture) *Visus per omnes sensus recurrit,* All the senses are called Seeing; as there is *videre & audire,* S. *Iohn turned to see the sound;* and there is *Gustate, & videte, Taste, and see, how sweet the Lord is;* And so of the rest of the senses, all is sight. Employ then this noblest sense upon the noblest object, see God; see God in every thing, and then thou needst not take off thine eye from Beauty, from Riches, from Honour, from any thing. [8:221, 9:62]

Donne quotes Revelation 1:12 at least one other time, and again he notices and draws attention to the juxtaposition of the faculties of seeing and hearing:

> See him, as St. *John* did, who turned to see a voice: see him in the preaching of his Word; see him in that seal, which is a Copy of him, as he is of his Father, see him in the Sacrament. [4:129, 3:1500]

To speak of spiritual sight is to Donne the most convenient way of expressing the effect of preaching. One does well to remember this fact, for it is at times obscured by Donne's traditional terminology when he speaks of the word and "essential Word." Although there are some impressive passages stressing the idea of the sacramental power of the word,[250] Donne holds that God's first language addressed itself to the eye:

When the holy Ghost fell upon the waters, in the Creation, God spoke so, in his language of *Workes,* as that all men may understand them. For, in this language, the language of *workes,* the *Eye* is the *eare, seeing* is *hearing.* How often does the holy Ghost call upon us, in the Scriptures, *Ecce, quia os Domini locutum, Behold, the mouth of the Lord hath spoken it?* he calls us to *behold,* (which is the office of the *eye*) and that that we are to behold, is the *voice* of God, belonging to the eare; seeing is hearing, in Gods first language, the language of *works.* [10:110, 4:255]

Of course Donne knows, and repeats several times, that faith comes through hearing.[251] But there is an element of incompleteness about this sense: hearing is good and necessary, but seeing is better. Bernard, with whose sermons on the psalms Donne was well acquainted,[252] best expressed this idea of the relative importance of the senses:

The Psalmist says, "I trust to see the goodness of the Lord in the land of the living." That is, he desires to have the upper windows of the body opened wide to the light of God, longing to walk by sight rather than by faith. Faith comes by hearing, not from sight. It is the substance of the things hoped for, the evidence of the things that do not appear. Consequently, in faith, just as in hope, the eye fails us, and it is the ear alone that can profit us. The prophet says "The Lord God has opened my ear. But the day will come when He shall also open my eyes." [253]

The mystic longs for the moment when "the eye shall take in more than the ear or even the mind takes in at present." [254] Some of Bernard's most lyrical and exalted passages are those treating of the bliss of that final vision when man will see God *sicuti est.*[255] This "fierce desire of the soul to see," [256] which Donne shares with Bernard, is the explanation of the density of a field of imagery in which the *oculus mentis* metaphor, the "interior eye" is the center, and it helps to explain the frequency of such metaphors in Bernard. Although what man can see here is *in aenigmate* and therefore, as Bernard explains, *totum in nocte*,[257] this inner vision is in a sense a foretaste, it is as close as one here can possibly come to that final blissful vision.

For Donne, similarly, the most convenient expression for representing eternal life is the "sight" of God:

> Darknesse is that, by which the holy Ghost himselfe hath chosen to expresse *hell;* hell is *darknesse;* and the way to it, to hell, is *Excaecation* in this life, blindnesse in our spirituall eyes. Eternall life hereafter is *Visio Dei*, the sight of God, and the way to that here, is to *see God* here. [4:173, 6:372]

But although Donne's passages dealing with eternal vision are similar in attitude to Bernard's, they do not have Bernard's emotional intensity. The same concept is there but it is expounded in, and tempered by, theological terminology:

> That which is our end, *salvation*, we use to expresse in Schooles by these two termes, we call it *visionem Dei*, the sight of God, and we call it *unionem*, an union with God; we shall *see* God, and we shall be *united* to God . . . we shall see him *Sicuti est*, as he is. [5:168, 8:9]

Donne knows, as he points out in at least one passage (quoted earlier), that even that final mode of vision will be spiritual, although, as in the passage above, that theological distinction is sometimes obscured. The density of the field of imagery in which understanding is presented as perception, insight as sight, is a gauge of the depth of his longing that partial spiritual vision *nunc* may be replaced by complete insight *tunc*.

One of the rhetorical advantages of this field of imagery has always been the fact that tropes within it may be graduated according to some scale (usually clarity of vision). Reference to more specifically optical processes such as focusing and multiplying allows Donne to control firmly the imagination of his listeners. I hope I have shown beyond doubt that such so-called optical imagery does not introduce foreign material into the ser-

mon. If such tropes are not repetitions of formulae well established in homiletic tradition, they constitute, through new processes
of reflection, focusing, and magnifying, new developments in an
old field of imagery.

# Extended Metaphor

I have shown in the previous section that Donne's *theatrum mundi*
metaphors are within the field of imagery of spiritual vision.
Similarly, I pointed out earlier that for Donne the *mare-mundus*
theme derived its meaning from its relation to the concept of
life as a pilgrimage. These relations are evidence that fields of
imagery can overlap and that they can include smaller structures.
The existence of substructures, while attesting to the fact that
in living language fields of imagery are not tidily discrete, poses
some problems for the examination of imagery. Some subjective
element in the identification of fields cannot be quite excluded.
Nor can there be a uniform method of analyzing them except
for a preliminary description of their scope. However, the exam-
iner makes his choices in terms of the kinds of tropes he finds
and in terms of their numbers. The structures that result should
ultimately justify the choices.

The fields of imagery I have examined were chosen because
the tropes belonging to them were particularly numerous, but
there are of course others, of which I want to sketch out the
more important.

In a number of tropes Donne presents life as warfare. "Our
life," he says, "is a warfare; other wars, in a great part, end in
mariages: Ours in a divorce, in a divorce of body and soule in
death" (10:176, 7:634). The field of imagery is furnished with
tropes referring to various techniques of contemporary warfare,
sentinels, ammunition, and so on. Donne expresses the central

analogy in a formula that, by its terseness, could suggest that it is taken right from his own commonplace book. He says, "*Militia, vita;* our whole life is a warfare," and indicates the scriptural source as being Job 7:1 (6:108, 4:487). The same analogy could be derived also from a number of metaphors in Paul's epistles.[258]

The theme of sickness is also presented in terms of war. Rugoff has observed that such tropes are frequent in the *Devotions*,[259] of which sickness is the occasion, but they can be found in the sermons, too. There Donne indicates that one source of the analogy is Bernard: "It is true, that in bodily Sickness, *Tua dimicant contra te arma*. It is a discomfortable war, when thou fightest against thy self" (3:56, 1:315).

Another field of imagery in Donne's sermons that reflects his reading of Bernard is the one presenting the relation between God and man as marriage. The traditional interpretation of the Song of Songs, in which Christ is the Spouse, is explicated by many of Donne's tropes, and Donne does not hesitate to develop passages that are very obviously sexual. Thus he ends a sermon with a quotation from Songs 8:3:

> Wee end all, with the *valediction* of the *Spouse* to *Christ: His left hand is under my head, and his right embraces mee,* was the *Spouses valediction,* and *goodnight* to *Christ* then, when she laid her selfe downe to sleepe in the strength of his *Mandrakes,* and in the power of his *Spices,* as it is exprest there; that is, in the *influence* of his *mercies.* Beloved, every good *Soule* is the *Spouse* of *Christ.* [8:92, 2:1077]

The discussion of the typological dimension of such passages must be postponed until the next chapter. Here I only stop to note that in Donne's sermons this field is denser than the two just briefly mentioned. Often he develops the legal implications of the metaphor; his tropes elaborate the ideas of promise, betrothal, widowhood, and divorce. Without Christ, he says, for instance, with reference to 1 Timothy 5:6, "the soul is a Widow, and no Dowager, she hath lost her husband" (2:211, 9:513).

Some particularly elaborate analogies can be found in a sermon that Donne preached before the king. There he comments on the frequency of biblical tropes that belong to this field of imagery by saying, "God is *Love*, and the *Holy Ghost* is amorous in his Metaphors" (7:87, 2:524). He attributes to such metaphors both psychological and rhetorical intent:

> As *Christ* in his *Parable* comprehends all excuses, and all backwardnesses in the following of him, in those two, *Marriage* and *Purchasing* (for one had bought the Land and *stocke,* and another had married a Wife) So *God* expresses his love to Man, in these two too, He hath married us, he hath bought us; that so he might take in all dispositions, and worke upon Uxorious Men, men soupled and entendred with Matrimoniall love, and upon wordly men, men kneaded and plaistred with earthly love. [7:91, 2:670]

His admiration for the rhetorical effectiveness of the two biblical metaphors may help to explain his elaboration of the two fields of imagery, spiritual marriage and Redemption, of which they are the center. It is in this context that I would like to understand the widely publicized observation that Donne expresses religion through human love.[260]

Tropes belonging to the field of imagery of spiritual food are not rare in Donne's sermons but are generally quite traditional. Even the food mentioned is often biblical, as when he says that "God hath his panier full of Manna, and of Quailes" (7:140, 4:814). Degrees of nutritive value and of digestibility are the traditional co-ordinates between which metaphors are plotted in this field, which Lange has described in detail.[261] Donne does not go beyond the "milk for babes" (6:136, 6:159) that is traditionally at one end of the scale in homiletic literature; "bone" or simply "solid meat" at the other end is not less topical, as when he says, speaking of the mystery of the Incarnation, "the mysteries of all the Religions in the World, are but Milke in respect of this Bone, but Catechismes in respect of this Schoolepoint, but Alphabets in respect of this hard Style" (3:297, 14:205).[262] Some of the tropes of this field have a typological dimension and will be discussed in that context.

The idea of co-ordinates, or at least of a scale, within a field of imagery calls for a final consideration. The fields presented here were constructed by collecting scattered tropes that were identified as explicating some central analogy. Every field has its particular shape, and I have tried to show Donne's focal points and his favorite distinctions. Such structures, obtained by pulling together various metaphors, are of the nature of a paradigm: the bare structures exist, although they are not overtly present as such anywhere in the spoken sermon or on the printed page. As to their psychological existence, one may to some degree compare them to the old bard's hoard of formulae: the preacher had at his disposal a large number of analogies such as the *vita-militia* one, which he could explicate at any point if the context required it.

However, the field of imagery has also an equivalent on the syntagmatical level: the extended analogy. Donne believed that "a continued *Metaphor* is an *Allegory*, and holds in more" (7:72, 2:Dedication). In his sermons, extended metaphors are numerous. Several tropes of one field of imagery lend themselves well to clarification through distinctions and gradations. Consider the following metaphors:

> One name of Man is *Ish;* and that they derive *à Sonitu;* Man is but a voice, but a sound, but a noise, he begins the noise himselfe, when he comes crying into the world; and when he goes out, perchance friends celebrate, perchance enemies calumniate him, with a diverse voice, a diverse noise. A melancholique man, is but a groaning; a sportfull man, but a song; an active man, but a Trumpet; a mighty man, but a thunderclap. [9:61, 1:539]

Similarly the analogy man-worm allows the elaboration: "We, men of this world, wormes of this dunghil, whether Basilisks or blind wormes, whether Scarabs or Silkworms, whether high or low in the world . . ." (8:326, 14:514). To illustrate how Donne uses extended analogies for arranging and rearranging grades and scales I quote one more example; differentiation and gradation is here expressed in terms of man as a field or garden:

> The naturall man . . . may relieve the poore, he may defend the oppressed. But yet, he is but as an open field; and though he be not absolutely barren, he bears but grasse. The godly man, he that hath taken in the knowledge of a great, and a powerfull God, and enclosed, and hedged in himselfe with the feare of God, may produce actions better then the meere naturall man, because he referres his actions to the glory of his imagined God. But yet this man, though he be more fruitfull, then the former, more then a grassy field; yet he is but a ploughed field, and he bears but corne, and corne, God knowes, choaked with weeds. But that man, who hath taken hold of God, by those handles, by which God hath delivered, and manifested himselfe in the notions of Father, Sonne, and holy Ghost; he is no field, but a garden, a Garden of Gods planting, a Paradise in which grow all things good to eate, and good to see. [9:51, 1:159]

There is nothing so special about this passage from a sermon of 1629 that it might not occur in any other sermon. However, figurative passages belonging to one field of imagery become more frequent in Donne's later sermons. This observation is borne out by the fact that it becomes increasingly difficult to quote shorter passages without disrupting their imagery. Earlier I quoted a passage in which Donne defined his attitude toward secular learning by saying that "sheep-pastures" could be planted with trees only in the "hedge-rowes" and not all over, otherwise the pastures would lose their function. This occurs in a sermon in which the word of God is consistently presented as the "grasse" in agreement with the topical metaphors of "pastor" and "congregation." [263]

Inversely, it appears that in his later sermons Donne resorts less frequently to the method of illustrating one point by a number of different analogies. In an early sermon Donne warns against ill-suited company thus: "And howsoever, in some cases excuses might be found, what good Mariner would anchor under a Rock, and lie in danger of beating upon that? What Fish would chuse his food upon a Hook? What Mouse at a Trap? What man would mingle Sugar and Rats-bane together, and then trust his cunning to sever them again?" (1:202, 3:700). Similar is the passage on the depth of the mystery of the Incarnation in which Donne says that other mysteries are but milk to "this bone," catechisms to this "schoolepoint," alphabets to this "hard style." I will quote only one further example to illustrate a point that can easily be overstated. In his Christmas sermon of 1621, Donne uses the following analogies to prove what is more or less one point, the relative value of "outward things" in religion as exemplified by the need for a new chapel:

> *John Baptist* bore witnesse of the light, *outward things* beare witnesse of your faith, the exalting of our *naturall faculties* beare witnesse of the supernaturall. We do not compare the master and the servant, and yet we thank that servant that brings us to his master. We make a great difference between the *treasure* in the chest, and the *key* that opens it, yet we are glad to have that key in our hands. The bell that cals me to *Church*, does not catechise me, nor preach to me, yet I observe the sound of that bell, because it brings me to *him* that does those offices to me. The light of *nature* is far from being enough; but, as a *candle* may kindle a *torch*, so into the faculties of nature, well imployed God infuses *faith*. [3:368, 17:764]

The elements of this passage are illustrations of one central proposition. Donne could have concluded the series in the same way he ended a similar string of analogies elsewhere: "Thou canst not lack Examples" (1:177, 2:323).

In the vast corpus of Donne's sermons, it is fairly easy to find uses of tropes that contradict this observation, that is, to find in the early sermons interrelated images for one concept and in the later ones lists of images related only logically. But such exceptions do not obscure what seems a definite trend in the evolution of Donne's figurative technique, a trend that became apparent through a consideration of the difference between the abstract structure of a field of imagery and its concrete realization in an extended metaphor.

# 4. Imagery and Exegesis of Scripture

o far my examination of Donne's imagery has shown that in coining tropes he was aware of a scale ranging from high to low, and that he generally adjusted vehicles to tenors according to a hierarchical principle. His admiration for the Bible as a model for metaphor, expressed, for instance, in the remarks on the divine "purchase" and "marriage" cited earlier, is another element of his theory of imagery. Extending the analysis to patristic literature, as far as that was possible, I have shown that a large number of his figures derived from traditional fields of imagery, and I have described the way in which Donne developed them. The supposition was that recognition of both Donne's theory and his practice would be a help in understanding his sermons, and would qualify earlier judgments about discordant elements in his figurative discourse.

However, there are a number of tropes that are not yet sufficiently explained. When Donne calls Christ a "stone of rest" (2:186, 8:227), the choice of the metaphor can be justified neither by the principle of hierarchy nor by the existence of a conventional field of imagery. Although it might have been justified simply on the ground that the Christ-stone comparison was prominent in several biblical writers, and therefore Donne did not need to worry about its decorum, the added idea of "rest," suggesting Jacob's pillow stone, indicates that a factor we have not yet considered was operative here, namely, typology, or allegorical reading, a matter I will take up in the final section of this chapter.

I do not overlook the fact that Donne usually spoke disparagingly of allegorical interpretation, nor do I disagree with Helen Gardner's observation that Donne, like most post-Reformation exegetes, stressed the importance of the letter.[1] It must be said, however, that answers to the questions of how Donne thought about allegorical readings of Scripture, what he understood by the various senses of Scripture,[2] and what his stand was concerning certain controverted interpretations—interesting as such problems may be—are of only very limited help when one comes to examine Donne's tropes. The rhetorical level has its own validity, and I will show that certain semantic theories that were the basis of conventional biblical exegesis supplied a pattern for what otherwise often appears only abstruse, overingenious, or shrewd. Whether, beyond that, a metaphor based on biblical allegory had the special "truth value" for Donne that it had for the medieval exegetes is a different question, which I intend to discuss only in passing.

If a trope like "stone of rest" for Christ is not indecorous, the reason is first of all that it is securely tied into the structure of a sermon on Matthew 21:44, "Whosoever shall fall on this stone . . ." It is part of a larger whole, and Donne's method of setting up the sermon helps to integrate it there. Therefore I will begin with a note on sermon structure.

# Word-by-Word Exegesis

In accordance with the advice of such theorists as Keckermann, Donne began most of his sermons with a *praecognitio textus*, in which he acquainted the hearers with the text his sermon would treat. The short and often schematic divisions of the first sermons were extended to longer sections in the sermons at St. Paul's, but the number of main parts was usually limited to two or three. Sometimes—more rarely in the very early sermons—he created an image for the structure of his *divisio*, for instance, a tree. Thus the parts are not abstract branches, but the whole is a tree with branches of different sizes, from which fruits are to be reaped. He might also present the *divisio* as a construction consisting of various rooms, which he then proceeded to furnish. In the early sermons such passages were merely a technical device for structuring the *divisio;* later they became invested with more meaning. The tree, for instance, was seen as analogous to the "tree of knowledge" and the "tree of life" (8:131, 5:54).[3] The *divisio* was followed by the main body of the sermon, which was finally rounded off by the conclusion.

Except for a small number of sermons, mostly early ones, constructed on the basis of the senses of Scripture or divided into two parts, a "historical" interpretation and an application, Donne usually extracted the main idea of the text from Scripture by means of grammatical *claves* (questions identifying the important elements of the sentence analyzed), or by such categories as *modus* (the manner), *res* (the matter), and *sedes* (the place or location). Sometimes he first separated "subject" from "action" and then applied this *modus eruditus*, that is, the categories just mentioned, to the analysis of them.[4] Although in the later sermons he rarely used technical terms, his procedure remained essentially the same. Another and less frequently used way of ordering the sermon consists in unfolding a number of aspects of a single theme.[5]

It is hardly possible to give a clear-cut structural typology of the sermons[6] since, as I have already indicated, all these methods of dividing and ordering may appear in combination: the larger structure (the two or three parts constituting the sermon) may be arranged according to one principle of order, the substructures according to another; or the main parts may be constructed according to different principles. With these varied methods of organization it is surprising that in the exposition Donne usually managed somehow to follow the word order of his text, so that the most general statement one can make about his principle of order is that it is *per verba*. Whether or not the preacher followed his text word by word, the order in which he treated his ideas, for instance, in the "actor-action" scheme, was in the overwhelming majority of sermons that of the passage he was interpreting.[7] Thus the text was not only left intact but was pointed to at the various steps of the exegesis.

This technique is of great importance for Donne's imagery. As he alters, in various ways, the meaning of a single term or of an expression that sums up a part of the sentence, the entire text becomes a metaphor.[8] Several times Donne preached on John 1:8, "He was not that light, but was sent to bear witness of that light," treating one by one the subject ("he," referring to John the Baptist), the verb ("bearing witness"), and the complement ("light"). He replaced these by terms with different meanings and proposed a reading after each substitution. In the sermon on light, he thus inserts various "lights" in the text and then offers a moral application. He introduces *lux essentiae, lux gloriae, lux fidei, lux naturae, lux aeternorum corporum, lux incensionum, lux depuratarum mixtorum,* and *lux repercussionum. Lux naturae,* for instance, is incorporated into the sermon in the following manner:

> *John Baptist was not the light,* he was not Christ, *but he bore witnesse of him.* The light of *faith,* in the highest exaltation that can be had, in the *Elect,* here, is not that very *beatificall vision,* which we shall have in heaven, but it beares witnesse of that light. The light of *nature,* in the highest exaltation is not *faith,* but it *beares witnesse* of it. The lights of *faith,* and of *nature,* are subordinate *John Baptists.* [3:367, 17:720]

The way in which the preacher starts from the consideration of the given text and, after transposing it to a different level of meaning, gives a new reading of the text, can be shown from another passage in the same sermon. In it Donne brings into his text the light of the heavenly bodies, by which he means, as he points out, the "Fundamentall articles of Faith" (3:371, 17:845):

> And a third payre of lights of *attestation*, that beare witnesse to the light of our Text, is *Lux aeternorum Corporum*, that light which the *Sunne* and the *Moone*, and those glorious bodies give from heaven . . . : both these beare witnesse of this light, that is, admit an application to it. [3:369, 17:776]

Another consequence of an interpretation that proceeds word by word is that the preacher is constantly made aware of the metaphorical structure of language. Often Donne remarked that he would now proceed to explain a mannerism (*idiotismus*) or a metaphor of the Holy Ghost.[9] He explained metaphors, and the explication often consisted of nothing more than the creation of new metaphors.[10] He introduced the theme of his third sermon on Psalm 38:4, "For mine iniquities are gone over mine head, as a heavy burden, they are too heavy for me," indicating the following procedure: "first, we pursue that which lies upon our selves, the *Burden*, in those four mischievous inconveniences wrapped up in that Metaphor" (2:132, 5:35). He concluded the first part of his explication with metaphors:

> And this is the first inconvenience, and mischief, implyed in this Metaphor which the holy Ghost hath chosen, *Mine iniquities are as a burden, Inclinant*, they bend down my soule, created streight, to an incurvation, to a crookednesse. [2:133, 5:85]

It was observed above that a whole sentence may be lifted to another, "metaphorical" level of meaning when one of its words is given a different meaning or is replaced by another word. There is yet another aspect of this "substitution technique": through constant repetition certain words of the Bible quotation may acquire a certain symbolic character, may be turned into "symbols."[11] In a sermon on Psalm 38:2, "For thine arrowes stick fast in me, and thy hand presseth me sore," Donne substitutes mankind for David ("me") and says:

> They stick, and they *stick fast; altè infixae;* every syllable aggravates our misery. Now for the most part, experimentally, we know not whether they stick fast or no, for we never goe about to pull them out: these arrows, these tentations, come, and welcome: we are so far from offering to pull them out, that we fix them faster and faster in us; we assist our tentations: yea, we take preparatives and fomentations, we supple our selves by *provocations,* lest our flesh should be of proof against these arrows, that death may enter the surer, and the deeper into us by them. And he that does in some measure, soberly and religiously, goe about to draw out these arrows, yet never consummates, never perfects his own work; He pulls back the arrow a little way, and he sees *blood,* and he feels *spirit* to goe out with it, and he lets it alone: He forbears his sinfull companions, a little while, and he feels a *melancholy* take hold of him, the spirit and life of his life decays, and he falls to those companions again. [2:63, 1:542]

In the various sections of the word-by-word exegesis of the quotation from Scripture, the arrows recur, often with their meaning changed. They are taken to mean sicknesses, pains of conscience, and temptations. Thus, in his explication of *manus* the preacher can say, "Gods hand is upon them, the *work* is his, the *arrows* are his, and the *sticking* of them is his, whatsoever . . . they be" (2:67, 1:691). Words that are in this way invested with a particular meaning and that acquire a certain symbolic character will no doubt stick in the memory of the hearer. Donne himself recognized how rhetorical efficacy relates to what I have called substitution: "Change the person, and wee shall finde a whole quiver of arrows. Extend this *Man* to all *Mankind;* carry *Davids* History up to *Adams* History . . . and we shall see *arrows* fly about our ears" (2:55, 1:231).

Donne probably chose this verse to preach on because it admits of such metaphorical exposition. In his word-by-word interpretation he devotes to the exposition of *arrows* more time than to other words, proceeding in accordance with the rules that had been established by the theorists since the Middle Ages. After adducing a number of passages in the Bible in which arrows are mentioned—the so-called concordance *in verbis*[12]—he replaces the arrows of the original biblical passage with the meanings that he assigns to four properties of arrows, one by one.

Throughout his preaching career Donne sometimes chose passages from Scripture containing metaphors or "concrete objects" allowing such an exposition,[13] but he did not by any means always do so. Sermons with such central metaphors as the arrow, the heart, or the stone on which the wicked shall fall are rare. How is the preacher to proceed if there is, in his text, no metaphor lending itself to the kind of treatment Donne gave the arrow? For such a situation Jean de Galles gave some advice that may be compared with Donne's practice:

> But if the object treated in the theme has either few properties, or many which, however, you do not know, or though many known ones, such as do not edify; then it is usual that the preacher applies himself to another object richer in properties and more edifying. For the edification of souls is more to be attended to than the continuity of the sermon.[14]

Although Donne normally took up the terms of the text he was preaching on, he allowed himself enough leeway to bring in and explicate whatever related term he pleased, thus often adding to the metaphorical density of a sermon. Preaching on Simeon's words in Luke 2:29 and 30, "Lord now lettest thou thy servant depart in peace, according to thy word: For mine eyes have seen thy salvation," he has a long passage on *columbae*, which he takes from the mention of the sacrificial offering of "a pair of turtledoves, or two young pigeons" in Luke 2:24. He adduces some conventional animal lore, points to the meaning of these animals as emblems, and finally gives several "uses"; that is, he applies them in detail to a moral.[15]

Perhaps a concern like Jean de Galles's with the importance of meaningful properties of things, a concern that overruled the rhetorical virtue of *sermonis continuatio*, helps to explain some passages in Donne that appear particularly "heterogeneous" or "metaphysical." I will attempt to answer this question as I examine the medieval conception of how scriptural words signify, a conception which is at the basis of such substitutions as *temptations* for *arrows*, or *man* for *David*.

# *Vox* and *Res*

It sometimes seems that Donne was overclever in elaborating the meanings of objects in his texts. In a sermon that is said to contain "some shrewd passages" [16] Donne took *honey* to signify, on the one hand, Christian religion and, on the other, poison and "temporal things." Elsewhere he called temptations, death, sickness, original sin, and even a sermon, "arrows," and greediness as well as the gospels, a "net." [17] It is evident that these metaphors were not obtained through free association. In some way or other they always derive from the text of Scripture he is preaching on, and his figurative usage rests on the example of a long line of exegetes for whom the words of the Bible were particularly invested with meaning, and who thought them to signify in a special way.

In the twelfth century Hugo of St. Victor expressed well this theory of signification when he said: "Holy Scripture excels by far secular knowledge in that in it not only the words [*voces*] but also the things [viz., those denoted by the words] have meaning." [18] Thus every word has first of all a literal sense: *arrow* (the *vox*) designates a projectile that is feathered and pointed (the *res*). Now it is the special and, at least originally, the unique mark of the Holy Scriptures that the "things" mentioned there, which in the normal process of signification are the *designata* and in which, therefore, signification ends, can in turn be carriers of meaning: they can signify. The meaning of the *vox* therefore has to be distinguished from the meaning that is proper to and closely linked with the *res*. It has even been argued that according to the medieval conception every "thing" that is made part of the language by the mere fact of being named points to a meaning of a higher order—that it is the sign of something spiritual.[19]

The thing does not have only one meaning as does the *vox* (unless a double meaning results from the special case of homonymy); it can have as many meanings as it has properties.[20] Peter of Poitiers took this principle even a little further when he explained: "For as many properties as a thing has, so many tongues does it have, which enunciate something spiritual and invisible, and through the diversity of which the meaning of the same word is varied." [21]

This conception of the biblical text was reflected in the intent of all philological scholarship of the Middle Ages to explore not only the nature of the *voces* (in the *trivium*), but also that of the *res* (in the *quadrivium*). Medieval exegetes were overdiligent in their search for meaningful qualities or properties of things —Moore has pointed out that when Peter of Poitiers commented on the reality of *oleum*, for example, he remarked that material oil illuminates, cures sickness, floats on the surface of other liquids, and serves as a condiment for other foods, and that the olive from which it is extracted is the symbol of peace. Although I cannot develop the history of the conception, it is probably safe to say that the same idea is *in nuce* contained in Augustine's *De doctrina*, which deeply influenced later exegetes of Scripture, and which, according to Donne, taught "a use of all Arts in Divinity" (10:148, 6:296). Augustine says:

> In addition, an imperfect knowledge of things causes figurative passages to be obscure; for example, when we do not recognize the nature of the animals, minerals, plants, or other things which are very often represented in the Scriptures

for the sake of an analogy. It is well known that a serpent exposes its whole body, rather than its head, to those attacking it, and how clearly that explains the Lord's meaning when he directed us to be "wise as serpents." We should, therefore, expose our body to persecutors, rather than our head, which is Christ. Thus the Christian faith, the head so to speak, may not be killed in us, as it would be if, preserving our body, we were to reject God! There is also the belief that, having forced itself through a small opening in disposing of its old skin, the serpent gains renewed vigor. How well this agrees with imitating the wisdom of the serpent and stripping off the "old man." . . . A knowledge of the nature of the serpent, therefore, explains many analogies which Holy Scripture habitually makes from that animal; so a lack of knowledge about other animals to which Scripture no less frequently alludes for comparisons hinders a reader very much.[22]

Here Augustine expresses his view that a knowledge of the language in which the original text is written is not sufficient for the interpretation of the Bible: knowledge of "things" has to supplement it.

It can be shown that some tropes in Donne's sermons reflect this traditional conception of the word. In them the *vox* is used to denote one of the significant properties of the *res* that it names. Developing the arrow metaphor, he introduces a passage by saying: "Another quality that tentations receive from the holy Ghosts Metaphore of *arrows* is, *Quia veloces*, because this captivity to sin, comes so swiftly, so impetuously upon us" (2:58, 1:341). He explains at length that arrows, like temptations, are "*vix visibiles*, hardly discernible" (2:59, 1:382), and that they wound deeply. He further uses "arrow" to mean original sin, since man is hit by sin as suddenly as by an arrow. An examination of a clavis such as the one by (pseudo-) Melito, which lists properties of things and their meanings, confirms the supposition that Donne was very close to tradition when he developed metaphors in this manner. There one finds such qualities as the swift-ness of the arrow, its power to wound deeply, and its relative invisibility (signifying *tentatio occulta* as opposed to a *tentatio manifesta*) as they were applied to Scripture by Gregory, Rha-banus Maurus, Petrus Capuanus, and others. However, the arrow had for them many more properties than Donne made use of in this sermon, for instance, its wood, metal point, and feathers.[23]

Similarly, in a sermon on Genesis 32:10, Donne concludes his consideration of the staff with which Jacob passed over the Jor-dan with the following remark:

> Hath this then been thy state with *Jacob*, that thou hast not onely been without the staff of bread, plenty, and abun-dance of temporal blessings, but without the staff of defence, that when the world hath snarl'd and barked at thee, and that thou wouldst justly have beaten a dog, yet thou couldst not finde a staff, thou hadst no means to right thy self? yet he hath not left thee without a staff of support, a staff to try how deep the waters be, that thou art to wade through, that is thy Christian constancy . . . : use that staff aright, and as Christ, who sent his Apostles without any staff of defense once, afterward gave them leave to carry swords, so . . . he will make thy staff, a sword. [1:280, 7:436]

In this passage Donne maps out only part of the wide realm of meaning belonging to *baculus;* more meanings follow: "a lead-ing staff, a competency," "his own natural faculties, his [i.e., man's] own staff, The imaginations of his own heart." He adduces all these meanings although he states that the staff of his text is primarily not a metaphor, but the very concrete object that supported the wanderer. Transcending the meaning that he finds in the quotation on which he is preaching, Donne thus creates new staff metaphors in his "application"; he multiplies the staffs by adducing other properties of the *res*, such as its usefulness as a weapon of defense. Jacob's *baculus sustentans*, which never-theless remains real and intact in its concreteness, serves him as a point of departure for presenting to his auditors the wide range of meaning of *baculus*. The range of meaning, of course, was largely established in tradition. In the clavis of Melito, for instance, one reads, "Baculus multiplex est et multa significat," after which follows a list of a number of staffs with their meanings.[24]

Since a thing has as many meanings as it has properties, and since some things may have good as well as bad qualities, it follows that some things have both good and bad meanings or, as the compilers say, those *in bonam partem* and those *in malam partem*. The lion, because it sleeps with open eyes, may signify Christ, who, dead as the Son of man, yet lived as the Son of God. Because of the lion's natural bloodthirstiness it may signify the devil, for it walks about roaring, seeking whom it may devour (1 Pet. 5:8). The lion may signify the righteous because of its boldness (Prov. 28:1), and it may also signify the heretic because of the foul smell of its teeth, a smell that comes from its mouth just as the words of blasphemy flow from the mouth of the heretic.[25]

These interpretations are not given here as oddities gleaned from the curiosity shop of medieval exegesis. As a matter of fact, Donne used figures that operated very much in the same way. Thus he comments on the fact that both *lion* and *serpent*[26] can stand for Christ as well as for the devil and contrasts the multiple signification of these words with the meaning of *light*, which can never be used *in malam partem*:

> In all the Scriptures, in which the word *Light* is very often metaphorically applyed, it is never applyed in an ill sence. Christ is called a *Lyon;* but there is an ill Lyon too, that *seeks whom he may devour.* Christ is the serpent that was exalted; but there is an ill serpent, that did devour us all at once. [4:103, 3:503]

This comment would suggest that he had before him some kind of clavis.[27] In another sermon we find:

> If it were the *Lion,* the Lion of the tribe of *Iuda,* is able to perform his promises; but there are more then Christ, out of this world, that beare the Lion; the *devill* is a *Lion* too,

that *seeketh whom he may devoure:* but he never seales with
that *Lambe*, with any impression of *humility*. [5:104, 4:315]

His argument rests on the fact that the two metaphors, lion-devil
and lion-Christ, are based on two different qualities of the lion,
and therefore are not incompatible.

It has to be noted at this point that although the *res* lion could
cover the whole range from Christ to the devil, the context
would usually determine for the medieval exegete which property of the *res* was relevant in a specific passage. Not all of the
wide range of properties would be operative in a given sentence;
in a specific context, one lion would not mean both Christ and
the devil. Proper selection of the significant qualities was the
object of spiritual interpretation.

Although the context will usually reveal whether *lion* means
Christ or the devil, spiritual meaning is sometimes more difficult
to determine. In such a case the exegete will multiply and test
out the various meanings based on the qualities of a thing.[28] This
is the method used by Donne in a sermon on Proverbs 25:16:
"Hast thou found honey? . . ." The allusions in this sermon to
the contemporary political scene have been examined well by Gifford,[29] but it has not been noticed that the instrument by which
Donne conveys his meanings is the theory of signification that I
have just outlined. He measures in detail the range of meaning
of the *res* honey, sometimes adducing the meaningful qualities
mentioned in other scriptural passages, at other times invoking
some apicultural knowledge. In the course of this process honey
is "favour in great persons," "glory," and also, according to Proverbs 24:13-14, the fruit of wisdom; it is the fruit of the bee's
diligence and also of its purity. More than this, he can even say
that "His word, the sincerity of the Gospel, the truth of his Religion is our honey and honey combe" (3:238, 10:494). Then, as
he unfolds the metaphor in which "is wrapped up . . . all that
is delightfull in this life" (3:231, 10:235),[30] he suddenly turns
around and, adducing Pliny for more information about the *res*,
says that honey is only *coeli sudor:*

God shall give thee the sweetnesse of this world, honour, and ease, and plenty, and hee shall give thee thy honey-combe, with thy honey, that which preserves thy honey to thee, that is, a religious knowledge, that all this is but hony; And honey is the dew of the flowres, whence it is drawne, is but *Coeli sudor*, a sweaty excrement of the heavens, and *Siderum saliva*, the spettle, the fleame of the starres, and *Apum vomitus*, the casting, the vomit of the Bee. And though honey be the sweetest thing that wee doe take into the body, yet there it degenerates into gall, and proves the bitterest. [3:233, 10:285]

It is on the basis of passages such as this that the editors of the *Sermons* remark in their introduction that the sermon is marred by the preacher's intent to parade his knowledge. Yet it had been precisely the function of all natural science in the Middle Ages to help explain the Scriptures. All the bestiaries, lapidaries, dictionaries of plants, and all general encyclopedias were designed to fulfill this purpose.[31] Donne's effort to make use of knowledge about the *res*, weird as it may sometimes appear to the modern reader, has to be viewed against the backdrop of this tradition. Pliny, whom Donne uses here, was the single most important source of such knowledge, and his remarks on honey were traditionally used to explicate passages of Scripture. During the Renaissance Cornelius à Lapide quoted extensively from Pliny, with exact references to book and chapter, when he explained a *mel* passage from Ecclesiasticus.[32] Characteristically, that quotation gives not only the virtues of honey but also its detrimental effects: honey inflates the stomach, creates gall, and so on. Melito's *Clavis* shows that honey used *in bonam partem* and *in malam partem* has a venerable history in biblical exegesis.[33]

The passage quoted from Donne may be compared with one from Hooker, who equally depends on tradition when he takes his analogies from honey and gall:

The light would never be acceptable, were it not for the usual intercourse with darkness. Too much honey doth turn into gall; and too much joy even spiritually would make us wantons. Happier a great deal is that man's case, whose soul by inward desolation is humbled, than he whose heart is through abundance of spiritual delight lifted up and exalted above measure.[34]

Whereas Donne, through his definitions taken from the natural sciences, lays the stress on opposite views of the same thing, Hooker alludes loosely to oversaturation: it is only "too much" honey that turns into gall. He does not insist on the analogy from the natural world, the world of the *res*, but is concerned with the moral level. Whereas Donne consistently uses different aspects of the same thing as tools to get at the meaning of the metaphor, Hooker casually refers to an analogy which is already morally framed. Overstressing the difference somewhat, one might say that Donne takes over a method of interpretation while Hooker alludes to a topical analogy.

Donne's method of unfolding the properties of the *res*, in which process he creates new metaphors, is particularly noticeable in his early sermons. This is natural, since the beginner will follow traditional examples more closely. Thus, in an early sermon, after citing Abraham's confession, "I know I am but dust and ashes," (Gen. 18:27), he quotes Augustine's gloss on this passage and then explicates it:

> *Vere pulvis omnis homo*, saies he [Augustine]; truly every man is truly dust; for as dust is blown from one to another corner by the wind, and lies dead there till another wind remove it from that corner; so are we hurried from sin to sin, and have no motion in our selves, but as a new sin imprints it in us: so *vere pulvis*, for our disposition to evil we are truly dust; and *vere cinis*, we are truly dry ashes; for ashes produceth no seed of it self, nor gives growth to any seed that is cast into it. [1:315, 9:524]

Elsewhere Donne refers to the Fathers in general, when he gives a traditional explanation of Psalm 58:4, here adduced in the course of an elaborate concordance *in verbis* of *audire* and *auris:*

Here is none of that action which was in S. *Stephens* persecutors, *Continuerunt aures,* they withheld their eares,
. . . neither is there any of their actions, *Qui obturant aures,*
as the Psalmist sayes, the Serpent does, who (as the Fathers
note often) stops one ear with laying it close to the ground,
and the other with covering it with his tail. [2:174, 7:385]

The Psalmist mentions that the adder stops its ear to resist the
charmer; however, the way in which this is done is lifted from
the physical world of the *res.* It goes without saying that this
world need not be scientific in the modern sense of the word,
but includes a good deal of the legendary.

I mentioned earlier the passage in which Donne explains the
sacrificial offering of a turtledove or a pigeon at the presentation
in the temple. The starting point for his application of the
scriptural passage to the political scene is the solitariness and
chastity of the turtledove ("I thinke we finde no Bigamy in the
Turtle" [7:282, 11:112]), standing for the contemplative life, and
the sociability and fecundity of the pigeon, representing the active life. These properties, with their meanings, are mentioned
in the medieval texts collected in Melito's *Clavis.*[35]

The model of former exegetes is even more prominent in a
sermon on Psalm 32:9: "Be not as the horse, or the mule, who
have no understanding." Although the meaning of the animals
is explained in the psalm itself, he invokes the authority of the
"Fathers and other Expositors" for a more detailed spiritual reading of their properties; he hesitates, however, to call their various
readings of the respective natures of horse and mule "interpretations," and settles on "at least, severall Allusions" (9:376, 17:194).
He refers to the sterility of the mule and its "low" descent, and
notes that Jerome "thinks fiercenesse and rashnesse to be presented in the Horse, and sloth in the mule," then reports, without
disapproval, that Augustine "carries these qualities farre." Finally,
he takes up the following equally traditional reading: "Here we
may contract it best, if we understand Pride by the Horse, and
Lust by the Mule" (9:377, 17:221). This is only the beginning

of the exposition proper, which makes use of more properties, distinctions, and scriptural passages about horses, asses, whipping, and bridling. There is more than a superficial similarity between his method and the conception behind the elaborate chapters in Melito on the properties (and their meanings) of horse, mule, and ass;[36] for Donne makes it quite clear as he closes the sermon that he has not been indulging his ingenuity through specious allusions, but has been defining the meaning of the text:

> And therefore, as God would have us conserve the dignity of our nature in his Image, and not descend to the qualities of these Beasts, Horse and Mule, specified by the Holy Ghost, to represent to us those two sins, which are the wombes and mothers of very many others, Pride and Lust . . . so would he have us doe it for this also, that he might not be put to a necessity of bitting and bridling us. [9:390, 17:706]

His method of unfolding the meaning of the text consisted in exploring the actual properties of the *res*. In one sermon, for instance, he elaborates the various qualities of a net, and in the course of his explanation expressly refers to a *"res nodosa"*:

> The Gospel of Christ Jesus is a net; It hath leads and corks; It hath leads, that is, the denouncing of Gods judgements, and a power to sink down, and lay flat any stubborne and rebellious heart, And it hath corks, that is, the power of absolution, and application of the mercies of God, that swimme above all his works, means to erect an humble and contrite spirit, above all the waters of tribulation, and affliction. A net is *Res nodosa*, a knotty thing; and so is the Scripture, full of knots, of scruple, and perplexity, and anxiety, and vexation, if thou wilt goe about to entangle thy selfe in those things, which appertaine not to thy salvation; but knots of a fast union, and inseparable alliance of thy soule to God, and to the fellowship of his Saints, if thou take the Scriptures, as they were intended for thee. . . . A net is a large thing, past thy fadoming, if thou cast it from

thee, but if thou draw it to thee, it will lie upon thine arme. [2:308, 14:758]

While there can be hardly any doubt about the nature of such tropes, especially here, where the preacher stresses the method by which he derives the various analogies,[37] their resemblance to another kind of figure has yet to be considered. Following Mario Praz's suggestion, Albert Schöne has pointed out that the *subscriptio* of an emblem is practically identical with a literary conceit.[38] The practice of relating point by point the various parts of an emblematic picture to some spiritual meaning is not unlike the procedure outlined above. On a purely rhetorical level, this similarity to an emblem might be claimed for the more elaborate figures of the kind examined here.

If the *res* was quite commonly used as a metaphor, it was sometimes seen to be unnecessary if not impossible to list its properties. Thus Petrus Cantor, Petrus Capuanus, Rhabanus, and other expositors could content themselves with listing only the various meanings (based on a combination of properties) of *cor* ("heart") and *gazophylacium* ("treasure").[39] Accordingly, Donne's procedure in such a case would consist in selecting and discussing these meanings in the way described above. Thus he preaches an extremely regular and well-structured sermon on Matthew 6:21, "For where your treasure is, there will your heart be also," treating in its two parts, first, several "hearts," then, several "treasures." As an organizing figure he chooses the letter *Y*, which, as Joan Webber points out, "he made an emblem of the two courses of life open to men."[40] Donne evidently has this structure in mind when he assigns two kinds of treasure to the two arms of the *Y*:

> one broader, but on the left hand, denoting the Treasures of this World; the other narrower, but on the right hand, Treasure laid up for the World to come. Be sure ye turn the right way: for, *where your Treasure is, there will your Heart be also.* [9:174, 7:48]

However, for the other part of the sermon, on the heart, the symbolical letter is used in a different way. The good heart, *cor fixum*, is its stem; two opposing hearts, *cor nullum* ("heartlessness") and *cor duplex* ("irresolution") are its arms. But then he wants to add a third heart, *cor vagum* ("inconstancy"), and so ends up with only a loose correlation between emblem and idea, the bottom and the top of the *Y* representing merely the one and the many, the steady heart versus "three Enemies to that fixation and intireness of the Heart" (9:176, 7:113). The attempt to give the sermon an emblematic shape somewhat conceals the fact that the underlying distinction in both parts of the sermon is that between the two kinds of meanings of heart and treasure: *in bonam partem* and *in malam partem*. Whereas he begins the series of hearts with the good meaning, his usual practice of concluding on a consoling note demands that he take up the bad treasures (*thesaurus malorum, thesaurus Dei hic*, and *thesaurus Dei in futuro*) before treating the good ones (*thesaurus bonorum* and *thesaurus Dei erga hic*). These kinds of treasure can be found listed in traditional handbooks, although not in precisely the same terms. Of "good" treasures especially there are many. Donne may be somewhat unusual in stressing the negative meanings, although the *Liber distinctionum monasticarum* also lists a *thesaurus vitiorum* (comparable to Donne's *thesaurus malorum*) and a *thesaurus poenarum* (comparable to Donne's "treasures" of God's punishments on earth and in the future life).[41]

If the case for tradition is made here, this does not necessarily belittle Donne's originality. The recognition of traditional elements may be a necessary help in determining individual traits of a work of literature. With the tradition in mind, one can notice how elegantly Donne turns the old metaphor of the pearl [42] to a new use in the opening of a sermon:

> When our Saviour forbids us to cast pearl before swine, we understand ordinarily in that place, that by pearl, are understood the Scriptures; and when we consider the naturall generation and production of Pearl, that they grow bigger and bigger by a continuall succession, and devolution of dew, and other glutinous moysture that fals upon them, and there

condenses and hardens, so that a pearl is but a body of many shels, many crusts, many films, many coats enwrapped upon one another, To this Scripture which we have in hand, doth that Metaphor of pearl very properly appertain. [2:311, 15:1]

Although the metaphor might be called nothing more than a pleasant conceit, Donne makes a point of deriving it from Scripture, and develops it in the manner in which medieval exegetes explicate metaphors, isolating the trope and exploring the *res* without paying much attention to the context; of course in this sermon he is not interested in pursuing the meaning of the entire statement, in which Christ warns his listeners not to give what is valuable to the unholy (Donne does not mean to disparage his congregation).

Some characteristics of Donne's use of figures can be seen more clearly when it is compared with that of his contemporaries. In the following passages Donne and Andrewes obviously use the same source, and yet the effects they achieve are not the same. The first quotation is from Andrewes's sermon, "Of the Sending of the Holy Ghost" (marginal: "In the shape of a Fowle"):

What shape then? of what creature? All things quick in motion, as angels, as the wind, whereto He is elsewhere compared, are set forth with "wings"—"the wings of the wind." Of one with wings then, as most apt to express the swiftness of His operation, in all His works; but specially in this. None of the other kind of creatures, though never so light of foot, can sufficiently set forth the quickness of His working. He goes not, He flies, He; *Nescit tarda molimena;* that He doth, He is not long in doing; therefore, *in specie volatilis,* "in the shape of a thing flying".[43]

To add evidence to his interpretation, which stresses the speed of the bird, Donne adduces the same quotation and identifies its source as Ambrose:

We may easily see that verified in S. *Peters* proceeding, which S. *Ambrose* sayes, *Nescit tarda molimina Spiritus sancti gratia,* The holy Ghost cannot goe a slow pace; It is the devill in the serpent that creeps, but the holy Ghost in the Dove flyes. [5:37, 1:69]

Elsewhere he invokes other metaphors for the motions of the Spirit:

(to speak humanely) the Holy Ghost had an extraordinary, a perverse ambition, to goe downewards, to inlarge himselfe, in his working, by falling; *He fell.* [5:36, 1:47]

But the Holy Ghost, (as mysterious in his actions, as in his Essentiall, or in his Personall beeing) fell so from heaven, as that he remained in heaven, even then when he was fallen. [5:48, 1:475]

This Dove sent from heaven, did more then that Dove, which was sent out of the Arke; That went and came, but was not in both places at once. [5:48, 1:478]

Donne proceeds very much as Andrewes does: he shows that the shape and the movement of the "thing" are meaningful. Yet his passages are "wittier" because he deliberately builds up para-doxes. He draws his analogies from the natural world less in order to explain the divine than to infer by his carefully worked out paradoxes the supernatural quality of the event. His phrase "to speak humanely" indicates his awareness that he might be close to overstepping the limits of decorum. In the first quota-tion, the speed of the bird is shown to be meaningful in the tradi-tional manner. In the second, Donne applies his method of in-terpretation to the direction of the flight, thus bringing out the intended paradox. Another paradox is pointed out in the third, where the mysterious nature of the Holy Ghost is also stated in abstract terms. Through a concordance *in verbis* the preacher, in the last quotation, stresses the import of the foregoing para-dox, which ultimately calls into doubt any attempt at fully un-veiling a divine truth clothed in metaphor.

The distinction between *vox* and *res* is at the basis of particularly "witty" passages. The preacher may compare the properties of things and derive an argument from their likeness: "The Holy Ghost is a Dove . . . The Dove is *animal sociale* . . . And Christ is a Sheep, *animal gregale*, they flock together" (4:349, 14:149). Part of the tension in this figure seems to result from the fact that it is the properties of the *res* (the *specifica* of the definitions) rather than the things themselves that are comparable. Sometimes Donne—at least seemingly—disregards the difference between the literal meaning of a word and the particular metaphorical meaning. Bringing together a number of scriptural references, he shapes them into superficial paradoxes that, as Joan Webber remarks, serve to capture the attention of the auditor:[44]

> The Church of God should be built upon a Rock, and yet *Job* had his Church upon a Dunghill; The bed is a scene, and an embleme of wantonnesse, and yet *Hezekiah* had his Church in his Bed; The Church is to be placed upon the top of a Hill, and yet the Prophet *Jeremy* had his Church *in Luto,* in a miry Dungeon; Constancy, and setlednesse belongs to the Church, and yet *Jonah* had his Church in the Whales belly; The Lyon that roares, and seeks whom he may devour, is an enemy to this Church, and yet *Daniel* had his Church in the Lions den; *Aquae quietudinum*, the waters of rest in the Psalme, were a figure of the Church, and yet the three children had their Church in the fiery furnace. [2:216, 10:116]

Donne pretends that the conventional rock on which the church is built (meaning faith or, on another metaphorical level, Christ himself) is comparable to Job's literal ashheap. Further, he disregards the difference between the lion as the devil and the lion whose den became the place of Daniel's prayer. On the basis of their identical *voces* he combines Peter's metaphorical lion and Daniel's flesh-and-blood lions. This wordplay is not simple punning, it is analogous to the stylistic features of the medieval hymns Father Walter Ong has so admirably analyzed.[45] The paradoxes serve to prove Donne's point that any place, whatever its degree of comfort or its conventional reputation, can be made a place of worship, of intimate contact with God; they also help to "focus the attention of his auditors on a spiritual truth." [46]

# The Senses of Scripture

By calling the replacement of David by mankind (in Donne's explication of Ps. 38:2) a substitution, and by focusing on the difference between word and thing, I have tried to remain within the range of linguistically demonstrable facts and to avoid complicating the discussion at too early a stage with the intricate problem of the various senses of the Bible. Their basis, however, is exactly this distinction between the meaning of *vox* and *res*. The *vox* indicates the historical or literal sense; the *res*, through its properties, the spiritual meaning. Starting from this difference, medieval exegetes could make certain finer distinctions between kinds of meaning of these properties. Thus, inquiring more closely into the spiritual or mystical meaning, Nicholas of Lyra says that "in general this meaning is threefold," and then gives the well-known allegorical, tropological, and anagogical senses.[47] The divine authorship of the Bible makes the things mentioned there signify other things, not in the sense of mere symbolism, however, but in the sense of an actual prophecy in the history of Salvation. It lies outside the scope of this study to retrace the history of this conception, which rests on the conviction that the Old and the New Testaments form one fundamental unity and that the Old Testament is meaningful only with reference to the salvation fulfilled in Christ.[48] In the allegorical interpretation, an event of the Old Testament is seen as a figure in relation to the fulfillment in Christ or his Church (*caput et membra*);[49] the tropological interpretation of the event shows its relevance as a sign of what we ought to do—that is, the moral sense is unveiled; and the anagogical interpretation of the event unfolds its significance for the world to come. As early as the fourth century, Augustine, to prevent excesses of spiritual interpretation, formulated the principle, "figura nihil probat," and pointed out that the literal sense is always holy:

> Above all, brethren, we admonish you in the name of the Lord as much as we can, and instruct you that when you hear expounded the Sacrament of the Scriptures telling what has happened, you first of all believe that what has been read to you happened just as it has been read; so that you do not try without the foundation of history to build in air.[50]

Donne's thorough acquaintance with these traditional methods of interpretation hardly needs demonstration. As I have shown, he was familiar with the underlying distinction of *vox* and *res*. When he disagreed with Lyra it was only for a shift of emphasis: "And as *Lyra* notes, being perchance too Allegoricall and Typick in this, it [the Bible] hath this common with all other books, that *words* signifie *things;* but hath this particular, that all the *things* signifie other *things*." [51] Quinn has rightly suggested that it may be the "all" that Donne wished to qualify, but he has also noticed that Lyra did not say "all," although he may easily be held to imply that in every case the thing is a sign of another thing.[52] It is clear that Donne wanted to restrict and not to eliminate biblical allegory.

Several times in his sermons and essays[53] Donne commented on the exegesis according to three senses of Scripture—literal, allegorical, and tropological. He did not usually consider a separate anagogical sense. In accord with Protestant and most Catholic exegetes of the century that followed the Council of Trent,[54] Donne attributed weight in theological argumentation to the *sensus litteralis* alone. Like Thomas Aquinas and, later, the Protestant Keckermann,[55] he followed Augustine when he said, "Figura nihil probat" (3:144, 5:375); and like Keckermann[56] and most exegetes, who in this followed Thomas Aquinas, he defined the literal sense as the principal intention of the Holy

Ghost (6:42, 2:4).[57] This *sensus litteralis,* however, need not be the meaning of the letter; it may be expressed through metaphor.

Helen Gardner is right in rejecting the view that for the men of the seventeenth century every statement in Scripture, whether narrative, psalm, prophecy, parable, or visionary exhortation, had a spiritual meaning. She points to the fact that since the Middle Ages more and more spiritual nourishment had been drawn from the letter.[58] Yet the more the growing literalism of the age is emphasized, the more those elements that link Donne to tradition stand out. Not only, in contrast to a Protestant like Keckermann,[59] did he think the senses of Scripture useful for exposition, but in certain controversial interpretations he objected to Calvin's tendency to reject Old Testament foreshadowings of Christ.[60] Of course it is hardly surprising that Donne constantly had to qualify his opinion, that the preacher had to be on his guard, as it were, to counter criticism. In one such qualification he echoes Augustine's admonition not to neglect the foundation of history, and Augustine was, after all, one of the important developers of scriptural exegesis according to the senses. Donne says:

> And therefore though it be ever lawfull, and often times very usefull, for the raising and exaltation of our devotion, and to present the plenty, and abundance of the *holy Ghost* in the *Scriptures,* who satisfies us with the marrow, and with fatnesse, to induce the *diverse senses* that the Scriptures doe admit, yet this may not be admitted, if there may be danger thereby, to neglect or weaken the *literall sense* it selfe. [3:353, 17:176]

As was pointed out, a few of Donne's sermons, mostly early ones, have as their structural principle an exegesis according to the senses of Scripture, a device for sermon making that comes down from the Middle Ages.[61]

> . . . Which words we shall first consider, as they are our present object, as they are historically and literally to be

understood of *David;* And secondly, in their *retrospect,* as they look back upon that first *Adam,* and so concern *Mankind collectively,* and so *you,* and *I* . . . ; And thirdly, we shall consider them in their *prospect,* in their future relation to the *second Adam.* [2:75, 2:113]

He refers to "some of our Expositors" for justification of his procedure. In the exegesis of the psalm from which he takes his text (Ps. 38:3), he proceeds mainly word by word, linking the presentation of the literal sense with the moral application; finally he considers the entire psalm to be spoken of Christ and reviews briefly the main parts of the quotation. His division of the next sermon is similar: "First then, all these things are *literally* spoken of *David;* By *application,* of us; and by *figure,* of *Christ. Historically, David; morally,* we; *Typically,* Christ is the subject of this text" (2:97, 3:96). In the last sermon of the series on this psalm Donne says:

Nowe the conclusion of all, accordinge to our custome held in the parts of this psalme, shalbe a short application of some of the most important passages to the person of Christ, of whome many ancient expositors have understood this psalme to have byn principally intended. [2:161, 6:624]

Though this is not so apparent from the mere structure of the exposition, there are a number of typological interpretations in Donne's sermons. He cleverly adapts to his purpose certain traditional references in a sermon on Matthew 21:44, "Whosoever shall fall on this stone shall be broken: but on whomsoever it shall fall, it will grinde him to powder." In the manner in which he treated the arrow and the staff, discussed earlier, he first unfolds some properties and functions of the stone, which stands for Christ; firmness, for example, is given as meaning "the constancy and the perseverance of the love of Christ Jesus" (2:183, 8:134); then he takes the stone as cornerstone and as foundation stone. These stones not being sufficient, he adds Jacob's stone and David's stone. With regard to the latter, Donne refers to Augustine: "*Davids* sling was a type of the Crosse, and the stone was a type of Christ" (2:187, 8:260). It is apparent that the primary function of such figures is signification; the allegorical interpretation is mainly concerned with meanings. Jacob's stone is the stone of peace, David's stone is the stone of victory. The principle of hierarchy, which underlies many of Donne's figures, did not apply to tropes based on meaningful properties of the *res*. Therefore it was not at all strange for the medieval poet to compare Christ to a nut.[62] In Donne's sermons, however, there is seldom any dissonance as a result of disregard for hierarchy, since the congregation is made aware of the method by which these meanings are derived from Scripture.

In the first part of his exegesis, following the first part of his scriptural text, Donne develops the image of the *lapis* in such a way as to show that Christ is a stone over which man must stumble if he is to become aware of the state of his soul and to repent. For every stone that we find in this sermon, Donne sets exactly the limits of the metaphor and controls its meaning, never leaving its implications to the hearers to interpret in one way or the other, nor allowing the hearers to be carried away by its sensuous quality: ". . . this *stone*, (no harder, sharper, ruggeder than this . . .)" (2:193, 8:492). In the last part of the sermon he accumulates more stones mentioned in Scripture, and points out how, at the Last Judgment, they will grind the sinner to pieces. The rhetorical effect of the accumulation is intended: "All these stones shall fall upon him, and to add weight to all these, Christ Jesus himselfe shall fall upon his conscience, with unanswerable questions, and grinde his soule to powder" (2:196, 8:585).

Lancelot Andrewes's Easter sermon of 1611 affords an interesting parallel. Exegetically, if one accepts the Protestant premises, Donne may seem to have a better stand than Andrewes, who preaches on Psalm 118:22: "The stone, which the builders refused, the same stone is become the head of the corner." On the surface, this text does not yield to interpretation as readily as Donne's; but it serves Andrewes well because, as the New

Testament writers had already discovered, the properties and functions of the cornerstone, which here designates David, are easily applied to Christ. Before he interprets these properties in detail, he has to vindicate the identification of this stone with Christ. Referring to Acts 4:11 he says:

> It is the Holy Ghost's own application by the mouth of St. Peter, we may boldly make it ours. But though this be the chief sense, yet it is not the only. The chief it is, for "the spirit of prophecy" is in it, which "is the testimony of Jesus." Yet not the only, for according to the letter we cannot deny, but that originally it was meant of David.[63]

Finally, when Andrewes moves on to the third, the tropological, sense of the text, he readily admits: "And I confess, I chose it the rather for this third."

Donne is so familiar with biblical allegory that he can use the word *type* figuratively: the transfiguration of Christ is a "type" of the transfiguration that will occur in the general resurrection (3:120, 4:224), the natural man is "a convenient type" of the spiritual man (3:85, 2:448). Not only does he see a relation between the feast that Matthew, leaving his worldly job as tax collector, gave for Christ and Abraham's feast for his son on the day young Isaac was weaned, but also he sees Matthew's feast as "a feast that was a Type of a Type, a prevision of a vision, of that vision which S. *Peter* had after, of a sheet, with all kinde of meats clean and unclean in it . . ." (7:148, 5:251).

Donne uses chiefly well-known and widely accepted typological interpretations: Adam, Jacob, and David as types of Christ (1:278, 7:390), Joshua as deliverer of his people pointing forward to the Savior (3:301, 14:356),[64] and the ark as a type of the Church (3:246, 11:204). For Donne, as for the Christians of the preceding millenium, the person mentioned in Isaiah's prophecy (Isa. 63:3) as treading the winepress alone in his red apparel is Christ, "apparelled in our flesh, and his apparell dyed red in his owne blood" (3:297, 14:201). Although Donne disagrees with Irenaeus's view that Christ "is sowed in every furrow, in every place of the Scripture," he finds it so elegantly expressed that "it is almost pity, if it be not true" (3:140, 5:239). As for the Book of Isaiah (and secondarily the Psalms), "no booke of the Old Testament is so like a Gospel, so particular in all things concerning Christ" (6:292, 15:18).

In his sermon to the Company of the Virginian Plantation Donne made use of an interpretation that became central in the American Puritans' understanding of their history: "Be you content to carry him over these *Seas*, who dryed up one *Red Sea* for his first people, and hath powred out another *red Sea*, his owne bloud, for them and us" (4:265, 10:8). The parallel drawn also served to lend a quality of sacramental depth to the sea that the merchants have to cross, and to assign them a role in God's plan of salvation.

It is true of love images, as of all images that use biblical allegory, that they tend to have a grotesque effect if their basis is not immediately recognized. Donne once said: "There is a marriage, and Christ marries me." He continued, referring to Deuteronomy 21:12:

> As by the Law a man might mary a captive woman in the Warres, if he shaved her head, and pared her nails, and changed her clothes: so my Saviour having fought for my soul, fought to blood, to death, to the death of the Crosse for her, having studied my soul so much, as to write all those Epistles which are in the New Testament to my soul, having presented my soule with his own picture, that I can see his face in all his temporall blessings, having shaved her head in abating her pride, and pared her nails in contracting her greedy desires, and changed her clothes not to fashion her self after this world, my soul being thus fitted by himself, Christ Jesus has maried my soul. [3:251, 11:359]

The passage is taken out of the context of a marriage sermon in which Donne indicates as early as the *divisio* his intention to deal with the temporal, the spiritual, and finally with the eternal marriage in heaven—a kind of typological scheme of his own.

He begins his first section by talking about Adam and Eve, and then extends his remarks to men and women in general, represented by the young couple before him. The terms he has used to exemplify and to elucidate the meaning and purpose of the human marriage (*in ustionem, in prolificationem, in adjutorem*) are taken up again in the following parts: the persons here are Christ and his bride, the Church, and finally the Lamb of God and the soul.[65]

As in the sermon for the Virginia Company, Donne places those to whom he speaks in the large context of the history of salvation. Miss Webber rightly says that the marriage of the two people before him becomes a symbol invested with universal spiritual meaning.[66] More specifically it becomes a foreshadowing of future happiness. What Donne had to say on marriage in this world is not particularly inspiring, since he stressed, quite in the medieval fashion, its remedial function. The entire sermon culminates in the anagogical union with the Lamb of God. With Erich Auerbach, one might say that for Donne the marriage of the young couple before him was real, but incomplete. It pointed forward to something spiritual that was yet to come and that would be the final and complete event. In this sense it was not a symbol, but rather *umbra* and *figura* of a future *veritas*.[67]

I mentioned earlier that for Donne the analogy between human and divine love had a typological dimension stemming from the traditional reading of the Song of Solomon. Passages in which the Church or the soul was presented as the Spouse with reference to the Song of Solomon are numerous. Christ is the bridegroom whose death is his marriage (6:288, 14:287). The Church is "a Garden walled in" (5:351, 17:468) full of spices, the *hortus conclusus* of the Song (4:12). The soul has "a spikenard, a perfume, a fragrancy, a sweet savour in her selfe" (5:348, 17:359). The long tradition of typological exegesis of the Song of Solomon enabled Donne, as I noted in the preceding chapter, to adduce even obviously sexual passages without a breach of decorum.

The love imagery had become a conventional code used by the preacher to spell out a tropological sense:

> It was the safety of the Spouse, *That his left hand was under her head, and his right hand embraced her:* And it might well be her safety; for, *Per laevam vita praesens, per dextram aeterna designatur,* says S. *Gregory,* His left hand denotes this, and his right the other life: Our happinesse in this, our assurance of the next, consists in this, that we are in the hands of God. [9:292, 12:665]

Although Donne's own contribution consists in the general application expressed in the last sentence, this application, as is often the case with tropology, rests on typology.

Donne's position between an unreflective affirmation of spiritual allegory on the one hand and a flat rejection of it on the other becomes clearer when we consider two interpretations that Donne documents with an unusually large number of authorities.

In 1627 Donne chose as text for his Christmas sermon Exodus 4:13, "O my Lord, send, I pray thee, by the hand of him whom thou wilt send." This is a passage that had stirred up some controversy, the question being why Moses was reluctant to follow God's order and whom he would rather have had sent in his stead. In his comment on this verse Cornelius à Lapide listed a number of exegetes and their interpretations. He mentioned Lyra, who thought Moses was asking God to send his brother Aaron, and Rabbi Moses, according to whom Moses was thinking of Joshua. Then he turned to the group of writers with whom he agreed: "Secondly, many Fathers, such as St. Justinus, Tertullian, Cyprian, Eusebius, who write against the Jews, think that Moses asked for the coming of the Messiah." [68] According to these and some other exegetes (Basil, Gregory, Jerome) whose views Cornelius took from the commentary of his fellow Jesuit, Pereira, Moses was asking God to send soon the Messiah who had been promised for later, so that He could at the same time both redeem mankind and deliver his people from Egypt.[69] Cornelius, who generally tended toward literal interpretations, added: "This sense is very likely and fitting, whatever Abulensis may object and however much Eugubinus may cry out insolently against the Fathers."[70]

Calvin and Piscator (Johann Fischer), whom Donne thought to be "of the most rigid sub-division in the Reformation" (8:144, 5:519), flatly rejected the possibility that Moses might have thought of the Messiah. Calvin says:

> Those who interpret this passage as alluding to Christ, as though Moses said, that His power was needed to accomplish so mighty a task, introduce a forced and far-fetched sense, which is contradicted by the context, for God would not have been so aroused to anger by such a prayer. I see not why others should suppose it to be spoken of Aaron; for there is no weight in their conjecture, that Moses preferred his brother to himself. The third sense is more probable, viz., that God should stretch forth his hand to direct whomsoever he destined for the work.[71]

In the passage quoted below, Donne shows his knowledge of Calvin's position, but he seems to ignore Calvin's reasons. Donne agrees with "the ancient Fathers, with *Iustin Martyr*, with S. *Basil*, with *Tertullian*, with more, many, very many more . . ." (8:151, 5:771). The fact that the more recent exegetes with whom he agrees all belong to the Catholic side spurs him to a rhetorical slalom between the various commentators. If he agrees in the matter with the Jesuits Pereira and Cornelius à Lapide (from whom he takes most of his information), he still disagrees at least with their manner:

> Of our later writers, *Calvin* departs from the Ancients herein, so farre, as to say, *nimis coacta*, it seemes somewhat a forced, somewhat an unnaturall sense, to interpret these words of the comming of Christ; but he proceeds no farther. But another, of the same subdivision [Piscator], is, (as he uses to

be) more assured, more confident; and he saies, *est omni-
moda & praecisa recusatio;* It is an absolute refusall in *Moses*,
to obey the commandement of God: And that truly, needed
not to have beene said. Now, when wee consider the exposition in the Roman Church, when their great *Bishop*, (I
mean their great writing Bishop [Tostatus]) departs from the
Ancients, and does not understand these words of the comming of Christ, a Jesuit [Pererius] is so bold with that Bishop,
. . . as to tell him, *levis objectio*, that he departs from a good
foundation, the Fathers, and that upon a light reason. And
when another Author in that Church [Eugubinus] proceeds
farther, to so much vehemence, so much violence, as to say,
that it is not only an incommodious, but a superstitious sense,
to interpret these words of the comming of Christ, two Jesuits
[Pererius, Cornelius] correct him, almost in the same words,
(for in the waies of contumely and defamation, they agree
well) and say, *audacter obstrepit*, he does but sawcily bark,
and kick against the ancient Fathers. [8:151, 5:775]

Donne further mentions the readings of Lyra and Rabbi Moses,
both of which he may have taken from one of the Jesuit commentators, and then comes to the expositor with whom he can
wholeheartedly agree, Johann Wild. Although the Franciscan
Wild (or Ferus, as Donne calls him) does not say anything about
this passage that is different from what one finds in Cornelius or
Pereira, Donne may have thought his authority more acceptable
to his congregation since Wild was highly regarded by Protestants, who counted him among the "witnesses to truth." [72] His
writings had been put on the Index in 1590. Paraphrasing Wild,
Donne summarizes his own position:

But, with the Ancients, and later devout men, wee piously
beleeve *Moses* in these words to have extended his Devotion
towards his Nation, and the whole world together, as farre,
as one of them [Ferus] hath extended the Exposition; *quid
prodest ex Egypto exire, & in peccatis manere,* saies he; what
shall they bee the better, for comming out of the pressures of

> Egypt, if they must remaine still, under the oppression of a
> sinfull conscience? And that must be their case, if thou send
> but a *Moses*, and not a Christ to their succour. [8:152, 5:819]

He stood with the Fathers on this question, despite Calvin's quite
reasonable objection. Although Donne would have claimed that he
was, with the help of Ferus,[73] defining the literal meaning of his
text, his interpretation shows how broad his conception of the
"literal" meaning was by comparison with a deliberate literalist like
Calvin.

The second of the two Old Testament interpretations to be
considered in detail has already received some critical attention.
In a brief analysis of Donne's exposition of the passage about the
appearance of the three men to Abraham (Gen. 18:1-25), Helen
Gardner has rightly stressed the clear distinction Donne draws
between the literal or historical sense and the other levels of
interpretation that the preacher can, but need not, use to inten-
sify devotion.[74] She notes that Donne turns to Luther, and beyond Luther to Augustine's *Figura nihil probat*, to which Aquinas
had also referred. Donne is in fact maneuvering very cautiously
as he tries to define his position with regard to the controversial
matter of allegorical interpretation. But his is as outspoken a plea
for the use and usefulness of scriptural allegory as one could
expect from a Protestant pulpit. For a proper perspective on
Donne's position, one will do well to bear in mind Calvin's interpretation of the passage.

Donne's discussion of the passage mainly centers on the two
problems that are also discussed in the commentaries of Cornelius
à Lapide and Pereira:[75] since Abraham addressed in the singular
the angels who appeared to him in the shape of men, could it
be that one of them was Christ? or did they in some manner
represent the Trinity? In his commentary on these verses of
Genesis, Calvin's opinion concerning the second point is unequivo-
cal—the first possibility he does not even deign to mention:

> The mystery which some of the ancient writers have en-
> deavoured to elicit from this act; namely that Abraham

adored one out of the three, whom he saw, and, therefore, perceived by faith, that there are three persons in one God, since it is frivolous and obnoxious to ridicule and calumny, I am more than content to omit.[76]

As to the question whether one of the three was Christ, Donne notes that "this very many, very learned among the Ancients, did not onely aske by way of Probleme, and disputation, but affirme Doctrinally, by way of resolution" (3:140, 5:236). In Cornelius and Pereira Donne would have found examples of such opinions,[77] but he would also have found Augustine's refutation, which he explains at length in his own sermon. With Augustine arguing against such a view, and such modern commentators as Cornelius and Pereira agreeing with him, it would have been indeed unusual for Donne to see in one of the three angels Christ prefigured or even Christ in person.

Naturally in this sermon, preached on Trinity Sunday, his answer to the second question must be different. He says:

But yet, betweene them, who make this place, a distinct, and a literall, and a concluding argument, to prove the Trinity, and them who cry out against it, that it hath no relation to the Trinity, our Church hath gone a middle, and a moderate way, when by appointing this Scripture for this day . . . it declares to us . . . it is a refreshing . . . of that former knowledge which we had of the Trinity, to heare that our onely God thus manifested himselfe to *Abraham* in three Persons. [3:143, 5:345]

Donne refrains from telling us in this case what the poles are between which he is steering. Possibly Calvin is one pole (or the Jews, as Luther says); it is harder to see who he thinks has taken the passage as a literal proof of the Trinity. Augustine could be interpreted so;[78] however, Donne would have been familiar with Luther's view that "nowhere in the writings of the fathers will you find that Abraham regarded these men as the three Persons of the Deity."[79] In other passages in which

Donne sets forth the Anglican middle way he thinks of a position between radical Reform and Catholicism. Here he would have his congregation believe that the Catholic position is the extreme opposite of the rejection of the trinitarian interpretation. It seems that he used the Jesuit Pereira extensively in preparation of this sermon (his reference to Philo's reading of the three angels would be lifted right out of Pereira); but although Pereira reports the traditional opinion that the three angels shadow forth (*adumbrare*) the Trinity, he makes it quite clear that he does not think this to be the literal sense of the passage.[80]

The allegorical reading of the "three men" is thus presented by Donne as the wise avoidance of two opposite and mistaken literal readings; and it is furthermore buttressed by an unimpeachable authority, Martin Luther. He reports Luther to have said that the historical sense of the passage is nothing but a recommendation of hospitality. Although it does not prove the Trinity, we may use it to exercise our devotion (3:144, 5:365).[81] Then Donne continues:

> He [Luther] pursues it farther, to good use: The story doth not teach us, That *Sarah* is the *Christian Church* [Gal. 4:24], and *Hagar* the *Synagogue;* But S. *Paul* proves that, from that story; he proves it from thence, though he calls it but an *Allegory.* It is true that S. *Augustine* sayes, *Figura nihil probat,* A figure, an Allegory proves nothing; yet, sayes he, *addit lucem, & ornat,* It makes that which is true in it selfe, more evident and more acceptable. [3:144, 5:372] [82]

The two passages I have analyzed in some detail have shown that Donne was very careful about drawing support from sources that might suggest unorthodox leanings. Luther seemed to him the best and most acceptable authority to support his view of a limited usefulness of biblical allegory, although Donne failed to define clearly the positions he was eschewing. His interest in biblical allegory as a problem, however, was less theological than exegetical. His pronouncements about allegory were not dictated by a desire to abolish it, but were attempts to secure, with the help of exegetes acceptable to his congregation, a realm in which he could freely edify them with the spirit of the letter.[83]

In the preceding section of this study I have shown some of the ways in which Donne exercised this freedom, and my remarks on tropology, which was often the chief objective of his sermons, can therefore be brief. His method was that of the medieval exegete, who, in the service of allegory and tropology, measured out the spiritual meaning. If pursued to the particulars of one's contemporary scene, tropology becomes application. A sermon like the one on the spiritual honey shows that there was for Donne no clear line between the spiritual and the useful. Quinn has observed that "the most 'allegorical' of Donne's sermons are ones which deal with the text in the light of contemporary events." [84] The statement is true if by *allegorical* we understand "spiritual" or "tropological." It indicates that the method I have described is not a mere leftover from the Dark Ages, but that it has to be seen within the entire practice of the preacher's choosing and adapting a text to an occasion. John King gave an interesting description of how he came to choose a passage from the Psalms (46:7–11) for a sermon commemorating the anniversary of the Gunpowder Plot:

> My travaile for the choice of my text parallel to this daies worke, was as the flying of Noahs doue or floting of his arke; the one had no footing til it came to the arke againe, the other noe restinge place but on the mountaines of *Armenia*, nor I where to settle my divided thoughts, til I fel vpon this Psalme: here I met with manie vniformities.[85]

His text, King explains in the same sermon, serves him "to noe other vse then as a seal, or stamp, or mould."

It is true that Donne's high conception of Scripture forbade him to make any such statement, although his practice was often quite similar. On Guy Fawkes Day of 1622 Donne preached a sermon on Lamentations 4:20, in which he said: "If the breath be soure, if it bee tainted and corrupt, (as they would needs thinke in this case) is it good Physick for an ill breath, to cut off the head?" (4:256, 9:714).[86] While on other occasions Donne had often unfolded the moral meaning by putting himself in the place of the speaker—"Let me be the man of this Text . . ." (4:175, 6:463)—he in this case works out the application with particular ingenuity: "Historically" Jeremiah lamented the death of his king, "prophetically" he lamented the destruction of his nation because of the death of Christ. In the application[87] Josiah, the king of the Jews and "breath of [their] nostrils" (Lam. 4:20), becomes King James, who had escaped death at the hands of the plotters. "Prophetically" Donne interprets the lamentation as pointing to the disaster that would have followed the murder of King James. The designation of "ill breath" for a bad king occurs in this mesh of an allegorical relation between Josiah and Christ, and the "tropological" link made between Josiah (or Christ) and James. If one views the metaphor in this context, that is, if one follows the subtle argumentation concerned with meanings, the image will not appear excessively quaint or even homely.

Thomas Adams clearly expressed the fact that the recognition of the properties of things is at the heart of application. Preaching on Jeremiah 8:22, "Is there no Balme at Gilead . . . ," he says in the course of his interpretation of *balm:*

> Now though the Balme heere, wherunto the *Word* is compared, is more generally taken for the iuyce, now fitted and ready for application; yet without pinching the Metaphore, or restraining the libertie of it, I see not why, it may not be likened, both for generall and particular properties.[88]

It may seem that Donne sometimes "pinched" the biblical metaphor. But I have tried to show that for many of his tropes that are neither decorous according to the Renaissance principle of hierarchy nor situated within an established field of imagery there is behind his practice a traditional method based on the *vox-res* distinction, that is, the medieval theory of the special signification of the word of Scripture.

# 5. Conclusion

THIS study has attempted to find suitable historical and linguistic contexts for the imagery of Donne's sermons. Particular attention was given to classical charges of heterogeneity and dissonance in the sermons of the metaphysical preacher. In the second chapter I tried to measure Donne's tropes by some Renaissance theories of metaphor that are usually presented in the context of the principle of decorum. Quite within the Aristotelian tradition of rhetoric, contemporary *artes concionandi* discouraged remoteness in the choice of a vehicle for a tenor. The "distance" was conceived in terms of relative position on some scale of value, or some hierarchy of being, or both. One theoretical treatise spells out the very elementary rule that a base or evil tenor requires a similar vehicle, and a good tenor, a good or exalted vehicle, and gives examples of such subjects and corresponding vehicles. Although it cannot be proven that Donne was familiar with any such treatises, his comments suggest that he had in mind hierarchical levels, which he expressed in terms of "high" and "low." Such comments are often elicited by figures in which he comes close to overstepping the rules of decorum, a fact indicating that his use of tropes is controlled by that principle. In cases of difference in rank between tenor and vehicle, the trope is usually employed for the purpose of heightening or diminishing. The methods of heightening and diminishing are more obvious than in his poetry, since his prose presents, as it were, a slow-motion picture of a no less radical application of the same technique.

Radical diminution can be followed by radical amplification in the same sermon, the same section, or even the same paragraph.

Renaissance theory, however, does not go beyond judging the individual trope and its relation to the particular speaking situation. Whether a figure is bold, conspicuous, prosaic, or farfetched, or produces an effect of dissonance is very much dependent on context. A metaphor standing alone in a text of an abstract nature will be more striking than one that is integrated into the context by other tropes in its neighborhood, by similar tropes used or expected in the genre, or by the whole structure of a work. Moreover, if it belongs to a conventional field of imagery, it can hardly be bold or striking. In the third chapter my aim has been to establish a few such fields, which have not been sufficiently recognized in literary criticism. The possibility cannot be excluded that a figure in which Donne compares God's piercing of our souls to a surgeon's anatomizing may show some respect on Donne's part for the practitioner of surgery. In the analysis proposed here, however, the comparison is first of all related to the biblical and patristic concept of the Divine Physician. The fact that a field of imagery can be viewed as spelling out a concept shows the interdependence of vehicle and subject matter and makes it impossible to exclude theological questions entirely from rhetorical analysis.

W. Fraser Mitchell writes that it is difficult to determine where Donne is original.[1] The present analysis, which attempts to combine a synchronic with a diachronic view, proposes a partial answer to the question of Donne's originality. Originality within a field of imagery is apparently different from originality outside such a field; they compare as do generation and creation. I have described how Donne elaborates certain fields of imagery: he finds new symptoms for sin, if not a new therapy. Tropes that invoke contemporary ideas about medicine, the Paracelsian *balsamum naturale*, for example, do not form islands of foreign matter in his sermons, since they are linked to a field, in this example to the biblical idea of a spiritual balm. The field of the spiritual voyage is furnished with the nautical terms of contemporary seamanship. The tropes elaborating the analogy between book and world are motivated by the didactic intent Curtius has found in early homiletic literature, but besides using metaphors invoking the process of printing Donne combines the concept of the book of the world with the idea of systems of books (a book within a book), an idea probably derived from profane literature. The field of the sacraments as seals receives a similar systematic expansion, in which God's image is seen as sealed and restamped in man. Donne's elaboration of Bernard's tropes in this field has theological significance since he could hardly have been ignorant of Calvin's objection to the traditional distinction between image and likeness, upon which these tropes are based.

While Donne's tropes on spiritual sealing have gone unnoticed, his figures invoking contemporary business life have occasioned shock at this "profane" coupling of the "worldly" and the "spiritual." I have tried to show that many such tropes are elaborations of figures of the church fathers and that any shock is at least tempered by the recognition that they belong to the traditional field of imagery of Salvation as a purchase. Similarly, Donne's figures belonging to the field of spiritual vision have to be seen in relation to certain biblical metaphors, although tradition, that is, the history of the field, which has attracted the attention of Bultmann and others, is of even greater importance. Donne works in a homiletic tradition in which the so-called optical imagery is well established. He expands the field of spiritual vision somewhat by introducing new processes of reflection, focusing, and magnifying. If originality has any meaning as applied to the imagery of a preacher of the seventeenth century, notably to Donne, that meaning resides partly in the elaboration of such fields.

These fields of imagery are not exhaustive, but they summarize to some extent the metaphorical universe of Donne as preacher. I suggested that they can be compared to the word-hoard of the Old English bard: in a sermon certain topics will call up basic and highly traditional analogies, which the preacher will then elaborate. Although the field of imagery thus conceived is an abstract construct (as abstract as a grammatical paradigm), it can have an equivalent in the text: if the analogy at its base is sustained, the result is rhetorical allegory or possibly a conceit. Since the individual trope in such a series is thus prepared for by similar ones in its textual environment, it will hardly ever be audacious.

In the fourth chapter I have dealt with a number of tropes that are neither part of a conventional field of imagery nor decorous according to the Renaissance principle of hierarchy. Some of these tropes, in which similarity of rank between tenor and vehicle is disregarded, have led to the view that metaphysical preaching is characterized by unusual and whimsical images derived from a background of remote learning. Many of these tropes, however, rely on the medieval theory of signification of the word of Scripture, that is, the distinction between the meaning of a *vox* and the meanings of the various qualities of the *res* it designates. There can be no doubt about Donne's familiarity with traditional methods of scriptural exegesis. His contemporary Dr. C. B. of O. writes in his elegy "On Doctor Donne" that he possessed "Divinity great store, above the rest; / Not of the last Edition, but the best."[2] In his explanation of biblical metaphor Donne can be observed to create new metaphors by adducing meaningful properties of the *res*. His sounding of the import of the biblical word is mostly for the purpose of application. When he measures out in this way the various qualities of a thing, he is not giving free reign to a peculiar temperament, but following the practice of earlier preachers and the advice of *artes concionandi* since the time of Augustine. The learning that Donne uses in such figures is very much a part of the genre in which he is writing.

Notes
Bibliography
Index

# Notes

[*Full bibliographic information is given only for titles not listed in the bibliography.*]

## 1. Introduction

1. Evelyn M. Simpson and George R. Potter, eds., *The Sermons of John Donne* (hereafter cited as *Sermons*). All quotations are from this edition. The numbers that follow each quotation indicate the relevant volume, page, and sermon number, and the line on which the quotation begins—volume:page, sermon:line.

2. *Contrary Music*. See p. 3: "I think it is fair to say that in the pulpit Donne achieved his fullest artistic expression, and came even closer than in his poetry to reflect the spirit of the age." Frederick A. Rowe writes similarly in *I Launch at Paradise*, p. 223: "In this century the Monarch of Wit has greatly extended his fame, and many have come under his imperious rule. He has taught us much. But he would have us chiefly know that it was the taking of orders that was his coronation; and that the pulpit was his throne."

3. Rosemond Tuve, *Elizabethan and Metaphysical Imagery*; Louis L. Martz, *The Poetry of Meditation*.

4. W. Fraser Mitchell, *English Pulpit Oratory from Andrewes to Tillotson*, p. 7.

5. Douglas Bush, *English Literature in the Earlier Seventeenth Century, 1600–1660*, p. 310.

6. Samuel Johnson, *Lives of the English Poets*, 1:20.

7. Milton Allan Rugoff, *Donne's Imagery*.

8. Dietrich Arno Hill, *The Modus Praedicandi of John Donne*; Dennis B. Quinn, *John Donne's Sermons on the Psalms and the Traditions of Biblical Exegesis*; William Gifford, "Time and Place in Donne's Sermons"; and Robert Sorlien, *John Donne and the Christian Life*.

9. Webber, *Contrary Music;* Janel Mulder Mueller, "John Donne's *Ars Praedicandi.*"

10. Mary Ellen Williams, *John Donne's "Orbe of Man . . . Inexplicable Mistery.*"

11. Ibid., p. 8.

12. Compared with these general reservations it is only a minor matter that the critic sometimes digresses from her subject, the archetype of roundness. However, in her remark that Donne compares "the two great virtues," thankfulness and repentance, to silver and gold (p. 337), or that Donne used the image of gold metal in the form of too thin gold leaf or gold dust (p. 341), the critic is not analyzing archetypal images but is describing "metal images" in the manner of Spurgeon and Rugoff.

13. William R. Mueller, *John Donne: Preacher.* Mueller's book as a whole is not a study of imagery, but in one chapter he proposes to study "passages in which comparisons are made . . . between the religious experience and some familiar area of secular experience," and also "the way in which references to various parts of the body are used metaphorically and symbolically" (p. 115). As he conducts the analysis, it seems that almost any comparison derived from a physical object may be seen as exemplifying Donne's use of concrete and familiar images. Similar comments are also found in the otherwise excellent introduction to the Simpson-Potter edition; see *Sermons,* 1:83, where we are told that Donne surprised and shocked in his prose as well as in his verse.

14. *Style in the French Novel,* pp. 210 f.

15. For an excellent report on the present state of research, see Hugo Meier, *Die Metapher;* reviewed by H. H. Lieb in *Zeitschrift für Romanische Philologie* 82 (1966):187–94.

16. "Bewusstseinslage der doppelten Bedeutung" ("Zur Psychologie und Statistik der Metaphern," p. 321). Translations into English here and elsewhere in the text are by the author, unless otherwise indicated.

17. "Der metaphorische Ausdruck steht jedesmal *in einer gewissen Spannung mit dem Zusammenhang*" (ibid.).

18. The *"Art" of Rhetoric* (ed. and trans. J. H. Freese) 3. 11. 5. Cf. Aristotle's famous praise of metaphor in *Poetics* 22. 16.

19. *Rhetoric* 3. 11. 6.

20. Reported by Stählin, "Zur Psychologie," p. 361, n.

21. Harald Weinrich, *Linguistik der Lüge,* pp. 42 f. For the classic presentation of information theory see C. Shannon and W. Weaver, *The Mathematical Theory of Communication.*

22. Cicero *De oratore* 3. 160.

23. Ibid. 163.

24. "Semantik der kühnen Metapher," p. 325.

25. *The Philosophy of Rhetoric*, pp. 96–101.

26. "Semantik der kühnen Metapher," p. 329.

27. The history of the idea (of a scale, ladder, or chain of being) has been sketched out by Arthur O. Lovejoy, in *The Great Chain of Being*, particularly chaps. 2 and 3.

28. The argument has been borrowed from Weinrich, "Semantik der kühnen Metapher," p. 340).

29. "Nicht die durch keine Determination eingeschränkte Zufälligkeit des Bedeutungserlebnisses ist das Normale, sondern das durch Situation und Zusammenhang wirksam bestimmte Bedeutungserlebnis" ("Zur Psychologie," p. 320).

30. "Eine Metapher, und das ist im Grunde die einzig mögliche Metapherndefinition, ist ein Wort in einem Kontext, durch den es so determiniert ist, dass es etwas anderes meint als es bedeutet" ("Semantik der kühnen Metapher," p. 340).

31. *Mimesis*, p. 337.

32. Tuve, *Elizabethan and Metaphysical Imagery*, chap. 9.

33. Ferdinand de Saussure, *Cours de linguistique générale*, pp. 112 f.

34. Adam of St. Victor, in J.-P. Migne, *Patrologiae cursus completus ... series Latina* (hereafter cited as *PL*) 196. 1433.

## 2. Imagery and Decorum

1. Rosemond Tuve, *Elizabethan and Metaphysical Imagery*, p. 192.

2. Ibid., p. 247.

3. C. S. Lewis, *English Literature in the Sixteenth Century*, p. 540.

4. Ibid.

5. Ibid., p. 541. The author adds: "We must never suppose that they are writing from a sensibility in which the decorous dissociations of high from low or the strange from the familiar did not exist. . . . Decorum was in their bones."

6. Ibid.

7. Dorothea Roth, *Die mittelalterliche Predigttheorie und das Manuale Curatorum des Johann Ulrich von Surgant.*

8. See J. M. Connor's article "Preaching, II (Homiletic Theory)," *New Catholic Encyclopedia.*

9. In 1623 he began a letter to the Duke of Buckingham, who was then in Madrid, thus: "Most honoured Lord,—I can thus far make

myself believe that, I am where your Lordship is, in Spain, that in my poor Library where indeed I am, I can turn mine eye towards no shelf, in any profession from the mistress of my youth, Poetry, to the wife of mine age, Divinity, but that I meet more authors of that nation than of any other. Their authors in Divinity, though they do not show us the best way to heaven, yet they think they do. And so, though they do not say true, yet they do not lie, because they speak their conscience" (quoted from Edmund Gosse, *The Life and Letters of John Donne* 2:176). Cf. Geoffrey Keynes, *A Bibliography of Dr. John Donne*, p. 207. His list of books from Donne's library includes only one Spanish text, but there are some others by Spanish authors, though written in Latin.

10. This outstanding Dominican was praised by the Jesuit Rapin as the very model of a preacher. His book, first published in 1576, was recommended even by Bellarmine and Berulle (*New Catholic Encyclopedia*, s.v. "Preaching, II"). I have used the edition published in Verona in 1732.

11. "Quatuor sunt autem, quae praecipue observare debet, qui apte dicere cupit, nempe ut oratio tum dicenti, tum audienti, tum rebus ipsis, quas tractat, et officio, quod gerit, maxime conveniat. Hoc est, quis dicat, cui dicat, et quid potissimum dicendo consequi velit. In his igitur omnibus, quid maxime deceat, considerandum est; quod quidem non ad artis praecepta solum, sed ad prudentiae iudicium quod sicut rerum omnium gerendarum, ita dicendarum moderator est, praecipue pertinet. Inter eius autem officia, et maximum, et difficillimum est, quid ubique deceat, intelligere. Hinc enim decorum illud nascitur, quod omnibus in rebus captandum est" (*Ecclesiastica rhetorica*, bk. 5, chap. 17, pp. 186 f.).

12. "Unde et doctor quisque, ut in una cunctos virtute charitatis aedificet, ex una doctrina, non una eademque exhortatione tangere corda audientium debet" (*Regula pastoralis*, pt. 3, prologue [*PL* 77. 49]).

13. Roth, *Mittelalterliche Predigttheorie*, p. 29.

14. "Aliter enim dividendum est cum clero, aliter cum populo praedicatur, cum ab illis acutius, ab istis tardius capiatur," quoted from Roth, p. 67.

15. "Non solum quis dicat, sed apud quos etiam dicat, considerandum esse ratio ipsa monet. Aliter enim apud rusticos et agrestes homines, aliter apud eruditos, aut nobiles, aut principes viros, et delicatas aures dicendum est. Apud hos enim sublimis et elaborata oratio, apud illos vero concitatior esse debet. Praeterea aliter apud monachos et virgines Deo dicatas, hominesque rerum divinarum et

contemplationi addictos, aliter apud eos, qui sine ullo divini Numinis metu in omnia scelera ruunt" (Luis de Granada, *Ecclesiastica rhetorica,* bk. 5, chap. 17, p. 188).

16. Bartholomew Keckermann, *Rhetoricae ecclesiasticae, sive artis formandi et habendi conciones sacras libri duo,* bk. 2, chap. 10, passim.

17. *The "Art" of Rhetoric* (ed. and trans. J. H. Freese) 3. 2. 8.

18. Cf. Keckermann, *Rhetorica ecclesiastica,* bk. 1, chap. 10, p. 112, and Luis de Granada, *Ecclesiastica rhetorica,* bk. 5, chap. 6, p. 147.

19. "Haec de tropis dicta sint: quae, ut ante diximus, ornamenti plurimum orationi conciliant: quorum omnium una est ratio atque natura: nempe pro noto et propio alicuius rei nomine aliud subrogare, quod vel ornatius, vel significantius sit, vel etiam vim habeat probationis et argumenti" (*Ecclesiastica rhetorica,* bk. 5, chap. 6, p. 147).

20. "Simplicium verborum ornatus est in Tropis, ex quibus metaphora potissimum concionator utetur; siquidem tropus is est omnium florentissimus, et ad movendum delectandemque accomodatatus" (*Rhetorica ecclesiastica,* bk. 1, chap. 10, p. 112).

21. "Metaphora multum habet perspicuitatis et iucunditatis" (ibid., p. 113).

22. "In translationibus autem fugienda est dissimilitudo, qualis est in illo Ennii, Caeli ingentes fornices" (Luis de Granada, *Ecclesiastica rhetorica,* bk. 5, chap. 6, p. 143).

23. "Sed cavendum est, quod etiam in illo capite per Exempla monet Aristotles, ne Metaphorae sint durae, longuius petitae, abjectae, et leves . . ." (*Rhetorica ecclesiastica,* bk. 1, chap. 10, p. 112).

24. "Quod si vereare ne paulo durior translatio esse videatur, mollienda est proposito saepe verbo: ut . . ." and "Diligenter etiam cavendum est, ne omnia, quae Poetis permissa sunt, convenire orationi putemus . . ." (*Ecclesiastica rhetorica,* bk. 5, chap. 6, p. 143).

25. "Vitandum etiam hic illud nimium, ne totam concionem faciamus metaphoricam aut allegoricam, prout videmus factum ab Origene et aliis nonullis; et hodie fit a Pontificis non paucis" (*Rhetorica ecclesiastica,* bk. 1, chap. 10, p. 113).

26. "Haec igitur prima admonitio sit, ut cum alicuius rei tractatione auditorium animos afficere volumus, eam rem maximam in suo genere ostendamus, eamdemque, si natura rei patitur, velut oculis spectandam proponamus" (Luis de Granada, *Ecclesiastica rhetorica,* bk. 3, chap. 10, p. 98).

27. The Franciscan exegete Didacus Stella (Diego of Estella, d. 1578) is the author of the widely used *De ratione concionandi, sive rhetorica ecclesiastica* of 1576. I have used the edition published in Verona in 1782.

28. "Propterea, in toto vel in parte, ipsa collatio, et res, quae fertur, communicent, velut ea, quae natura symbolizant, sive bonum, sive malum illud sit. Nedum si sit opus diversa creaturarum genera tam turpis, seu nocivae qualitatis, quam boni genii, et naturae, ut completa ipsa comparatio fiat, vel in parte inquirat. In data exemplo inveniemus subiectum quod est homo, et illud est qui bonum: Et praedicatum quod est peccatum, et illud est quid malum, sive nocivum. Modo ad aliquod malum comparandum, pleraque sunt turpis naturae, et qualitatis, quae in toto, vel in parte assimilantur. Ea sunt lutum, toxicum, aspis, venenum, captivitas, ulcus, limus, basiliscus, etc. Ut hominem frugi significemus pleraque sunt eximiae naturae: quibus salutem in parte licet comparare. Ea sunt Sol, aether, Princeps, et huiusmodi cetera, quae bonum in toto, vel in parte dicunt" (*De ratione concionandi*, chap. 12, p. 31).

29. See Introduction, n. 1.

30. George Puttenham, *The Arte of English Poesie*, p. 241.

31. Ibid. Parable and fable share the characteristic that they are "inuented for doctrine sake by wise and grave men."

32. "¿No habéis visto cuando un rufiancito anda por una mujer, rodeándole la puerta, y pasando malas noches por ella, y dice en su corazón: 'Yo haré que paséis lo que yo pasé, y que andéis vos tras mí como y anduve tras vos'? Pues ansí pasa, aunque la comparacíon ne sea muy al pelo, por la persona ser mala acá y buena acullá. Ansí dice Jesucristu: 'Dejalda, que lo que me hizo pasar por traella a mí, agora me lo pagará, que yo haré que sepa por experiencia lo que yo pasé por ella. *Ego ostendam illi quanta oporteat eum pati pro nomine meo.* Porque por muchas veces que llamé y no me oyeste, tú llamarás y parecerte ha que no te oyo'" (Juan de Avila, *Obras completas*, 2:308).

33. Quoted above, pp. 19–20.

34. "Quod autem ad docendi aut discendi spectat, id ex dialecticis et rhetoricis est petendum. Nemo est tam perspicax ingenio, qui non infoelicissimè, omnia opera lusa, vel discat vel doceat, neglecta Dialectica et Rhetorica" (*De sacris concionibus formandis compendiaria formula*, D).

35. For instance, the Spanish Jesuit Gerónimo Nadal, "De ministerio verbi Dei," p. 658: "et concionator in librum referat et locos communes, qui vtiles postea illi possint." See also Francisco de Borgia, *Tratado breve del modo de predicar*, p. 194: "Tenga para esto [embellishments, arrangement] lugares comunes con abundanzia y riqueza de sentencias. . . ." Concerning the *loci* see Sister Miriam Joseph, *Shakespeare's Use of the Arts of Language*, chap. 1, and Edgar Mertner, "Topos und Commonplace," p. 186.

36. "Comparatio maioris est, quotiens id, quod minus est, maiori comparatur. Ab hoc loco sic argumentabimur. Ioan. 15. Nõ est seruus maior domino suo. Si me persecuti sunt, & vos persequentur. Si sermonē meũ seruauerunt, & vestrum seruabunt. Argumentum à comparatione maioris. Maxima propositio. Quod in re maiore valet, valeat in minore. Item, si maius adest, etiam id quod minus.

"Minoris comparatio est, quotiens maior res confertur minori. Ex eo capitur argumentum hoc modo: Ad Hebraeos. 9. Si enim sanguis hircorum, & taurorum, & cinis vitulae aspersus, inquinatos sanctificat ad emundationem carnis, quantò magis sanguis Christi, qui per Spiritum sanctum semetipsum obtulit immaculatum Deo, emundavit conscientiam nostram ab operibus mortis ad seruiendum Deo viuenti. Locus à minore. Maxima propositio. Quod in re minore valet, valeat in maiore. Item si minus abest, & maius abesse videtur.

"Paria dicuntur, quae eiusdem conditionis sunt. Ab eo loco ita fit argumentum, prima ad Corinth. 9. Nunquid non habemus potestatem sororem mulierculam circunducendi, sicut & caeteri Apostoli, & fratres Domini, et Cephas? Aut solus ego, & Barnabas no habemus potestatem hoc operandi? Locus à comparatione parium. Maxima. Rerum parium idem esse iudicium" (Johann Reuchlin, *De arte concionandi*, p. Bi). For an English writer on the subject, see John Hoskins, *Directions for Speech and Style*, pp. 17 ff.

37. Robert Cawdrey, *A Treasurie or Store-House of Similies*, p. 80.

38. Bellarmine, *The Ascent of the Mind to God*, step 2, chap. 3, p. 28.

39. See Arthur O. Lovejoy, *The Great Chain of Being*, p. 91.

40. Bellarmine, *Ascent of the Mind*, step 2, chap. 1, p. 23.

41. See Tuve, *Elizabethan and Metaphysical Imagery*, p. 196.

42. "Decorum Ecclesiasticae orationis est, ut affecta sit, & morata, ut rebus, de quibus dicatur, conveniens; affecta autem erit, si eos motus, & sensus, ad quos orator auditorem adducere studeat, animo, & mente concipiat ipse: ut, cum in scaelera hominum, & flagitia invehendum est, quod saepe necesse est facere, acriter, concitate, vehementer dicat: si misericordia populi commovenda, si pauperum incommoda, & miseriae explicandae, si Christi passiones oratione exprimandae, presertim feria sexta hebdomadae sanctae, si B. Virginis, & illo tempore, & saepe alias dolorum & acerbitas & magnitudo commendanda: ut Eccl. orator verbis, sententiis, voce, vultu, collacrimando denique, sese ad ea, quae dicat, accomodet . . ." (*De ecclesiastica rhetorica*, bk. 3, chap. 40, p. 114).

43. T. A. H. McNaron, *John Donne's Sermons Approached as Dramatic "Dialogues of One."*

44. Puttenham, *Arte of English Poesie*, p. 219.

45. Louis L. Martz, *The Poetry of Meditation.*

46. Bellarmine, *Ascent of the Mind,* step 1, chap. 3, p. 6.

47. In her *Elizabethan and Metaphysical Imagery,* pp. 203 f., Rosemond Tuve mentions as examples "the used woman, a shell to fling away, the sun eclipsed with a wink, men as mere dishes for death."

48. *Arte of English Poesie,* p. 219.

49. Cawdrey, *Treasurie of Similies,* p. 353.

50. *Arte of English Poesie,* p. 219.

51. Ignatius, who is helping out Lucifer, is made to reply to Philippus Aureolus Theophrastus Paracelsus Bombast of Hohenheim: "You must not thinke sir, that you may heere draw out an oration to the proportion of your name: It must be confessed, that you attempted great matters, and well becomming a great officer of Lucifer, when you vndertook not only to make man, in your *Alimbicks,* but also to preserve him immortall" (*Ignatius His Conclave,* pp. 25–26).

52. E. R. Curtius, *European Literature and the Latin Middle Ages,* p. 159.

53. John Hoskins, *Directions for Speech and Style,* p. 17.

54. Ibid., p. 35.

55. Ibid., partly quoted by Tuve, *Elizabethan and Metaphysical Imagery,* p. 204.

56. "For the Preacher does not use amplification, to the intent to bring to passe, that the matter might appere either greater or lesser then it is of it selfe, or (as it is sayed) that of a flye might bee made an Elephante, or agayne of an Elephante a flye, in which point the *Rhetoritians* doe most chiefly laboure, couetinge withall to corrupte the iudgement of the hearers, and to withdrawe them from the right scope; but to the ends, it may bee acknowledged of all men to bee suche and so greate, as is meate and requisite that it should bee in deede which verily is no other thing, then to reclayme men erring from the truth, to a prudent and sincere iudgement" (Andreas Gerardus [Hyperius], *The Practis of Preaching,* p. 37a). Hyperius does not deal with tropes in particular since he supposes his ecclesiastical readers are sufficiently familiar with the subject.

57. "Multae autem sunt in translationum usu adhibendae oratori cautiones: primum ne a remotis sumantur: ut si quis dicat Christum serenissimum, quia rex, quia eo nomine reges appellantur: deinde ne ab ulla re turpi proficiscantur, ut siquis Deum Patrem Carnificem Christi nominet: iussit quidem, ut propter peccata hominum moreretur, ut illa morte divinae iustitiae satisfieret, et caeli ianua aperiretur fidelibus: non ideo tamen appelari debuit carnifex, atque, ut paucis dicam, translationes faciles, a rebus pulchris desumptae, et iudicio, quod succum

prudentiae sapientes homines appellarunt, adhibito, illuminant orationem" (Valerio, *De ecclesiastica rhetorica*, bk. 3, chap. 8, p. 93).

58. Bellarmine, *Ascent of the Mind*, step 7, chap. 3, p. 125.

59. Walter J. Ong, S.J., "Wit and Mystery."

60. Maurice F. Reidy, S.J., *Bishop Lancelot Andrewes, Jacobean Court Preacher*, p. 63.

61. *Obras completas*, 2:834.

62. Cf. the following striking passage derived from Ps. 56:8: "*As he put all thy teares into his bottles*, so he puts all the graines of thy dust into his Cabinet, and the windes that scatter, the waters that wash them away, carry them not out of his sight" (4:66, 2:97).

63. "Vis divina pilam ludens jaculatur ab alto, / Et salit, resilit: tollitur, atque cadit. / Tolleris in Coelum, Princeps, cave culmina praeceps. / Divinis manibus si es pila, ludus eris" (Juan de Solórzano Pereira, *Emblemata Centum*, p. 15). The first edition is dated 1635. This particular emblem therefore would not have been available to Donne.

64. The editors of the sermons note that the analogy is one that has found favor with atheistic philosophers, "but was hardly to be expected from the pulpit of St. Paul's" (*Sermons*, 1:98).

65. See M. A. Rugoff, *Donne's Imagery*, "Sports and Games," pp. 125–28.

66. Donne's relation to the company has been studied in detail by Robert Sorlien in his anthology *John Donne and the Christian Life*. The sermon is no. 10 in vol. 4.

67. There is a detailed study of two of Donne's sermons by William Gifford, "Time and Place in Donne's Sermons."

68. See 4:308, 12:203—"when I have spent my selfe to the last farthing, my lungs to the last breath, my wit to the last Metaphore . . ."

69. [Hyperius], *The Practis of Preaching*, p. 17a.

70. The notion of "sweetness" is common in Augustine, who takes it from Cicero; see *De doctrina Christiana* 4. 26. 56.

71. See 5:257, 13:440 and 9:88, 2:727.

72. See, e.g., Domenico Nanni Mirabelli, *Polyanthea, opus suavissimis floribus exornatum*.

73. Evelyn Simpson has drawn attention to passages occurring twice in the work of Donne which seem to illustrate this usage, *A Study of the Prose Works of John Donne*, p. 252. See also W. Fraser Mitchell, *English Pulpit Oratory*, pp. 83–85.

74. On the school exercise of theme writing in relation to the use of commonplaces, see Sister Joan Marie Lechner, *Renaissance Concepts of the Commonplaces*, pp. 156 f.

75. See Mitchell, *English Pulpit Oratory*, pp. 10, 100, 126.

76. Oliver Ormerod, *The Picture of a Puritane*, p. 64.

77. *The Devills Banket, Described in Sixe Sermons*, p. 328.

78. *The Faithfull Shepheard*, pp. 35, 38.

79. Ibid. p. 17.

80. See Barbara K. Lewalski, "Milton on Learning and the Learned-Ministry Controversy," and her chapter "Athens: Learning, Kingship, and Prophecy" in *Milton's Brief Epic*.

81. *The Arte of Prophecying*, p. 133.

82. See Mitchell, *English Pulpit Oratory*, p. 183.

83. John King, *A Sermon Preached in Oxon*, p. 27.

84. Donne quotes Augustine as admitting ornament "*ad ancillationem*" (10:147, 6:262).

85. See Lewalski, *Milton's Brief Epic*, p. 287.

86. "Illa quoque eloquentia generis temperati apud eloquentem ecclesiasticum, nec inornata relinquitur, nec indecenter ornatur" (*De doct. Christ.* 4. 26. 57 [*PL* 34. 117]).

# 3. Fields of Imagery

1. Stephen Ullmann, *Style in the French Novel*, pp. 210–17.

2. Henry W. Wells, *Poetic Imagery*.

3. An early but excellent description of some of Donne's themes is by Mary Paton Ramsay, *Les doctrines médiévales chez Donne, le poète métaphysicien de l'Angleterre* (London, 1917).

4. Because of this freedom, a writer's metaphors are taken to be of particular psychological interest. Rugoff explains: "His fancy is given free rein—the wonderful liberty of developing a parallel or analogy out of anything from heaven, earth or the infinite world of the mind. Given such freedom, he turns naturally and inevitably to those things which, for reasons that lie as deep as personality itself, he has found most interesting, most vivid, most memorable" (*Donne's Imagery*, pp. 13–14).

5. Ibid., p. 14. The kind of insight Rugoff intends to get is expressed in his introductory statement: "Thus, we may discover through the study of the sources of Donne's imagery not only that he has a compelling interest in, let us say, the sciences of his time but that the figures he draws from these are an essential part of that material whereby he transmutes passion into precise and objective terms and

achieves that intellectual apprehension of emotion that is so vital a characteristic of his work" (ibid., p. 18).

6. Ibid., p. 228.

7. L. H. Hornstein, "Analysis of Imagery." Noting Spurgeon's observation that Shakespeare, after *Anthony and Cleopatra*, uses very few food images, she asks: "Are we to conclude that during the last decade of his life Shakespeare neither enjoyed his food nor suffered heart-burn—or perhaps had stopped eating altogether?" (p. 650).

8. Wilhelm Stählin, "Zur Psychologie und Statistik der Metaphern"; see 1 Tim. 1:19.

9. Rugoff makes this comment after distinguishing "references" and "allusions," which are an integral part of subject matter, from proper "images": "But imagery has, as we have seen, no such restricted relation to subject matter; as soon as we begin to examine Donne's images we find that those from religion not only do not show a corresponding preponderance but actually occur no more often than the images from half a dozen other sources and not so effectively or analytically as those from two or three we have already considered.

"There are, however, two circumstances which suggest at least a partial explanation of this situation: at the time of his early writings Donne's all-engrossing interest in religion had not yet manifested itself, and in his later works the very fact that their subject matter was religion made it only natural that he should avoid religious imagery— only natural, I say, because Donne's imagery makes clear that he accepted fully the conception of an image as an illumination of an idea by another not related to it in subject matter" (*Donne's Imagery*, p. 83).

10. Thus, with Rugoff, the larger arrangement, from "Science and Learning" through "Man and His Environment" to the "World Outside" has some affinity with encyclopedic representations of the world, such as Rhabanus Maurus's *De universo*.

11. Harald Weinrich, "Münze und Wort," p. 516.

12. "Erst durch die Stiftung des Bildfeldes wird der eine Sinnbezirk zum bildspendenden Feld, der andere zum bildempfangenden Feld. Es wäre eine unzulässige und trügerische Abstraktion, das bildspendende Feld vom bildempfangenden Feld zu isolieren. Alle Metaphern aus dem Finanzwesen zusammen also bilden—gar nichts. Auch wenn man alle Metaphern *für* das Wortwesen zusammennimmt, erhält man gar nichts, jedenfalls keine sinnvolle Struktur. Solange man also nicht das bildspendende *und* das bildempfangende Feld gleichzeitig im Auge hat, ist von Metaphorik gar nicht die Rede" (ibid., pp. 515–16).

13. Matt. 9:12; Mark 2:17; Luke 5:31. Of course other passages such as the one on the healing of the leper (Matt. 8:3) are relevant here.

14. *Contrary Music*, p. 215, n. 20.

15. "Nam et aeger petit multa a medico, non dat medicus: non exaudit ad voluntatem, ut exaudiat ad sanitatem. Ergo medicum tuum pone Deum" (*Enarratio in Psalmum* 85 [PL 37. 1088]).

16. "Ergo non est exauditus; sed non ad insipientiam, sed ad sapientiam: ut intelligat homo medicum esse Deum, et tribulationem medicamentum esse ad salutem, non poenam ad damnationem. Sub medicamento positus ureris, secaris, clamas: non audit medicus ad voluntatem, sed audit ad sanitatem" (*Enarr. in Ps.* 21 [PL 36. 173]).

17. "Unde scis quam putre est quod secat medicus, agens ferrum, per putria? Nonne novit modum, quid faciat, quo usque faciat? Numquid ullulatus eius qui secatur, retrahit manus medici artificiose secantis? Ille clamat; ille secat" (*In Joannis evangelium* 7 [PL 35. 1443]).

18. "Sed perversus, et nesciens quo venisset, erat tanquam in statione medici curandus, et sana membra ostendebat, vulnera tegebat. Deus tegat vulnera; noli tu. Nam si tu tegere volueris erubescens, medicus non curabit. Medicus tegat, et curet; emplastro enim tegit. Sub tegmine medici sanatur vulnus, sub tegmine vulnerati celatur vulnus. Cui celas? Qui novit omnia" (*Enarr. in Ps.* 31 [PL 36. 266]).

19. Ibid.

20. "Non vides quanta homines patiantur sub medicorum manibus, spem incertam homine promittente? Sanaberis dicit medicus; sanaberis, si secuero. Et homo dicit, et homini dicit; nec qui dicit certus est, nec qui audit, quia ille dicit homini, qui non fecit hominem, et non perfecte scit quid agatur in homine: et tamen ad verba hominis plus nescientis quid agatur in homine credit homo, subdit membra, ligari se patitur, aut plerumque etiam non ligatus secatur aut uritur; et accipit forte salutem paucorum dierum, jam sanatus quando moriatur ignorans" (*Enarr. in Ps.* 85 [PL 37. 1088–89]).

21. "Quibus te medicamentis curet, ille novit; quibus sectionibus, quibus ustionibus, ille novit. Tu tibi aegritudinem comparasti peccando: ille venit non solum fovere, sed secare et urere" (ibid. [PL 37. 1088]).

22. Jean Courtès, "Saint Augustin et la médecine," p. 47.

23. Rudolf Arbesmann, O.S.A., "Christ the *Medicus Humilis* in St. Augustine," and "The Concept of *Christus Medicus* in St. Augustine."

24. Arbesmann, "The Concept of *Christus Medicus*," p. 7. One does well to bear this emphasis in mind when studying Donne's tropes, although it cannot be overlooked that the concept is quite frequent in

Augustine's *Confessions* (see, for instance, bk. 10), which Donne had read carefully.

25. John King, *A sermon of pvblicke thanksgiuing . . . preached . . . the 11. of Aprill, 1619* (London, 1619), p. 33.

26. Robert Burton reports in his *Anatomy of Melancholy*, 1:461: "*Laurentius, cap. 3. de melan.* thinks this kind of melancholy *hilare delirium*, which is a little adust with some mixture of blood, to be that which *Aristotle* meant, when he said that melancholy men of all others are most witty, which causeth many times divine ravishment, and a kind of *enthusiasmus*, (divine inspiration), which stirreth them up to be excellent Philosophers, Poets, Prophets, etc." For an excellent discussion of the problem, see Lawrence Babb, *The Elizabethan Malady*, pp. 58 ff.

27. Burton, *Anatomy of Melancholy*, 1:198.

28. Ibid., 1:200.

29. See Jean Starobinski, *Geschichte der Melancholiebehandlung von den Anfängen bis 1900*, pp. 16 f. and p. 41. Indiscriminate use of this treatment must have weakened many a melancholic, so that Burton (*Anatomy of Melancholy*, 2:275) writes: "Purges come last . . . because they weaken nature and dry so much."

30. Such a discussion would make the analysis of imagery the tool to explore something else which may be obtained more easily in other ways. Thus Don Cameron Allen, who has dealt with the subject, has studied also Donne's direct statements as contained, for instance, in his letters ("Donne's Knowledge of Renaissance Medicine"). One would also compare such statements with Donne's reading, for example, Joannes Mesua, *De re medica* (Paris, 1562), which according to Geoffrey Keynes's list was in Donne's library (*A Bibliography of Dr. John Donne*, p. 217). It would be hazardous to decide the question on the basis of imagery. Because of its function as a code in communication, imagery seems in fact unsuited to use as the basis for a conclusive argument. In relation to what he calls, drawing on Croce, the "preachable conceit" in the tradition of the baroque or metaphysical sermon, J. A. Mazzeo has rightly stressed the noncommittal character of Donne's figures drawing on alchemy and the occult sciences (*Renaissance and Seventeenth-Century Studies*, p. 89).

31. Quoted from Levin L. Schücking, *The Meaning of Hamlet*, p. 28.

32. Guillaume Du Bartas, *Works*, ed. U. T. Holmes et al. (Chapel Hill, N.C., 1938), 2:318. The editor's note is characteristic: "The word *emplastre* spoils for many of us the poetic beauty of the foregoing passage."

33. See n. 18, above.

34. See Pierre Hubert Nysten, *Dictionnaire de médecine* (Paris, 1855).

35. Rugoff, *Donne's Imagery*, p. 59.

36. Thomas Adams, *The Devills Banket, Described in Sixe Sermons*, p. 300.

37. Robert Cawdrey, *A Treasurie or Store-House of Similies*, p. 218.

38. See Allen, "Donne's Knowledge of Renaissance Medicine," pp. 325 f.; Rugoff, *Donne's Imagery*, pp. 50 f.; and Mazzeo, *Renaissance and Seventeenth-Century Studies*, p. 68. In *Sermons* see 5:347, 17:352 and 6:116, 5:88: "Every thing hath in it, as Physitions use to call it, *Naturale Balsamum*, A naturall Balsamum, which, if any wound or hurt which that creature hath received, be kept clean from extrinsique putrefaction, will heale of it self. We are so far from that naturall Balsamum, as that we have a naturall poyson in us, Originall sin."

39. Jer. 8:22.

40. Bernard of Clairvaux speaks of the *unctio* of the Divine Physician (*Sermones de tempore*, In vigilia nativitatis Domini 6. 2 [*PL* 183. 109–10]).

41. See Thomas Adams, "Physicke from Heaven," in *Devills Banket*, p. 266 (dedication) and p. 311.

42. See also 6:87, 3:216.

43. "Probably the most fantastic analogy to issue from this source is that between the way God can use scandals and temptations to physic the spirit of man and the way apothecaries mix vipers and poisons to make 'sovereign treacles' " (Rugoff, *Donne's Imagery*, p. 52). The reference is to 3:170, 6:524: "Can an Apothecary make a Soveraign triacle of Vipers, and other poysons, and cannot God admit offenses, and scandals into his physick?"

44. For *amaritudo* versus *suavitas* ("bitterness" versus "sweetness"), see Augustine *Enarr. in Ps.* 85 (*PL* 37. 1085).

45. Cawdrey, *Treasurie of Similies*, p. 340.

46. Thomas Adams, "Physicke from Heaven," in *Devills Banket*, p. 326.

47. The identification is of course only metaphorical. The line between sin and sickness was often discussed in the Middle Ages, in particular with reference to melancholy; see Starobinski, *Geschichte der Melancholiebehandlung*. If melancholy was a physiological distemper, how could it be a sin? The fact that Donne speaks of the relation of sin to sickness with reference to melancholy suggests the influence

of the old discussion. Cf. 3:270, 12:515, where Donne says that "inordinate sorrow growes into sinfull melancholy" and 3:286, 13:434: "Let no man therefore think to present his complexion to God for an excuse, and say, My choler with which my constitution abounded, and which I could not remedy, enclined me to wrath, and so to bloud; My Melancholy enclined me to sadnesse, and so to Desperation, as though thy sins were medicinall sins, sins to vent humours."

48. "medicus qui novit quibus sectionibus, quibus ustionibus te curet" (*Enarr. in Ps.* 85 [*PL* 37. 1088]).

49. "manus medici artificiose secans," and "agens ferrum per putria" (*In Joannis evangelium* 7. 1 [*PL* 35. 1443]).

50. "venit non solum fovere, sed et secare et urere" (*Enarr. in Ps.* 85 [*PL* 37. 1088]).

51. Allen, "Donne's Knowledge of Renaissance Medicine," p. 339.

52. "For home-bred medicines are both more easie for the Parsons purse, and more familiar for all mens bodyes. So, where the Apothecary useth either for loosing, Rubarb, or for binding, Bolearmena, the Parson useth damask Roses for the one, and plantaine, shepherds purse, knot-grasse for the other, and that with better successe" (*Works*, p. 261).

53. Rugoff, *Donne's Imagery*, p. 220.

54. For *febris* see *PL* 35. 1443.

55. Allen, "Donne's Knowledge of Renaissance Medicine," p. 327. The passage is 2:81, 2:329.

56. "et ipsa recordatio sabbati, et nondum retentio, facit me nondum gaudere, et agnoscere nec sanitatem esse in ipsa carne, neque dici debere, cum comparo istam sanitatem illi sanitati quam habebo in requie sempiterna, ubi corruptibile hoc induet incorruptionem, et mortale induet immortalitatem (I *Cor.* xv, 53); et video quia in illius sanitatis comparatione, ista sanitas morbus est" (*Enarr. in Ps.* 37 [*PL* 36. 399]).

57. He quotes, for instance, "Sanitas hujus vitae, bene intelligentibus, sanitas non est" (2:80, 2:304) and "Medicamentum famis cibus . . . fatigationis somnus" (2:80, 2:307). Both passages are from *Enarr. in Ps.* 37 (*PL* 36. 398).

58. "Sicut etiam ille qui medetur vulneri corporis, adhibet quaedam contraria, sicut frigidum calido, vel humidum sicco, vel si quid aliud hujusmodi . . . sic sapientia Dei hominem curans, seipsum exhibuit ad sanandum, ipsa medicus, ipsa medicina. Quia ergo per superbiam homo lapsus est, humilitatem adhibuit ad sanandum" (*De doctrina Christiana* 1. 14. 13 [*PL* 34. 24]).

59. *The Meaning of Hamlet*, pp. 27 f.

60. Ollivier Dezeimeris, *Dictionnaire historique de la médecine ancienne et moderne* (Paris, 1831), 1:750.

61. See 6:198, 9:444, quoted above, where Donne speaks of the purging of melancholy.

62. Both quotations in this paragraph are from Allen, "Donne's Knowledge of Renaissance Medicine," p. 322.

63. "Totum hoc in corde humano, tamquam vermibus corruptionis hujus scatet. Exaggeravimus morbum, laudemus et medicum" (*Enarr. in Ps.* 102 [*PL* 37. 1320]).

64. "Das Arztbild ist bei Calvin . . . völlig aus dem Problemkreis herausgenommen, in dem es die kirchliche Sprache seit alters verwandte: der Gnadenerfahrung oder Rechtfertigung" (Erwin Mülhaupt, *Die Predigt Calvins*, p. 56).

65. "Quod enim pateris tribulationes, manus est secantis medici, non sententia judicis punientis" (*Sermones de sanctis* 278. 5 [*PL* 38. 1271]).

66. Quoted from Miss Wallerstein's notes, published posthumously, *Studies in Donne*, p. 354.

67. Helen C. White, *The Metaphysical Poets*, p. 133.

68. William R. Mueller, *John Donne: Preacher*, p. 117.

69. After enumerating Donne's travels and referring to a storm that drove his ship back to Plymouth, Rugoff writes: "Such in brief was Donne's experience with ships. It is enough to prepare us for one of the main currents of his imagery from this source—the tendency to recall the more unpleasant aspects of sea travel and to consider all such travel as symbolizing progress through any medium beset with countless and inexorable perils" (*Donne's Imagery*, p. 130).

70. But not in all languages, as Benjamin Lee Whorf has shown in his *Language, Thought, and Reality*, ed. J. B. Carrol (New York, 1956). The importance of the biblical concept of life as a journey, especially for American literature, has been recognized in some recent studies; see Paul Gerhard Buchloh, "Vom 'Pilgrim's Progress' zum 'Pilgrim's Regress,' " and Klaus Weiss, *Das Bild des Weges*.

71. See Joseph Pieper, "Bemerkungen über den *status viatoris.*"

72. Heb. 11:13 and 1 Pet. 2:11.

73. See, e.g., Chrysostom *In epistolam II ad Timotheum* 4, in J.–P. Migne, *Patrologiae cursus completus . . . series Graeca* (hereafter cited as *PG*) 62. 623: "Cum agonotheta venerit, quanto fruetur honore? Apud alienos hospes erat, hospes et peregrinus, et tantae habetur admirationi; cum in patria erit, quo non fruetur bono?" and *In epistolam ad Colossenses* 7 (*PG* 62. 346): "Sive ergo contumelia

afficiamur, ne doleamus; sive quodvis patiamur: non est enim nostra vita haec vita: hospites enim et peregrini sumus."

74. "Nec nata nobis sunt inter quae nati sumus, quia propter illum renati sumus. Sint haec ad necessitatis usum, non ad charitatis affectum: sint tanquam stabulum viatoris, non tanquam praedium possessoris. Refice, et transi. Iter agis, attende ad quem venisti; quia magnus est qui ad te venit. Discedendo de hac vita, locum facis venienti: stabuli est ista conditio: cedes, ut alius accedat" (*Sermones de scripturis* 177 [*PL* 38. 954]).

75. Bernard *Serm. de temp.*, In quadragesima 7 (*PL* 183. 183c).

76. D. C. Allen, "Donne and the Ship Metaphor," p. 309.

77. "In omnibus tamen quae fecit Dominus, admonet nos quemadmodum hic vivamus. Nemo quippe in hoc saeculo non peregrinus est: quamvis non omnes ad patriam redire desiderent. Ex ipso autem itinere fluctus tempestatesque patimur: sed opus est vel in navi simus. Nam si in navi pericula sunt, sine nave certus interitus. Quantasvis enim vires habeat lacertorum qui natat in pelago, aliquando magnitudine maris victus absorbetur et mergitur. Opus est ergo ut in navi simus, hoc est, ut in ligno portemur, ut mare hoc transire valeamus. Hoc autem lignum, quo infirmitas nostra portatur, crux est domini, in qua signamur, et ab hujus mundi submersionibus vindicamur. Patimur fluctus: sed ille Deus est, qui opituletur nobis" (*Sermones de tempore* 75 [*PL* 38. 475]). The passage is quoted by Allen.

78. Henri Rondet, S.J., "Le symbolisme de la mer chez saint Augustin." Hugo Rahner's series of articles on the *antenna crucis* in *Zeitschrift für katholische Theologie* is also relevant: "I. Odysseus am Mastbaum," *ZkTh* 65 (1941):123–52; "II. Das Meer der Welt," *ZkTh* 66 (1942):89–118; "III. Das Schiff aus Holz," *ZkTh* 66 (1942):196–227 and 68 (1943):1–21; "IV. Das Kreuz als Mastbaum und Antenne," *ZkTh* 75 (1953):129–73; "V. Das mystische Tau," *ZkTh* 75 (1953): 385–410; "VI. Der Schiffbruch und die Planke des Heils," *ZkTh* 79 (1957):129–69.

79. These uses do not amount to a meaningful structure, for as Mueller himself concludes (*John Donne: Preacher*, pp. 141–42), the sea "is used with favorable and unfavorable connotations." Whether the fact that Donne uses such analogies to make a spiritual point is psychologically significant is questionable. The words, for instance, that Mueller quotes from Donne, "all our words are sea, all our words are sin" (4:286, 16:113), follow after a long passage developing the analogy between the swelling of our concupiscences and the swelling of a river, which will first fill the various channels and then overflow

the whole field. This moral analogy is not original with Donne; it is contained in Cawdrey's *Treasurie of Similies* (p. 144). Donne's figure, which heightens the topical river into a sea, tells little about how he thinks about the ocean.

80. It is not unlikely that Donne was familiar with the sermons of a well-known convert to Protestantism, Marco Antonio de Dominis, whose *Rockes of Christian Shipwracke* was published in London in 1618.

81. Cf. 4:227, 8:648 and 8:64, 2:52.

82. See F. J. Dölger, *Sol Salutis*, pp. 272–85.

83. *The Spirituall Navigator Bound for the Holy Land*, pp. 26–27.

84. Ibid., p. 27.

85. Bernardino Ochino, *Certaine Godly Sermons of Faith, Hope and Charitie*, p. 40.

86. See also 7:440, 18:218.

87. Mary Ellen Williams, *John Donne's "Orbe of Man . . . Inexplicable Mistery,"* p. 296.

88. *Georgics* 2. 41. The metaphor has been studied by E. R. Curtius, *European Literature and the Latin Middle Ages*, pp. 128–29.

89. Jerome *Commentaria in Osee* 3 (PL 25. 905a) and *Commentaria in Ezechielem* 12 (PL 25. 369d).

90. Mueller, *John Donne: Preacher*, p. 140.

91. *Latin Middle Ages*, p. 319.

92. *Donne's Imagery*, p. 109.

93. *Contrary Music*, p. 125.

94. Ibid., p. 129.

95. *Latin Middle Ages*, p. 320.

96. *PL* 176. 644d ff., cited in Curtius, p. 320.

97. According to Curtius, *Latin Middle Ages*, p. 320.

98. Ibid., p. 321.

99. "Qué seran luego todas las criaturas deste mundo, tan hermosas y tan acabadas, sino unas como letras quebrades y iluminadas que declaran bien el primor y la sabiduría de su autor? . . . Así nosotros . . . habiéndonos vos puesto delante este tan marabilloso libro de todo el universo, para que por las criaturas dél, como por unas letras vivas, leyesemos la excelencia del Criador" (ibid., p. 320).

100. Ibid.; the reference is to Bernard Silvestris.

101. *Contrary Music*, p. 128.

102. Ps. 69:28.

103. Curtius, *Latin Middle Ages*, pp. 320–21.

104. This has been noted by Joan Webber, *Contrary Music*, p. 125.

105. *Latin Middle Ages*, p. 321.

106. "das ist das recht buch, aus dem die anatomia folgen sol, das der mensch wisse der elementen und microcosmi substanz, proportiones etc. zuvergleichen. nicht das gnugsam sei, so der cörper gesehen wird der menschen, item aufgeschnitten und aber besehen. . . . das sehen ist alein ein sehen wie ein baur, der ein psalter sieht, alein die buchstaben; da ist weiter nichts mer von im zusagen" (Paracelsus, *Sämtliche Werke*, Abt. 1, 11:184).

107. Ibid., p. 174.

108. Ibid., p. 172.

109. "*Invisibilia Dei*, Apostolo teste, *a creatura mundi, per ea quae facta sunt, intellecta conspiciuntur*. Ea est velut communis quidam liber, et catena alligatus, ut assolet, sensibilis mundus iste, ut in eo sapientiam Dei legat quicunque voluerit. Erit tamen cum coelum plicabitur sicut liber, in quo utique nemo deinceps legere habeat necesse, quoniam erunt omnes docibiles Dei (*Joan*. vi, 45) et quemadmodum creatura coeli, sic et creatura mundi, jam non per speculum et in aenigmate, sed facie ad faciem Deum videbit, et sapientiam ejus ad liquidum contemplabitur in se ipsa. Interim vero opus habet humana anima velut quodam vehiculo creaturae, ut ad cognitionem Creatoris assurgat" (Bernard of Clairvaux *Sermones de diversis* 9. 1 [*PL* 183. 565c]).

110. Cf. Alain de Lille (*PL* 210. 579): "Omnis mundi creatura, / Quasi liber, et pictura / Nobis est, et speculum." The passage is quoted by Curtius, *Latin Middle Ages*, p. 319.

111. "the man in whom God imprints these beames of Blessedness" (9:265, 11:547).

112. See Augustine *Enarr. in Ps.* 40 (*PL* 36. 459): "quod tam recenti sermone impressum est auribus et cordibus vestris."

113. The metaphorical extension is again helped by the wide meaning of the Latin *imprimere*.

114. Rev. 5:1 and elsewhere.

115. Wilhelm Michaelis, "Zeichen, Siegel, Kreuz," pp. 505–25.

116. Rev. 7:2.

117. Rev. 13:16; 14:9; 20:4.

118. Michaelis discusses the question; see "Zeichen, Siegel, Kreuz," pp. 519 f.

119. *The Seal of the Spirit*, p. 235.

120. Ibid., p. 241.

121. "Luge eos qui nihil ab infidelibus differunt, qui sine illuminatione, sine signaculo decesserunt" (Chrysostom *In epistolam ad Philippenses* 3. 4 [*PG* 62. 203]).

122. "Non dat sancta canibus: sed ubi probam conscientiam videt,

illic salutare et admirabile sigillum confert" (Cyril of Jerusalem *Catechesis* 1. 3 [*PG* 33. 374a]).

123. *PG* 33. 374, n. 4. Cornelius à Lapide is well acquainted with this custom; see *Commentaria*, 10:1235. Commenting on John 13:16 he writes: "Faciet omnes habere characterem in manu," and goes on to explain: "Sic olim milites signabantur stigmate in manu."

124. "Accedite ad mysticum signaculum, ut ab hero favorabiliter agnosci possitis. Sancto ac ratione praedito Christi gregi accenseamini, ut olim ad dexteram ejus segregati, paratam vobis vitam haereditate consequamini" (Cyril *Catechesis* 1. 2 [*PG* 33. 371b]).

125. See *PG* 33. 273, n. 4.

126. "Et vos oves Christi estis, characterem dominicum portatis in Sacramento quod accipitis; sed erratis et peritis" (*Epistulae* 173. 3 [*PL* 33. 754]).

127. "Sic enim error corrigendus est ovis, ut non in ea corrumpatur signaculum Redemptoris" (ibid. 185. 23 [*PL* 33. 803]).

128. "Puta te esse militarem: Si characterem imperatoris tui intus habeas, securus militas; si extra habeas, non solum tibi ad militiam non prodest character ille, sed etiam desertore punieris" (Augustine *In Joannis evangelium* 6. 15 [*PL* 35. 1432]); see also *De baptismo contra Donatistas* 3. 19. 25 (*PL* 43. 151).

129. "Durch diese beiden Bilder vom character militaris bzw. dominicus ist Augustins Tauflehre so epochemachend geworden" (Werner Jetter, *Die Taufe beim jungen Luther*, p. 12).

130. Ibid., p. 13.

131. "unde posuit duo pertinentia ad characterem, sicut *sigillum* et *custodiam*, in quantum ipse character, qui sigillum dicitur, quantum est de se, custodit animam in bono" (*Summa theologiae* 3. 66. 1 ad 1).

132. There is an interesting passage in which he deals with an ambiguous word of Cyprian's that became important in the controversy about confirmation. When Hooker quotes Cyprian's sentence, he leaves out the sealing phrase in question (*signaculo domenico consumentur*); see *Of the Laws of Ecclesiastical Polity: The Fifth Book*, ed. R. Bayne (London, 1902), chap. 66, sec. 5, p. 365. Donne, however, does not hesitate to multiply the "seals" (5:49, 1:526 and 5:52, 1:625). For Cyril, see also Lampe, *Seal of the Spirit*, pp. 170–74.

133. See Eph. 1:13–14, Eph. 4:30, 2 Cor. 1:22.

134. See Lampe, *Seal of the Spirit*, pp. 248 f.

135. "Quod autem per spiritum ad imaginem Dei fuerit obsignatus, ipse nos rursus docuit, his verbis: *Et inspirauit in faciem eius spiraculum vitae*. Simul enim et vitam creaturae Spiritus indidit, et

suos characteres diuinitus impressit" (*Commentarius in Ioannem*, in *Opera omnia*, 4:122B).

136. "Sicut enim Deus in Genesi creavit hominem ad imaginem suam, ita Christus hominem lapsum et perditum sua morte in baptismo reformavit, et quasi denuo creavit ad imaginem Dei, et suam" (Cornelius à Lapide, *Commentaria*, 9:666).

137. Lampe, *Seal of the Spirit*, p. 248.

138. Particularly the writers of the Alexandrian school developed the idea of the baptismal image as a restamping of the image of God; see Lampe, p. 250. Cyril is in fact singled out by Donne and praised for one of his similes in this field of imagery; see 9:80, 2:435.

139. "Nam quemadmodum si qua alicujus effigies in tabula aliqua depicta, injectis sordibus fuerit deleta, necesse est eum, cujus illa est effigies, iterum adesse, ut ejus imago in eadem materia possit restitui; ipsa enim materia propter expressam in se imaginem non projicitur, sed deleta effigies in ea renovatur: ita sanctissimus Patris Filius, qui Patris imago est, ad nos advenit, ut hominem ad sui similitudinem factum reficeret" (*De incarnatione Verbi* 14 [*PG* 25. 119]).

140. "Filius enim Dei et Patris signaculum est, totam eius, et perfectam similitudinem continens, et in proprio decore genitoris natura coruscans. In ipso porro quoque ad similitudinem suam nos signat Deus: siquidem in Christum transformati, velut imaginem Dei acquirimus. Signaculum igitur perfectum Dei et Patris, est Filius, et ipsum elegit, hoc est eligibilem reddidit, et electum" ("In Aggaeum commentarius" 20, in *Opera omnia*, 3:650).

141. "Deum quidem sanctos consignare per Filium credimus . . . Sigillo è ferro verbi gratia, vel auro sui similitudinem iis rebus imprimit quae eo insigniuntur, ita tamen vt suiipsius nihil amittat, sed solo impressionis actu ea in quibus recipitur insigniat: sic intellegimus signatum esse à Patre Filium, quippe qui nihil substantiae ipsius habeat, sed sola exacta similitudine fruatur, aliud ab ipso existit, non secus ac imago ratione archetypi" (*Commentarius in Ioannem* 3. 5, in *Opera omnia*, 4:302D).

142. "Tertius modus est iuxta characterem seu impressionem a sigillo, ubi deest consubstantialitas et potentiae efficientia" (*Summa theol.* 1. 42. 2 arg. 1).

143. "Where a thing is by its presence, its image is not required to supply the place of the thing, as where the emperor is the soldiers do not pay homage to his image. Yet the image of a thing is required together with its presence, that it may be reflected by the presence of the thing, just as the image in wax is perfected by the impression of the

seal (*sicut imago in cera perficitur per impressionem sigilli*)" (ibid. 3. 5. 4 ad 1).

144. *Sermons*, 1:95.

145. Lampe adduces examples from Gregory of Nyssa and Macarius, who, as he points out, could have found the simile in Philo; see *Seal of the Spirit*, p. 254.

146. "Recipe ergo similitudinem Dei, quam per mala facta amisisti. Sicut enim in nummo imago imperatoris aliter est, aliter in filio: nam imago et imago est; sed aliter impressa est in nummo, aliter in filio, aliter in solido aureo imago imperatoris: sic et tu nummus Dei es, ex hoc melior, quia cum intellectu et cum quadam vita nummus Dei es, ut scias etiam cujus imaginem geras, et ad cujus imaginem factus sis: nam nummus nescit se habere imaginem imperatoris" (*Serm. de script.* 9. 8 [*PL* 38. 82]).

147. Matt. 22:20; cf. Lampe, *Seal of the Spirit*, p. 254.

148. "Neque enim Spiritus sanctus pictoris instar in nobis diuinam essentiam depingit, aliud quippiam ab illa existens: neque hoc modo nos ad similitudinem Dei ducit sed quum ipse sit Deus et ex Deo procedat, in cordibus eorum qui ipsum suscipiunt, velut cera inuisibiliter instar sigilli imprimitur: et naturam nostram per communicationem similitudinemque sui, ad archetypi pulchritudinem depingit, Deique imaginem homini restituit" (*Thesaurus de sancta et consubstantiali Trinitate*, in *Opera omnia*, 5:360B).

149. Cornelius à Lapide, *Commentaria*, 8:957.

150. Ibid.

151. Ps. 4:6.

152. "Ama signaculum tuum, et imaginem tuam; utque expressior in te forma tui Creatoris appareat, ei qui charitas est, te fide et charitate conforma . . . Amator tuus ad hoc exhortatione prophetica te invitavit: *Pone me*, inquit, *ut signaculum super cor tuum*, et *super bracchium tuum dexterum* (*Cantic.* viii, 6). Ac si dicat: Pone me memoriale tuum in corde et bracchio, id est, in cogitatione et opere, ut deposita imagine terreni hominis, coelestis imaginem portes (I *Cor.* xv, 49), attendens divinae dilectionis argumenta, quae refelli non possunt. Pone me super cor tuum, ut fidei signaculum, ut amoris exemplum. Tale signaculum ante praevaricationem suam in se angelus apostata exprimebat, testimonio Ezechielis dicentis: *Tu signaculum similitudinis, plenus sapientia, et perfectus decore* (*Ezech.* xxviii, 12). Angelus siquidem in sua creatione tanta Deo conformitate unitus est, ut esset potius signaculum similitudinis, quam simile vel signatum. De sigillo quippe talis, similitudo imaginaliter exprimitur, qualis in eodem sigillo essentialiter habetur: et haec homini competit. Angelus vero pro sua subtilitate Deo

expressiori similitudine adhaerebat, quia totus et tantummodo spiritus erat. Nos vero luteo inclusos carcere, et in habitatione terrena depressos, charitas ad dignitatis angelicae statum reparat: et licet corpus, quod corrumpitur, aggravet animam, et deprimat terrena cogitatio sensum multa cogitantem (*Sap.* ix, 15), tamen peccato deformatos, novum diligendi mandatum ad Dei similitudinem nos reformat" (*De charitate* 21. 68 [*PL* 184. 617]).

153. *Studies in Donne*, p. 342. "The image of God can burn in hell, but it cannot be consumed."

154. "Imago siquidem in gehenna ipsa uri poterit, non exuri; ardere, sed non deleri" (*Serm. de temp.*, In festo annuntiationis 1. 7 [*PL* 183. 386c]).

155. *Institutes of the Christian Religion* 1. 15. 3: "Also, there is no slight quarrel over 'image' and 'likeness' when interpreters seek a nonexistent difference between these two words, except that 'likeness' has been added by way of explanation" (The Library of Christian Classics, vol. 20, p. 187).

156. Cf., for instance, Augustine *De spiritu et littera* 28 (PL 44. 230).

157. *Corpus reformatorum* 86. 75. On Calvin's "legal imagery," see Mülhaupt, *Die Predigt Calvins*, pp. 42–44.

158. Eph. 4:30.

159. "Spiritu sancto signati, et quasi sigillo obsignati . . . estis, non quasi pecudes in corpore, uti signati sunt Judaei signe circumcisionis: sed quasi filii promissionis et quasi regali grex Christi et Spiritus sancti, signati estis in anima" (*Commentaria*, 9:546).

160. See Origen *In Genesim homilia* 3. 3 (PG 12. 177a).

161. "Postquam diversas productiones testium, legum, oraculorum, prophetarum, signorum, tandem proprium sanguinem allegavit, obtinuit allegatio illa tuae sententiam libertatis; super calculo sententiali scriptae sunt litterae in membrana capitis crucifixi, et confirmatae a saeculo misericordiae et veritatis, pacis et iustitiae obviantium sibi. Denique impressum est sigillum, plaga scilicet lateris, quam in pretium redemptionis nostrae et placationem continuam jugiter exhibet ante oculos Patris" (*De charitate* 20. 64 [*PL* 184. 615]).

162. 1 Kings 21:20: "Thou hast sold thyself to work evil."

163. Isa. 51:3.

164. Martin Herz has studied some such metaphors in the language of the liturgy: *Sacrum Commercium*.

165. See ibid., p. 195; Herz notes the interesting fact that Augustine uses the term only in his homiletic writings, and not in *De civitate Dei* or *Confessiones*, written in the Latin of the educated. This is of course

a particular consideration of decorum. Donne is, as I will show, fully aware of the rhetorical effectiveness of this concept as addressed to a certain audience.

166. See 1 Pet. 1:18; 1 Cor. 6:20; Eph. 1:7.

167. "Mortuus est Deus, ut compensatio fieret coelestis cuiusdam mercimonii, ne mortem videret homo" (*Serm. de script.* 80. 5 [*PL* 38. 496]).

168. "Cum ergo Deus esset et homo, volens nos vivere de suo, mortuus est de nostro. Unde enim ipse moreretur non habebat: sed nec nos unde viveremus" (ibid.).

169. "Qualia commercia! quid dedit, et quid accepit?" (ibid.).

170. "Mais il est bien évident que ces comparaisons commerciales et financières ne comportent, par elles-mêmes, aucune signification doctrinale. Un orateur chrétien ne peut-il, à la suite de l'Ecriture, parler de 'rachat,' voire même poursuivre l'analogie aussi loin que le lui permet sa virtuosité, sans qu'il faille aussitôt lui demander en quoi a consisté le prix et où se trouve le vendeur qui l'a perçu? *Intelligenti pauca*" (*Le dogme de la Rédemption chez saint Augustin*, p. 108).

171. "Mercantes homines veniunt ad commercia, ad res mutandas. Nam antiqua commercia rerum mutatio fuit . . . postremum alius dat plumbum, ut accipiat argentum; sed multum dat plumbum contra parum argentum . . . Et quis enumerat omnia? Tamen nemo dat vitam, ut accipiat mortem" (*Serm. de script.* 80. 5 [*PL* 38. 496–97]); quoted by Herz, *Sacrum Commercium*, p. 169.

172. See Herz, *Sacrum Commercium*, p. 210.

173. "Empti enim estis pretio magno" (1 Cor. 6:20); "Pretio empti estis" (1 Cor. 7:23). Cf. also 2 Pet. 2:1: "Eum, qui emit eos, Dominum negant."

174. "Vide commercium emptionis nostrae. Christus pendet in ligno: vide, quanto emit et sic videbis quid emit. Empturus est aliquid; ipsum aliquid nondum scis. Vide, vide quanti, et videbis quid. Sanguinem fudit, sanguine suo emit, sanguine Agni immaculati emit, sanguine unici Filii Dei emit. Quid emptum est sanguine unici Filii Dei? Adhuc vide quanti. Propheta dixit longe antequam fieret: *Foderunt manus meas et pedes meos, dinumeraverunt omnia ossa mea* (Ps. xxi, 17). Magnum pretium video, Christe, videam quid emisti: *Commemorabuntur et convertentur ad Dominum universi fines terrae* (Ps. xxi, 28). In uno eodemque psalmo emptorem video, et pretium et possessionem! Emptor Christus est, pretium sanguis, possessio orbis terrarum" (*Enarr. in Ps.* 147. 16 [*PL* 37. 1925]).

175. "Redempta est enim vita tua de corruptione: jam securus

esto: initus est bonae fidei contractus; nemo fallit redemptorem tuum, nemo circumvenit, nemo premit. Egit hic commercium, jam pretium solvit, sanguinem fudit" (*Enarr. in Ps.* 102. 6 [*PL* 37. 1321]).

176. *Serm. de temp.*, In epiphania Domini 1. 2 (*PL* 183. 143). Cf. Augustine, *PL* 36. 178–79.

177. Lancelot Andrewes, *Ninety-Six Sermons*, 1:15. Cf. also Luke 12:48.

178. For example, 1:241, 5:193.

179. See 3:240, 10:558; 3:255, 11:521; and 8:173, 6:585.

180. S. Lyonnet, S.J., "De notione Redemptionis."

181. *Enarr. in Ps.* 147. 16 (*PL* 37. 1925).

182. See Heb. 2:14; Col. 2:15; John 12:31, 14:30; 2 Cor. 4:4; 2 Pet. 2:19.

183. See Jean Rivière, *Le dogme de la Rédemption*, particularly chap. 2, "Le 'droit' du Démon"; references to the most relevant passages in the Fathers can be found in Rivière's article "Rédemption," in *Dictionnaire de Théologie Catholique*.

184. *Dictionnaire de Théologie Catholique*, s.v. "Rédemption," vol. 13, col. 1939.

185. Augustine *Enarr. in Ps.* 125 (*PL* 37. 1658).

186. Augustine *Enarr. in Ps.* 95 (*PL* 37. 1231).

187. See Herz, *Sacrum Commercium*, p. 212.

188. See ibid., p. 173.

189. Rom. 5:12–21; 1 Cor. 15:21–22, 45–49.

190. "Convenit recordari quemadmodum de paradiso in desertum Adam primus ejectus sit (*Gen.* iii, 24), ut advertas quemadmodum de deserto ad paradisum Adam secundus reverterit. Videte enim quemadmodum suis nodis praejudicia resolvantur, et suis divina beneficia vestigiis reformentur. Ex terra virgine Adam (*Gen.* ii, 7), Christus ex virgine; ille ad imaginem Dei factus (*Gen.* i, 27), hic imago Dei. . . . Mors per arborem, vita per crucem" (*Expositio Evangelii secundum Lucam* 4. 7 [*PL* 15. 1614]).

191. *Enarr. in Ps.* 125 (*PL* 37. 1658); cf. Herz, *Sacrum Commercium*, p. 214.

192. "Evacuatum est igitur generale illud venditionis nostrae et lethale chirographum, et pactum captivitatis in jus transiit Redemptoris" (Leo *Sermones* 61. 4 [*PL* 54. 348a]).

193. "Sanguis tuus, qui fusus est ut deleret chirographum peccatorum. Unde enim superbiebat [diabolus] nisi quia cautionem contra nos tenebat? Hanc tu cautionem, hoc chirographum tuo sanguine delevisti" (*Enarr. in Ps.* 88. 11 [*PL* 37. 1126–27]).

194. Eph. 1:14. See also 2 Cor. 1:22 and 5:5.

195. "Juristische Formulierungen in den Gebeten der Kirche," p. 259.

196. Herz, *Sacrum Commercium*, pp. 206 f.

197. Walter Dürig, "Der Begriff *pignus* in der römischen Liturgie."

198. *Sacrum Commercium*, p. 207.

199. Augustine *Serm. de script.* 130. 2 (*PL* 38. 726).

200. "Die göttliche Tauschgabe, das Leben, wird uns mystisch-sakramental schon in der Gegenwart zuteil, ist aber zugleich der künftige Heilsbesitz. Der 'wunderbare Tausch' ist Gegenwart und Zukunft zugleich, ein Heilsgeschehen, das sich im Glauben bewähren muss" (Herz, *Sacrum Commercium*, p. 207).

201. The degree of legalism in Donne's theology of salvation is a matter that goes too far beyond the scope of rhetorical analysis for me to attempt to discuss it for its own sake.

202. See Gen. 38:17–18.

203. Ambrose *De sacramentis* 5. 27 (*PL* 16. 453). See Herz, *Sacrum Commercium*, p. 213.

204. See n. 175 above.

205. "Like as if a man should be so farre in debt that he could not be freed, unless the suretie should be cast into prison for his sake; nay, which is more, be cruelly put to death for his debt, it would make him at his wits end and his very heart to bleed: So likewise is the case with us, by reason of our Sinnes; we are Gods debters, yea bankrupts before him, yet have we gotten a good suretie" (*Treasurie of Similies*, p. 141). Cawdrey then refers to Matt. 17:23 and Ezek. 12:10.

206. *Le dogme de la Rédemption*, p. 106.

207. The passage referred to by Donne may be from Jerome's *Commentaria in epistolam ad Galatas* (*PL* 26. 385), where he accuses the Marcionites of his time of disregarding the difference between *emere* and *redimere*. The passage does not, however, agree literally with the words quoted by Donne.

208. Rugoff, *Donne's Imagery*, p. 166. See also Evelyn M. Simpson, *A Study of the Prose Works of John Donne*, p. 236: "Sometimes Donne uses the homeliest phrases and imagery to drive home his meaning." She then quotes: "We have sold our selves for nothing; and however the ordinary murmuring may be true, in other things, that all things are grown dearer, our souls are still cheap enough, which at first were all sold in gross, for (perchance) an Apple, and are now retailed every day for nothing (*XXVI Sermons*, 11. 161)."

209. Simpson and Potter, *Sermons*, 1:97.

210. Rugoff, *Donne's Imagery*, p. 146.

211. Sonnet 15, "Wilt thou love God, as hee thee," lines 9–12, *The Divine Poems*, ed. Helen Gardner (Oxford, 1952), p. 11.

212. The term is used by R. A. Sayce to denote the "distance" between tenor and vehicle (*Style in French Prose*, pp. 62 f.). For a critical discussion of the term see H. Weinrich, "Semantik der kühnen Metapher," p. 328.

213. 1 Cor. 13:12.

214. "Illi oculos habebant, nos non habemus? Imo et nos cordis habemus; sed per fidem adhuc videmus, non per speciem. Quando erit species? Quando videbimus *facie ad faciem*, quod dicit apostolus" (*Enarr. in Ps.* 90 [PL 37. 1169]).

215. "Gloria Domino nostro . . . quia primo veritas carne operta venit ad nos, et sanavit per carnem suam oculum interiorem cordis nostri, ut eum postea facie ad faciem videre possemus" (*Enarr. in Ps.* 61 [PL 36. 673]).

216. "Apertum est nunc imagines videre per fidem, tunc res ipsas. (Greg.) Videamus Paulum quadam caligine quasi infantiae pannis obvolutum" (*Allegoriae in sacram Scripturam* [PL 112. 125]).

217. "Interdum tamen corporeus oculus, non adhuc festuca manente, sed jam sublata vel exsufflata, aliquandiu caligare videtur: quod quidem et ipsum in interiori oculo qui in spiritu ambulat, saepius experitur" (*De conversione* [PL 182. 851]).

218. "Quia quamdiu sumus in corpore, peregrinamur a Domino (II *Cor.* v, 6), longe sumus a facie Dei, a vultu gloriae, a contemplatione majestatis, nisi quia plerumque misericors et miserator Dominus illuminat vultum suum super nos. Hoc autem fit, cum remota nube illa, quae opposita erat ne transiret oratio, accedimus ad illum, et illuminamur, *revelata facie gloriam Domini speculantes* (II *Cor.* iii, 18). Non autem ita proprie *revelata facie* accipiamus, cum videamus adhuc per speculum et in aenigmate, et carcerali corpore teneamur: *Revelata* vero dicit, quantum ad caliginem corporum" (*Serm. de div.* 41 [PL 183. 659]).

219. The Latin can mean "to deceive" or simply "to escape the notice of."

220. "Caeterum sicut oculum simplicem duo ista faciunt bona, amor boni, et cognitio veri: sic nequam oculum duo e regione mala constituunt, caecitas, qua fit ut veritatem non agnoscat; et perversitas, qua fit ut diligat iniquitatem. Porro inter duo haec bona, quae nec fallere, nec falli sinunt; et duo illa mala, quae tam falli, quam fallere faciunt, duo sunt media: unum quidem bonum per quod oculus interior, etsi falli queat ignorantia veri, zelo tamen boni fallere penitus non consentit: alterum vero malum, quod licet veri notitiam non im-

pediat, amorem tamen boni prae malitia minime sentit" (*De praecepto et dispensatione* [PL 182. 881c]).

221. "Est qui bonum diligit, malum nescius agit. Hujus quidem bonus est oculus, quia prius: non tamen simplex quia caecus . . . Est e contrario qui bonum minime diligens, ex malitia quidem perversus est: sed sapiens ut faciat malum, per ignorantiam caecus non est" (ibid. [PL 182. 882]).

222. "Ecce haec sunt qui mundant oculum cordis, oratio et confessio" (*Serm. de sanct.*, In festo omnium sanctorum 1 [PL 183. 460]).

223. "Odibilis macula, quae beatam hanc nobis adimit visionem, et execrabilis negligentia qua dissimulamus interim illius oculi mundationem. Ut enim corporeus nobis visus aut humore interiori, aut exterioris injectione pulveris impeditur: sic et intuitus spiritualis interdum quidem propriae carnis illecebris, interdum curiositate saeculari et ambitione turbatur" (*De conversione* [PL 182. 851a]).

224. "Per speculum verò videre potest intelligi dupliciter: vel videmus in speculo resultantes similitudines hominum, arborum etc. vel ut videmus per vitra ocularia. Et utroque modo verificatur quòd videmus per speculum in aenigmate divina: nam et videmus Deum non in seipso, sed in eius similitudinibus quae sunt creaturae: nec ex harum inspectione similitudinum claram habemus de Dei, et coelestis patriae conditionibus notitiam, sed obscuram: et videmus ex parte nostri per species abstractas à sensilibus quasi ocularia specula, quae Dei, et coelestis sunt patriae cum difficultate et obscuritate" (*Opera omnia*, 5:134).

225. "Existimat Caetanus, per speculum videre sic intelligi posse, quomodo videmus per ocularia vitria, quae perspicilla vocantur; sed non est verisimile. Solent enim eiusmodi adhibere ad clarius videndum; ideoque haec similitudo seu metaphora non serviret rei propositae" (*Biblia maxima versionum*, 15:566a).

226. "Sensibile enim cognoscitur triplicer, vno modo per sui praesentiam in sensu, sicut lux videtur quae recipitur in oculo propter sui diaphaneitatem. Alio modo non per sui praesentiam, sed per speciem in sensu receptam tamen immediatè à sensibili deriuatam, sicut videtur color. Tertio modo per speciem non deriuatam immediatè à sensibile in sensu, sed in alio, sicut videtur aliquid in speculo. Consimilis habetur de Deo triplex cognitio naturalis. Vno modo per essentiam, quae soli Deo conuenit. Alio modo per similitudinem immediatè à Deo derivatam in cognoscento, et haec cognitio conuenit Angelo, cuius Deum. Tertio modo cognoscitur à nobis quasi in speculo, in quantum per creaturas à nobis cognitas sicut per speculum ducimur in Dei cognitionem" (ibid., p. 366c).

227. "Non proprie, clare distincte, sed quasi procul, obscure et confuse" (*Commentaria*, 9:322).

228. Tommaso de Vio, *Opera omnia*, 5:134.

229. 2 Cor. 3:18; cf. 8:222, 9:128.

230. Cyril of Alexandria *In epistolam II ad Corinthios* (PG 74. 931).

231. *Treasurie of Similies*, p. 488.

232. Ibid., p. 402.

233. "*Adam* . . . signifies but *Redness*" (2:78, 2:244).

234. *Latin Middle Ages*, pp. 138–44.

235. Quoted by Curtius, p. 138. From *Enarr. in Ps.* 127 (PL 37. 1686).

236. "Puto enim, quod Deus nos Apostolos novissimos ostendit tanquam morti destinatos, quia spectaculum facti sumus mundo et angelis et hominibus" (1 Cor. 4:9 [Vulgate]).

237. *OED*, s.v. "Spectacle" 5.

238. "Sed ideo sunt tanquam sincerissimum speculum proposita hominibus oracula coelestium paginarum, ut ibi quisque videat quodlibet peccatum quantum sit, quod forte magnum est, et male viventium caeco more contemnitur" (*Contra epistolam Parmeniani* 3. 9 [*PL* 43. 89]).

239. "Posuit tibi speculum Scripturam suam . . ." (*Enarr. in Ps.* 103 [*PL* 37. 1338]).

240. "Mandata Dei sive cum leguntur, sive cum memoria recoluntur, tanquam speculum intuendum est . . ." (*Enarr. in Ps.* 118 [*PL* 37. 1510]).

241. "Like as the Phisition seeing in a glasse by the water, the disease within the body, by skill and learning searches out the cause of the disease, and ministers good things for the same: Euen so wee, in looking into the glasse of God's word shall soone perceiue the diseases and sinnes which are in us, and the cause thereof, and so wholesomely minister some profitable and comfortable remedies for the same" (p. 61). See also p. 404: "but ourselves being open, and illuminate by the spirite and grace of our God, and taking the Glasse of the Law, therein to behold the state of our natur and our life, then we begin to know the great and grievous imperfections that are in us." On p. 451 Cawdrey gives an almost identical simile.

242. On "light" in Bible and liturgy, see the studies of the concept of *sol salutis* and *lumen Christi* by Franz Joseph Dölger: *Die Sonne der Gerechtigkeit und der Schwarze* (Münster, 1918), Literaturgeschichtliche Quellen und Forschungen, heft 14; *Sol Salutis*; and "*Lumen Christi*." A few others of lesser importance are Paula Seelthaler, "Das Licht in Schrift und Liturgie"; J. Daniel Joyce, "The New Testament

Witness to the Light," *Encounter* 21 (1960):3–20; Harold de Wolf, "Proclaiming Jesus Christ as Light: Ancient Message and Modern Meaning," *Encounter* 21 (1960):43–51.

243. An entire volume of *Eranos,* containing twelve lectures, was devoted to the subject: *Eranos-Jahrbuch* 10 (1943). Mircea Eliade, in whose bibliographical notes the other most relevant works can be found, has studied the mystical experience of "inner light" in various cultures and times; see "Significations de la 'lumière intérieure.' "

244. See Rudolf Bultmann, "Zur Geschichte der Lichtsymbolik im Altertum," p. 16.

245. Franz-J. Leenhardt, "La signification de la notion de la parole dans la pensée chrétienne," p. 268.

246. Ibid., p. 267.

247. Ibid., p. 286.

248. See Hans Leisegang's pages on "Das Auge der Seele" in his book *Der Heilige Geist,* vol. 1, pt. 1, pp. 215–22. Leisegang describes how Philon, trying to reinterpret the Old Testament tradition in the sense of Greek philosophy, replaces the ear by the eye. Also Bultmann, "Zur Geschichte der Lichtsymbolik," p. 16.

249. Plato *Republic* 6. 507C, 508A, trans. P. Shorey, Loeb Classical Library (London, 1963), pp. 97 f.

250. See Webber, *Contrary Music,* pp. 123 f.

251. For example: "The Organ that God hath given the Christian, is the *ear;* he hears God in his Word" (2:114, 3:696).

252. See, for instance, 5:42, 1:255.

253. "*Credo,* inquit, *videre bona Domini in terra viventium* (*Psal.* xxvi, 13). Supremas nimirum corporis sui fenestras supernae aperiri desiderat veritati, per speciem magis ambulare gestiens, quam per fidem. Sane fides ex auditu, non ex visu. Denique substantia est sperandarum rerum, argumentum non apparentium (*Hebr.* xi, 1). Et in fide ergo, sicut in spe, deficit oculus auris proficit sola. *Dominus Deus aperuit mihi aurem,* ait propheta (*Isai.* l, 5): sed quandoque etiam oculum revelabit" (*Serm. de temp.,* In psalmum xc . . . 8 [*PL* 183. 211a]).

254. "Nimirum tanta capiet oculus resurrectionis, quanta nec auditus, nec animus ipse nunc capiat" (ibid., 211b).

255. Cf. his *Meditationes piissimae* (*PL* 184. 487a) and *Serm. de div.* 22 (*PL* 183. 599b).

256. "Vehemens animae concupiscientia videndi" (*Serm. de temp.,* In psalmum xc . . . 8 [*PL* 183. 211b]).

257. *Sermones in Canticum Salomonis* 1. 3 (*PL* 184. 14b).

258. See 1 Tim. 1:18; Eph. 6:11; Rom. 13:12.

259. *Donne's Imagery*, p. 159.

260. See Rugoff, *Donne's Imagery*, pp. 82 f. and René Wellek and Austin Warren, *Theory of Literature* (New York, 1956), p. 197.

261. Klaus Lange, "Geistliche Speise."

262. Cf. Cawdrey, *Treasurie of Similies*, p. 64.

263. Vol. 10, no. 6. Because of a reference, Simpson and Potter suggest that this undated sermon is from the reign of King Charles (*Sermons*, 10:15).

# 4. Imagery and Exegesis of Scripture

1. *The Business of Criticism*, p. 136.

2. Dennis Quinn writes lucidly on the subject in the third chapter of his thesis, *John Donne's Sermons on the Psalms and the Traditions of Biblical Exegesis*. See also J. M. Mueller, "Donne's *Ars Praedicandi*," pp. 14–25.

3. On other divisions see Joan Webber, *Contrary Music*, p. 157.

4. See, for instance, vol. 1, no. 9.

5. See vol. 2, no. 16.

6. For such an attempt, see Webber, *Contrary Music*, p. 165.

7. The sermons constructed according to the three "senses" are an exception only insofar as the word-by-word exegesis is conducted separately for each sense.

8. Dennis Quinn aptly observes: "The imaginative advantage of Donne's word by word application of the text to the human condition is enormous. Every word becomes a metaphor: the whole text becomes an image" ("Donne's Christian Eloquence," p. 290); see also Quinn's thesis, *John Donne's Sermons*, p. 263.

9. See, e.g., 2:55, 1:219; 2:133, 5:90; 4:45, 1:22; 4:66, 2:114.

10. Rosemond Tuve has observed that among the "places of invention," definition is a rich spring of tropes (*Elizabethan and Metaphysical Imagery*, p. 299).

11. "Symbol" in the limited sense in which Wellek and Warren use this word, in *Theory of Literature* (New York, 1956), p. 178. They see recurrence as the primary characteristic of the symbol. An image may be invoked once as a metaphor, but if it persistently recurs, it becomes a symbol, may even become part of a symbolic system.

12. Etienne Gilson, "Michel Menot et la technique du sermon médiéval," in *Les Idées et les lettres*, p. 138.

13. Cf. *Sermons*, vol. 9, nos. 17, on Ps. 32:9, and 7, on Matt. 6:21.

14. "Si autem habet res tacta in themate paucas proprietates, aut si multas, tamen ignoras eas, vel si multas notas, tamen non aedificantes; non est mirendum, si transferat se praedicator ad aliam rem, in cujus proprietatibus magis abundet et plus aedificet. Magis enim amanda est animarum aedificatio quam sermonis continuatio" (*Ars concionandi*, 3:45. Quoted in Gilson, *Les Idées et les lettres*, p. 143).

15. *Sermons*, 7:283–84.

16. Ibid., 3:19.

17. Ibid., vol. 3, nos. 13 and 14.

18. "In hoc valde excellentior est divina Scriptura scientia saeculi, quod in ea non solum voces, sed et res significativae sunt" (*Excerptiones allegoricae* 2. 3 [*PL* 177. 205b]). Cf. Hugo's *Didascalion* 5. 3 (*PL* 176. 790c): "Sciendum est etiam, quod in divino eloquio non tantum verba, sed etiam res significare habent, qui modus non adeo in aliis scripturis inveniri solet." See Philip S. Moore, *The Works of Peter of Poitiers*, p. 67.

19. Friedrich Ohly, "Vom geistigen Sinn des Wortes im Mittelalter," *Zeitschrift für deutsches Altertum und deutsche Literatur* 89 (1958):1–23.

20. "Voces non plus quam duas aut tres habent significationes. Res autem tot possunt habere significationes, quot habent proprietates" (Hugo of St. Victor, *Excerptiones allegoricae* 2. 5 [*PL* 177. 205d]).

21. Quoted by Moore, *Peter of Poitiers*, p. 75 (the quotation is from MS Lat. 3186, fol. lvb, Bibliothèque nationale, Paris): "Quelibet enim res quot habet proprietates tot habet linguas aliquid spirituale nobis et invisibile insinuantes, pro quarum diversitate et ipsius nominis acceptio variatur."

22. "Christian Instruction," trans. J. J. Gavigan, O.S.A., in *Writings of St. Augustine*, vol. 4, The Fathers of the Church (New York, 1947), pp. 82–83 (*PL* 34. 47).

23. See J. B. Pitra, *Spicilegium Solesmense* (hereafter cited as Pitra), 2:307–9.

24. E.g., *baculus vindicans, baculus sustentans, baculus significans peregrinationem*, in Pitra, 2:386. The pseudo-Rhabanus explains Jacob's staff as signifying *iustitia;* see *Allegoriae in sacram Scripturam* (*PL* 112. 873a).

25. Pitra, 3:55 (from *Liber distinctionum monasticarum*): "Leoni propter foetorem dentium, comparatur haereticus, propter verba blasphemiae." Cf. Ohly, p. 7, and the example quoted by Moore, p. 75 (from Peter of Poitiers): "Verbi gratia, leo rex est ferarum, animal indomitum, avidus sanguinis, omnibus feris volens dominari. Similis est ei diabolus, quia rex est super universos filios superbie. Propter quod

nomine leonis quandoque intelligitur ut ibi: *Adversarius vester diabolus tanquem leo rugiens circuit* querens quem. devoret. . . . Leo fortissimus bestiarum ad nullius pavebit occursum, id est, Christus, fortior diabolo, cuius arma abstulit, eius occursum non pavet."

26. With reference to John 3:14–15.

27. In the *Liber distinctionum monasticarum* only "good" senses of light are listed. Petrus Capuanus, however, finds a "bad" sense—infernal light: "Lux tartarea dictur diabolus, qui se luci divinae comparavit, quando voluit sedem suam ponere ad aquilonem, ut esset similis Altissimo" (see Pitra, 2:102).

28. See Moore, *Peter of Poitiers*, p. 76.

29. William Gifford, "Time and Place in Donne's Sermons," pp. 391–94.

30. See also the meanings given for *mel* in *Alleg. in sacr. Script.* (PL 112. 997c).

31. See Ohly, "Vom geistigen Sinn des Wortes," p. 6.

32. Ecclesiasticus 39:31–33. "Sal, lac et panis similigineus et mel . . . hae omnia sanctis in bona, et peccatoribus in mala convertuntur" (Cornelius à Lapide, *Commentaria*, 5:876).

33. On the subject of *mel, favus,* and *cera,* see Melito's *Clavis*, in Pitra, 3:40–42.

34. Richard Hooker, *Works*, 3:475.

35. For *columba* see Pitra, 2:484–87; for *turtur* see Pitra, 2:490–92.

36. For *equus* signifying *superbia, vana gloria,* etc., see Pitra, 3:6–9; for *mulus*, meaning *sensus carnalis, luxoriosi,* etc., see Pitra, 3:9–10.

37. For the "net" (*rete, sagena*), see *Alleg. in sacr. Script.* (PL 112. 1039d and 1044c); also Pitra, 2:172.

38. Albert Schöne, "Emblemata," p. 199.

39. For *cor* see Pitra, 2:250–51; for *gazophylacium* see Pitra, 2:286–89.

40. *Contrary Music*, p. 130.

41. Pitra, 2:288.

42. See *Alleg. in sacr. Script.* (PL 112. 996).

43. Lancelot Andrewes, *Ninety-Six Sermons*, 3:255.

44. *Contrary Music*, p. 136.

45. "Wit and Mystery."

46. Webber, *Contrary Music*, p. 136.

47. "Habet tamen iste liber hoc speciale quod una littera continet plures sensus. Cujus ratio est quia principialis hujus libri auctor est ipse Deus: in cujus potestate est non solum uti vocibus ad aliquid significandum (quod etiam homines facere possunt et faciunt), sed etiam rebus significatis per voces utitur ad significandum alias res: et ideo

commune est omnibus libris, quod voces aliquid significent, sed speciale est huic libro quod res significatae per voces aliud significent. Secundum igitur primam significationem, quae est per voces, accipitur sensus litteralis seu historicus: secundum vero aliam significationem, quae est per ipsas res, accipitur sensus mysticus, seu spiritualis, qui est triplex in generali . . ." ("First Prologue" in *Glossa ordinaria* [PL 113. 28c]).

48. For a detailed account see Jean Daniélou, *Sacramentum Futuri;* Ceslaus Spicq, *Esquisse d'une histoire de l'exégèse latine au moyen âge;* Beryl Smalley, *The Study of the Bible in the Middle Ages;* Erich Auerbach, "Figura." The most thorough study is by Henri de Lubac, *Exégèse médiévale.* For a survival of biblical typology in Protestant literature, see B. K. Lewalski, *Milton's Brief Epic;* Ursula Brumm, *Die religiöse Typologie im amerikanischen Denken: Ihre Bedeutung für die amerikanische Literatur* (Leiden, 1963); Peter Nicolaisen, *Die Bildlichkeit in der Dichtung Edward Taylors;* J. A. Mazzeo, "Cromwell as Davidic King," in *Renaissance and Seventeenth-Century Studies,* pp. 183–208.

49. See H. de Lubac, *Exégèse médiévale,* pt. 1, 1:502.

50. "Ante omnia tamen, fratres, hoc in nomine Domini et admonemus, quantum possumus, et praecipimus, ut quando auditis exponi sacramentum Scripturae narrantis quae gesta sunt, prius illud quod lectum est credatis sic gestum, quomodo lectum est; ne subtracto fundamento rei gestae, quasi in aere quaeratis aedificare" (*Sermones de scripturis* 2. 6. 7 [PL 38. 30]).

51. *Essays in Divinity,* p. 8.

52. See Quinn, *John Donne's Sermons,* p. 207.

53. See, e.g., *Essays in Divinity,* p. 8 (quoted above) and p. 40.

54. See Maximilian Neumayr, *Die Schriftpredigt im Barock,* p. 31.

55. *Rhetorica ecclesiastica,* bk. 1, p. 69. Keckermann further quotes from Thomas: "Theologia symbolica non est argumentativa."

56. "eum [sensum] videlicet quem Spiritus sanctus principaliter intendit" (ibid.).

57. Also *Essays in Divinity,* p. 40. Compare Gardner, *Business of Criticism,* p. 139.

58. Gardner, *Business of Criticism,* p. 136.

59. "non est magni usus haec distinctio" (*Rhetorica ecclesiastica,* bk. 1, p. 68).

60. Of course Calvin accepts the commonly recognized types presented in the New Testament and recognizes "types" in the words of the prophets (see, for instance, *Institutes* 4. 18. 4). But wanting to

preserve the literal sense of Old Testament passages, he goes farther than most in objecting to typological and allegorical interpretations that he thinks would distort the sense or impose something farfetched. For his repudiation of biblical allegory see *Institutes* 2. 5. 19 and his commentaries on Gen. 2:8; Isa. 33:18; Jer. 31:24; Dan. 8:20–25 (where he disagrees with Luther); Dan. 10:6; and particularly on Gal. 4:22–26. Other reformers, notably Zwingli, were less radical; see Edwin Künzli, "Quellenproblem und mystischer Schriftsinn in Zwinglis Genesis- und Exoduskommentar." On Luther's position see Heinrich Bornkamm, *Luther und das Alte Testament*, pp. 74 ff., 176 ff., and 222 ff.

61. Smalley, *Study of the Bible*, p. 244.

62. Adam of St. Victor, *Sequentiae* (PL 196. 1433): "Nux est Christus, cortex nucis / Circa carnem poena crucis. / Testa, corpus osseum, / Carne tecta deitas, / Et Christi suavitas / Signatur per nucleum." For some brief but penetrating remarks on the sensibility on which such images are based see E. Mâle, *The Gothic Image*, pp. 30 ff.

63. Andrewes, *Ninety-Six Sermons*, 2:275.

64. With reference to Tertullian.

65. In the terms used earlier, it might be said that through the substitution of the persons, the action (*sponsare*) as well as the special terms discussed (*in ustionem*, etc.) acquire a metaphorical meaning.

66. *Contrary Music*, p. 174.

67. See Auerbach, "Figura."

68. "Secundo, multi Patres, ut S. Justinus, Tertull., Cyprian, Euseb. scribentes contra Judaeos, et Rupert. putant, Mosen hic petivisse adventum Messiae" (*Commentaria*, 1:383).

69. Ibid.

70. "Hic sensus valde probabilis et accomodatus est, quidquid objiciat Abulens. et audacter nimis tantis Patribus obstrepat Eugubinus" (ibid.).

71. Calvin, *Commentaries on the Four Last Books of Moses*, 1:93.

72. See *Wetzer und Welte's Kirchenlexikon*, 2d ed. (Freiburg, 1901), s.v. "Wild, Johann."

73. For the Wild passages that Donne quotes and paraphrases, see Johann Wild, *Annotationes . . . in Exodum, Numeros, Deuteronomium . . .*, pp. 59 f.

74. *Business of Criticism*, pp. 140 f.

75. Pereira's marginal subdivisions, "*An unus*," "*an illi tres*," etc., are very similar to Donne's. See *Commentaria in Genesim*, 3:320 f.

76. Calvin, *Commentaries on the First Book of Moses*, 1:470.

77. See Cornelius à Lapide, *Commentaria*, 1:183–84 and Benedictus Pereira, *Commentaria in Genesim*, 3:220–24.

78. See *De civitate Dei* 16. 29.

79. Luther, *Works*, vol. 3, *Lectures on Genesis*, p. 193.

80. Pereira, *Commentaria in Genesim*, 3:323, disagrees with Augustine's suggestion that Abraham's address in the singular might indicate that he recognized God's unity in the trinity of the messengers, saying: "Credibilius dictu est . . . cognouisse Abraham illum fuisse honoratiorem." This is also Calvin's opinion. Then Pereira reports: "Ex hac visione et facto Abrahae, atque ex omnium patrum qui super hac visione disputarunt expositione, nata est percelebris illa et peruulgata sententia: *Tres videt et unum adoravit:* quasi eo ipso quod tunc egit Abraham, mirifice adumbratum fuerit mysterium *Trinitatis:* neque enim id mysterij propalam exponi, et declarari eo tempore, vulgarique conueniebat."

81. Cf. Luther, *Works*, vol. 3, *Lectures on Genesis*, p. 193.

82. Cf. ibid., p. 192.

83. After the passage quoted above, Donne launches into a detailed exposition of Philo's reading, which is allegorical in the wide sense of the word, not figural. This allegorical interpretation and the reservations Donne has about its "truth value" can also be found in Pereira's commentary on the passage of the "three men."

84. *John Donne's Sermons*, p. 226.

85. John King, *A Sermon preached in Oxon*, p. 1.

86. Cf. Cawdrey, *Treasurie of Similies*, p. 425: "As breath is necessarie for the body of man: So also is a godly King to the people whome hee gouerneth."

87. "Our errand is to day, to apply all these branches to the day" (4:248, 9:404).

88. Adams, "Physicke from Heaven," in *The Devills Banket*, p. 271.

# 5. Conclusion

1. *English Pulpit Oratory*, p. 185.

2. *John Donne, Poems*, 1:374.

# Bibliography

ADAMS, THOMAS. *The Devills Banket, Described in Six Sermons.*
London, 1614.
——. *The Spirituall Navigator Bound for the Holy Land.*
London, 1615.
ALLEN, DON CAMERON. "Dean Donne Sets His Text."
*ELH* 10 (1943):208–27.
——. "Donne's Knowledge of Renaissance Medicine." *Journal of*
*English and Germanic Philology* 42 (1943): 322–42.
——. "Donne and the Ship Metaphor." *MLN* 76 (1961):306–12.
ANDREWES, LANCELOT. *Ninety-Six Sermons.* 4 vols. Oxford, 1874–78.
ARBESMANN, RUDOLF, O.S.A. "Christ the *Medicus Humilis* in St.
Augustine." In *Augustinus Magister: Etudes Augustiniennes,*
pp. 623–29. Paris, 1954.
——. "The Concept of *Christus Medicus* in St. Augustine."
*Traditio* 10 (1954):1–28.
ARISTOTLE. *The "Art" of Rhetoric.* Edited and translated by
J. H. Freese. London, 1926.
AUERBACH, ERICH. "Figura." *Archivum Romanicum* 22 (1938):438–89.
——. *Mimesis: The Representation of Reality in Western*
*Literature.* Translated by Willard R. Trask. Garden City,
N.Y., 1957.
AVILA, JUAN DE. *Obras completas.* Edited by L. S. Balust.
2 vols. Madrid, 1953.
BABB, LAWRENCE. *The Elizabethan Malady: A Study of Melancholia*
*in English Literature from 1580 to 1642.*
East Lansing, Mich., 1951.
BARNARD, RICHARD. *The Faithfull Shepheard.* London, 1607.
BELLARMINE, ROBERT. *The Ascent of the Mind to God: By a Ladder*
*of Things Created.* Edited by James Brodrick, S.J.
London, 1928.
*Biblia maxima versionum.* 19 vols. Paris, 1660.

BORGIA, FRANCISCO DE. *Tratado breve del modo de predicar*, in *Obras*. Edited by J. E. Nieremberg. Barcelona, 1882.

BORNKAMM, HEINRICH. *Luther und das Alte Testament*. Tübingen, 1948.

BUCHLOH, PAUL GERHARD. "Vom 'Pilgrim's Progress' zum 'Pilgrim's Regress': Der Fortschrittsgedanke in der englischen und amerikanischen Literatur." In *Die Idee des Fortschritts*, edited by E. Burck, pp. 153–78. Munich, 1963.

BULTMANN, RUDOLF. "Zur Geschichte der Lichtsymbolik im Altertum." *Philologus* 97 (1948):1–36.

BURTON, ROBERT. *The Anatomy of Melancholy*. Edited by A. R. Shilleto. 3 vols. London, 1923.

BUSH, DOUGLAS. *English Literature in the Earlier Seventeenth Century, 1600–1660*. Oxford, 1945.

CALVIN, [JOHN]. *Commentaries on the First Book of Moses Called Genesis*. Translated by J. King. 2 vols. Edinburgh, 1847.

———. *Commentaries on the Four Last Books of Moses*. Translated by C. W. Bingham. Edinburgh, 1852.

———. *Institutes of the Christian Religion*. Translated by Ford Lewis Battles. 2 vols. The Library of Christian Classics, vols. 20, 21. Philadelphia, 1960.

CAWDREY, ROBERT. *A Treasurie or Store-House of Similies: Both Pleasant and Delightfull, and Profitable, for all Estates of Men in Generall*. London, 1600.

CORNELIUS À LAPIDE. *Commentaria in Scripturam sacram*. 10 vols. Paris, 1875.

COURTÈS, JEAN. "Saint Augustin et la médecine." In *Augustinus Magister: Etudes Augustiniennes*, pp. 43–51. Paris, 1954.

CROCE, BENEDETTO. *I predicatori italiani del seicento e il gusto spagnuolo*. N.p., n.d.

CURTIUS, ERNST ROBERT. *European Literature and the Latin Middle Ages*. Translated by Willard R. Trask. New York, 1953.

CYRIL [OF ALEXANDRIA].*Opera omnia*. Edited by Aubert. 7 vols. Paris, 1638.

DANIÉLOU, JEAN. *Sacramentum Futuri: Etudes sur les origines de la typologie biblique*. Paris, 1950.

DOEBLER, BETTIE ANNE. "Donne's Debt to the Great Tradition: Old and New in His Treatment of Death." *Anglia* 85 (1967):15–33.

DÖLGER, FRANZ JOSEPH. *Sol Salutis: Gebet und Gesang im christlichen Altertum*. 2d ed. Münster, 1925.

———. "*Lumen Christi*: Untersuchungen zum abendlichen Lichtsegen in Antike und Christentum." *Antike und Christentum* 5 (1936):1–43.

DOMINIS, MARCO ANTONIO DE. *The Rockes of Christian Shipwracke.*
London, 1618.

DONNE, JOHN. *Poems.* Edited by Herbert J. C. Grierson. 2 vols.
Oxford, 1912.

———. *Ignatius His Conclave.* Introduction by C. M. Coffin. New
York, 1941.

———. *Essays in Divinity.* Edited by Evelyn M. Simpson. Oxford,
1952.

———. *The Sermons of John Donne.* Edited by Evelyn M. Simpson
and George R. Potter. 10 vols. Berkeley and Los Angeles,
1953–62.

DÜRIG, WALTER. "Der Begriff *pignus* in der römischen Liturgie,"
*Theologische Quartalschrift* 129 (1949):385–98.

ELIADE, MIRCEA. "Significations de la 'lumière intérieure.' "
*Eranos-Jahrbuch* 26 (1957):189–242.

GARDNER, HELEN. *The Business of Criticism.* Oxford, 1959.

GERARDUS, ANDREAS [HYPERIUS]. *The Practis of Preaching....* Translated
by J. Ludham. London, 1577.

GILSON, ÉTIENNE. "Michel Menot et la technique du sermon médiéval."
In *Les Idées et les lettres,* pp. 93–154. Paris, 1932.

GIFFORD, WILLIAM. "Time and Place in Donne's Sermons." *PMLA*
82 (1967):388–98.

GOSSE, EDMUND. *The Life and Letters of John Donne, Dean of
St. Paul's.* 2 vols. New York, 1899.

HEGEMANN-SPRINGER, E. "Juristische Formulierungen in den Gebeten
der Kirche." *Liturgische Zeitschrift* 5 (1932):254–60.

HEPINUS, IOANNIS. *De sacris concionibus formandis compendiaria
formula.* London, 1570.

HERBERT, GEORGE. *Works.* Edited by F. E. Hutchinson. Oxford, 1941.

HERZ, MARTIN. *Sacrum Commercium: Eine begriffsgeschichtliche Studie
zur Theologie der römischen Liturgiesprache.* Munich, 1958.

HILL, DIETRICH ARNO. *The Modus Praedicandi of John Donne: A
Rhetorical Analysis of Selected Sermons of John Donne with
Regard Specifically to the Theory of Preaching Which He
Put into Practice.* Ann Arbor, Mich., 1962.

HOOKER, RICHARD. *The Works of ... Mr. Richard Hooker.* Edited by
John Keble. 3d ed. 3 vols. Oxford, 1845.

HORNSTEIN, LILLIAN HERLANDS. "Analysis of Imagery: A Critique of a
Literary Method." *PMLA* 57 (1942):638–53.

HOSKINS, JOHN. *Directions for Speech and Style.* Edited by Hoyt H.
Hudson. Princeton, 1935.

JETTER, WERNER. *Die Taufe beim jungen Luther: Eine Untersuchung über das Werden der reformatorischen Sakraments- und Taufanschauung.* Tübingen, 1954.

JOHNSON, SAMUEL. *Lives of the English Poets.* Edited by G. B. Hill. 3 vols. Oxford, 1905.

KECKERMANN, BARTHOLOMEW. *Rhetoricae ecclesiasticae, sive artis formandi et habendi conciones sacras libri duo.* Hanover, 1606.

KEYNES, GEOFFREY. *A Bibliography of Dr. John Donne, Dean of St. Paul's.* 3d ed. Cambridge, 1958.

KING, JOHN. *A Sermon preached in Oxon: the 5. of November 1607.* Oxford, 1607.

———. *A sermon of pvblicke thanksgiuing for the happy recouerie of his Maiesty, preached the 11. of Aprill, 1619.* London, 1619.

KÜNZLI, EDWIN. "Quellenproblem und mystischer Schriftsinn in Zwinglis Genesis- und Exoduskommentar: (2 Teil) Der mystische Schriftsinn." *Zwingliana* 9 (1949–53):253–307.

LAMPE, G. W. H. *The Seal of the Spirit: A Study in the Doctrine of Baptism and Confirmation in the New Testament and the Fathers.* London, 1951.

LANGE, KLAUS. "Geistliche Speise: Untersuchungen zur Metaphorik der Bibelhermeneutik." *Zeitschrift für deutsches Altertum und deutsche Literatur* 95 (1966):81–122.

LECHNER, SISTER JOAN MARIE. *Renaissance Concepts of the Commonplaces.* New York, 1962.

LEENHARDT, FRANZ-J. "La signification de la notion de la parole dans la pensée chrétienne." *Revue d'Histoire et de Philosophie Religieuses* 35 (1955).

LEISEGANG, HANS. *Der Heilige Geist: Das Werden der mystisch-intuitiven Erkenntnis in der Philosophie und Religion der Griechen,* vol. 1, pt. 1. Leipzig, 1919.

LEWALSKI, BARBARA KIEFER. "Milton on Learning and the Learned-Ministry Controversy." *Huntington Library Quarterly* 24 (1961):267–81.

———. *Milton's Brief Epic: The Genre, Meaning, and Art of "Paradise Regained."* Providence, 1966.

LEWIS, C. S. *English Literature in the Sixteenth Century, excluding Drama.* Oxford, 1954.

LOVEJOY, ARTHUR O. *The Great Chain of Being: A Study of the History of an Idea.* Cambridge, Mass., 1936.

LUBAC, HENRI DE, S.J. *Exégèse médiévale: Les quatre sens de l'Ecriture,* pt. 1. 2 vols. Paris, 1961.

LUIS DE GRANADA. *Ecclesiasticae rhetoricae, sive de ratione concionandi, libri sex.* Verona, 1732.

LUTHER, MARTIN. *Works*, edited by Jaroslav Pelikan and Helmut T. Lehman. 55 vols. Saint Louis and Philadelphia, 1955–68. Vol. 3, *Lectures on Genesis*, translated by George V. Schick, 1961.

LYONNET, S., S.J. "De notione Redemptionis," *Verbum Domini* 36 (1958):129–46.

MÂLE, ÉMILE. *The Gothic Image: Religious Art in France of the Thirteenth Century*. Translated by D. Nussey. London, 1961.

MARTZ, LOUIS L. *The Poetry of Meditation*. New Haven, 1954.

MAZZEO, JOSEPH ANTHONY. *Renaissance and Seventeenth-Century Studies*. New York, 1964.

MCNARON, T. A. H. *John Donne's Sermons Approached as Dramatic "Dialogues of One."* Ann Arbor, Mich., 1964.

MEIER, HUGO. *Die Metapher: Versuch einer zusammenfassenden Betrachtung ihrer linguistischen Merkmale*. Winterthur, 1963.

MERTNER, EDGAR. "Topos und Commonplace." In *Strena Anglica: Festschrift für Otto Ritter*, pp. 178–224. Halle, 1956.

MICHAELIS, WILHELM. "Zeichen, Siegel, Kreuz: Ein Ausschnitt aus der Bedeutungsgeschichte biblischer Begriffe." *Theologische Zeitschrift* 12 (1956):505–25.

MIGNE, J.-P., ed. *Patrologiae cursus completus . . . series Latina.* 221 vols. Paris, 1844–64.

———. *Patrologiae cursus completus . . . series Graeca.* 161 vols. Paris, 1857–66.

MIRIAM JOSEPH, SISTER. *Shakespeare's Use of the Arts of Language*. New York, 1947.

MITCHELL, W. FRASER. *English Pulpit Oratory from Andrewes to Tillotson: A Study of Its Literary Aspects*. London, 1932.

MOORE, PHILIP S. *The Works of Peter of Poitiers*. Washington, D.C., 1936.

MUELLER, JANEL MULDER. "Donne's *Ars Praedicandi*: The Development of the Methods and Themes of His Preaching." Ph.D. thesis, Harvard University, 1965.

MUELLER, WILLIAM R. *John Donne: Preacher*. Princeton, 1962.

MÜLHAUPT, ERWIN. *Die Predigt Calvins: Ihre Geschichte, ihre Form und ihre religiösen Grundgedanken*. Berlin, 1931.

NADAL, GERÓNIMO. "De ministerio verbi Dei," in *Epistolae Nadal*, 4:653–70. Monumenta Historica Societatis Jesu, vol. 27. Madrid, 1905.

NANNI MIRABELLI, DOMENICO. *Polyanthea, opus suavissimis floribus exornatum*. Savona, 1503.

NEUMAYR, MAXIMILIAN. *Die Schriftpredigt im Barock: Auf Grund der Theorie der katholischen Barockhomiletik.* Paderborn, 1937.

NICOLAISEN, PETER. *Die Bildlichkeit in der Dichtung Edward Taylors.* Neumünster, 1966.

OCHINO, BERNARDINO. *Certaine Godly Sermons of Faith, Hope and Charitie.* Translated by W. Phiston. London, 1580.

ONG, WALTER J., S.J. "Wit and Mystery: A Revaluation in Medieval Latin Hymnody." *Speculum* 22 (1947):310–41.

ORMEROD, OLIVER. *The Picture of a Puritane.* London, 1605.

PARACELSUS. *Sämtliche Werke,* Abt. 1. Edited by Karl Sudhoff. 14 vols. Munich, 1922–33.

PEREIRA, BENEDICTUS. *Commentaria in Genesim.* 4 vols. Rome, 1595.

PERKINS, WILLIAM. *The Arte of Prophecying.* London, 1607.

PIEPER, JOSEPH. "Bemerkungen über den *status viatoris.*" *Catholica: Jahrbuch für Kontroverstheologie* 4 (1935):15–20.

PITRA, J. B. *Spicilegium Solesmense.* 4 vols. Paris, 1855.

PUTTENHAM, GEORGE. *The Arte of English Poesie.* Edited by Gladys D. Willcock and Alice Walker. Cambridge, 1936.

QUINN, DENNIS B. *John Donne's Sermons on the Psalms and the Traditions of Biblical Exegesis.* Ann Arbor, Mich., 1958.

———. "Donne's Christian Eloquence," *ELH* 27 (1960):276–97.

RAHNER, HUGO. "*Antenna crucis:* (II) Das Meer der Welt." *Zeitschrift für katholische Theologie* 66 (1942):89–118.

REIDY, MAURICE F., S.J. *Bishop Lancelot Andrewes, Jacobean Court Preacher: A Study in Early Seventeenth-Century Religious Thought.* Chicago, 1955.

REUCHLIN, JOHANN. *De arte concionandi.* London, 1570.

RICHARDS, I. A. *The Philosophy of Rhetoric.* New York, 1936.

RIVIÈRE, JEAN. *Le dogme de la Rédemption chez saint Augustin.* 3d ed. Paris, 1933.

RONDET, HENRI, S.J. "Le symbolisme de la mer chez saint Augustin." In *Augustinus Magister: Etudes Augustiniennes,* pp. 691–791. Paris, 1954.

ROTH, DOROTHEA. *Die mittelalterliche Predigttheorie und das Manuale Curatorum das Johann Ulrich von Surgant.* Basel, 1956.

ROWE, FREDERICK A. *I Launch at Paradise: A Consideration of John Donne, Poet and Preacher.* London, 1964.

RUGOFF, MILTON ALLAN. *Donne's Imagery: A Study in Creative Sources.* New York, 1962.

SAUSSURE, FERDINAND DE. *Cours de linguistique générale.* Paris, 1949.

SAYCE, RICHARD ANTHONY. *Style in French Prose: A Method of Analysis.* Oxford, 1953.

SCHÖNE, ALBERT. "Emblemata." *Deutsche Vierteljahrsschrift für Literaturwissenschaft und Geistesgeschichte* 37 (1963):195–231.

SCHÜCKING, LEVIN L. *The Meaning of Hamlet.* London, 1937.

SEELTHALER, PAULA, O.S.B. "Das Licht in Schrift und Liturgie." *Benediktinische Monatsschrift* 33 (1957):33–43, 121–29.

SHANNON, C. E., and WEAVER, W. *The Mathematical Theory of Communication.* Urbana, Ill., 1949.

SIMPSON, EVELYN M. *A Study of the Prose Works of John Donne.* Oxford, 1924.

SMALLEY, BERYL. *The Study of the Bible in the Middle Ages.* 2d ed. Oxford, 1952.

SOLÓRZANO PEREIRA, JUAN DE, *Emblemata Centum.* Madrid, 1779.

SORLIEN, ROBERT P. *John Donne and the Christian Life: An Anthology of Selected Sermons Preached by Donne.* Ann Arbor, Mich., 1955.

SPICQ, CESLAUS, O.P. *Esquisse d'une histoire de l'exégèse latine au moyen âge.* Bibliothèque thomiste, vol. 26. Paris, 1944.

SPURGEON, C. F. E. *Shakespeare's Imagery, and What It Tells Us.* New York, 1936.

STÄHLIN, WILHELM. "Zur Psychologie und Statistik der Metaphern." *Archiv für die gesamte Psychologie* 31 (1914):279–425.

STAROBINSKI, JEAN. *Geschichte der Melancholiebehandlung von den Anfängen bis 1900 (Acta psychomatica,* no. 4). Basel, 1960.

STELLA, DIDACUS. *De ratione concionandi, sive rhetorica ecclesiastica.* Verona, 1782.

TUVE, ROSEMOND. *Elizabethan and Metaphysical Imagery: Renaissance Poetic and Twentieth-Century Critics.* Chicago, 1947.

ULLMANN, STEPHEN. *Style in the French Novel.* New York, 1957.

VALERIO, AGOSTINO. *De ecclesiastica rhetorica, libri tres.* Verona, 1732.

VIO, TOMMASO DE [CAJETAN]. *Opera omnia quotquot in sacrae Scripturae expositionem reperiuntur.* 5 vols. Lyons, 1639.

WALLERSTEIN, RUTH C. *Studies in Donne.* Edited by Barbara H. Davis. Ann Arbor, Mich., 1962.

WEBBER, JOAN. *Contrary Music: The Prose Style of John Donne.* Madison, Wisc., 1963.

WELLS, HENRY W. *Poetic Imagery, Illustrated from Elizabethan Literature.* New York, 1924.

WEINRICH, HARALD. "Münze und Wort: Untersuchungen an einem
Bildfeld." In *Romanica: Festschrift für Gerhard Rohlfs*,
edited by H. Lausberg and H. Weinrich, pp. 508–21. Halle, 1958.
———. "Semantik der kühnen Metapher." *Deutsche
Vierteljahrsschrift für Literaturwissenschaft und
Geistesgeschichte* 37 (1963):325–44.
———. *Linguistik der Lüge*. Heidelberg, 1966.
WEISS, KLAUS. *Das Bild des Weges: Ein Schlüssel zum Verständnis
des Zeitlichen und Überzeitlichen in T. S. Eliots "Four
Quartets."* Bonn, 1965.
WHITE, HELEN C. *The Metaphysical Poets: A Study in Religious
Experience*. New York, 1936.
WILD, JOHANN [FERUS]. *Annotationes . . . in Exodum, Numeros,
Deuteronomium. . . .* Cologne, 1571.
WILLEY, BASIL. *The Seventeenth-Century Background: Studies
of the Thought of the Ages in Relation to Poetry and Religion*.
London, 1946.
WILLIAMS, MARY ELLEN. *John Donne's "Orbe of Man . . .
Inexplicable Mistery": A Study of Donne's Use of Archetypal
Images in the Round*. Ann Arbor, Mich., 1964.

# Index